Sex, Lies and Handlebar Tape

Paul Howard is a writer and journalist who contributes frequently to cycling magazines and the national press. A keen cyclist, he rode the entire Tour route on his own in 2003, setting off as early as 4 a.m. on the day of each stage to avoid being caught by Lance Armstrong. His experiences are recorded in his book, *Riding High*, which was shortlisted for the National Sporting Club's Best New Sports Writer prize. In 2009, he became only the eighth Briton to successfully complete the Tour Divide, at 2,745 miles the world's longest mountain bike race, an adventure he recounted in his critically acclaimed book *Two Wheels on My Wagon*. Paul currently lives in West Sussex with his wife and four children.

SEX, LIES AND HANDLEBAR TAPE

THE REMARKABLE LIFE OF JACQUES ANQUETIL, THE FIRST FIVE-TIMES WINNER OF THE TOUR DE FRANCE

PAUL HOWARD

MAINSTREAM
PUBLISHING

EDINBURGH AND LONDON

To Lily Franklin, 1918–2006

This edition, 2011

First published in Great Britain in 2008 by
MAINSTREAM PUBLISHING COMPANY
(EDINBURGH) LTD
7 Albany Street
Edinburgh EH1 3UG

ISBN 9781845964610

A catalogue record for this book is available
from the British Library

Typeset in Folio and Palatino

Printed in Great Britain by
CPI Cox and Wyman, Reading RG1 8EX

Acknowledgements

NO BOOK, LET ALONE a biography, can be written without considerable help from a number of people. Therefore, this list of acknowledgements is unashamedly extensive, although if it is not comprehensive I ask those inadvertently overlooked to accept my apologies.

First of all, I must thank Sophie Anquetil, the daughter of Jacques, for her enthusiasm for my idea to write a biography of her father, for her openness in talking about her family life and for the provision of several of the photos that add so much to this book (as well as providing a long-awaited opportunity for me to visit Corsica). I must also thank her for making it possible to speak to her grandmother, her father's wife, Jeanine – and I would like to thank Jeanine directly for her own contributions.

Anquetil's last companion, Dominique, was also generous with her time in talking to me, for which I am grateful, as I am for the time afforded to me by Maurice Dieulois, Richard Marillier, Bernard Hinault, Raymond Poulidor, Guy Ignolin, Georges Groussard (and Mme Groussard for her hospitality and cuisine), Brian Robinson, Vin Denson, Chris Boardman, Jean Milesi, Rudi Altig and Walter Godefroot.

No cycling biography would be complete without a bike ride, so I extend my gratitude to Joël Hacquet, president of the AC Sottevillais, for arranging my ride in Anquetil's wheel tracks. I would also like to thank Lionel Fairier and his son Cedric for their hospitality when acting as my guides, and also to Lionel for taking pictures when my own photographic abilities failed me.

I have also received considerable assistance from various magazines and their archives, most notably *L'Équipe* and *France Dimanche* in France and *Cycling Weekly* in the UK. At *L'Équipe*, I would like to thank specifically Philippe Brunel for his insight into and knowledge of my subject and Philippe LeMen for his comparable insight into and knowledge of the darker arts of the paper's archiving system. Simon Richardson and Ed Pickering provided a similar service at *Cycling Weekly* – my thanks.

The arduous task of sorting through several thousand pictures was facilitated by Arnaud Jacob at *L'Équipe* in France, and their actual appearance in the book was made possible by Edd Griffin at Presse Sports / Offside in the UK; I am grateful to Lee Fullarton for creating such an eye-catching cover. My thanks also to Dominic Harman and my wife Catherine for assisting me with the coherence of my first draft, and to the editing skills of Paul Murphy, who reacted to the material submitted to him with great tact and sensitivity.

Finally, a considerable thank you to the anonymous taxi driver in Marseille who took as many risks as he did short cuts to ensure the late arrival of my plane from the UK didn't result in me missing the connecting ferry to Corsica – without him, the whole project could have been stillborn.

Contents

Prologue

IT'S A GREY AUTUMNAL day in Normandy. The keen wind and occasional showers make the weather a perfect match for the subdued mood just outside a small village near Rouen as a coffin begins the slow journey to its last resting place. Inside the coffin is the body of Jacques Anquetil, one of the greatest sports stars of his generation and of his sport, cycling. In his native France, he is still held by many to have been one of the greatest sports stars of all time.

The coffin and the body start their journey outside Anquetil's chateau, nicknamed 'Les Elfes'. Chateau is not too grand a title. There are dozens of rooms, a heated outdoor swimming pool and formal grounds of 28 hectares, not to mention many more of farmland. As befits someone of such stature, a police motorbike leads the procession of hearse and half a dozen cars towards Rouen's famous cathedral. Two more policemen are required to regulate the traffic around the entrance to the chateau.

At the cathedral, mourners start to arrive soon after the coffin at midday. Although the funeral service doesn't start until 2 p.m., the cathedral is soon full; many people have to stand outside. Those squeezed inside further underline Anquetil's prestige. Here a secretary of state for sport and a former prime minister; there half a dozen winners of the

Tour de France, including Eddy Merckx and Bernard Hinault. There are also erstwhile friends and rivals, such as Raymond Poulidor, Anquetil's would-be nemesis, three former world champions in Rudi Altig, André Darrigade and Jean Stablinski, and former teammates such as Guy Ignolin.

Pride of place, however, is taken up by his immediate family, the composition of which goes some way to revealing the complex character of Anquetil himself. Alongside his 87-year-old mother can be seen Dominique, his partner at the time of his death, and their 19-month-old son Christopher. Then there is Jeanine, Anquetil's first wife. Also present are her children: Alain, the former husband of Dominique; and Annie, the estranged mother of Anquetil's 16-year-old daughter Sophie, who is there by her side.

Tacitly acknowledging the domestic tribulations that had led to such an unlikely family group, Jean-Marie Leblanc, then a journalist with the French daily sports newspaper *L'Équipe*, soon to be director of the Tour de France, records the words of the priest conducting the funeral. After lauding the friendships and fraternity inspired by sport, Father Larcher adds, 'In the life of a man, there is the good and the less good. It's not up to us to judge.'

Certainly, none of the thousands gathered for the service in Rouen, nor the several hundred who accompany the coffin to a private blessing service in Quincampoix at the church where the young Anquetil received his First Communion, are inclined to do so. Another journalist, Anquetil's close friend Pierre Chany, wrote of the 'remarkable dignity' of those present: 'The sadness of those gathered was immense, and the religiously observed silence was testament to the depth of the emotion.'

Proceedings are brought to a close when Anquetil is finally laid to rest in the small churchyard beside his father. The coffin is adorned with a single lily-of-the-valley flower and a yellow jersey from André Darrigade. 'There were many of us, thousand and thousands, who returned home yesterday richer than we arrived, in spite of leaving a part of ourselves in a small patch of Normandy's rich soil,' concluded Chany.

But who was Jacques Anquetil? Who was the man behind the sportsman? What was it about him that inspired such devotion from such a large number of people in spite of an obviously scandalous family life?

And it certainly was scandalous. The public may not have become aware of the story until after he had died, but even now his domestic arrangements can still inspire shock, even disgust, possibly admiration. First, he seduced the wife of his doctor, at the time not just his physician but also a friend. Then, he lived happily with her for more than ten years, acting for at least part of this time as stepfather to her two children. Once retired from cycling, however, he desired a child – the problem being that his wife could no longer conceive. In an effort to keep the family unit together, his stepdaughter acted as a surrogate mother and bore him a daughter. More than this, though, she also became his mistress, and another dozen years were spent living in a *ménage à trois à l'Anquetil*. Inevitably, the set-up proved unsustainable. When this unique domestic arrangement eventually collapsed, Anquetil's final companion was the former wife of his stepson, a woman with whom he then had a son less than two years before he died, at the age of only 53, from cancer of the stomach.

In case it's not clear, it should be categorically stated that there was no incest. There may or may not have been an abuse of power – this is considered later in more detail and in the context of the contributions of those directly involved. There was certainly a unique and provocative story, involving a series of events at which even Casanova might have baulked. Had it been scripted as a storyline in either *Footballers' Wives* or *Desperate Housewives*, it would surely have been considered too unrealistic, too risqué even. Yet, as is so often the case, truth is stranger than fiction.

It was also a truth widely, if not universally, acknowledged. Everyone involved in the Anquetil clan, including friends, among whom were journalists, and Sophie, from whom the truth was never concealed, was aware of the domestic reality. Such attempts as were made to conceal the truth, such deceit as was practised, such lies as are implied by the title of this book, were only for the outside world, that much-feared, dangerous place that wouldn't understand what was perceived as normal in the Anquetil household.

Yet it's precisely because this normality was so at odds with the normality of the rest of society that it's essential to understand the man if we're not to be overwhelmed by the scandal. The purpose of this biography is to come to terms not just with the reality of Anquetil's family life, but also to reveal the man for whom it was all possible. 'I encourage you to do that, because when you paint the portrait of Anquetil you understand how he could do what he did,' asserts Philippe Brunel, chief sports writer at *L'Équipe* and a friend of Anquetil, in his later years, and his daughter Sophie. 'If you don't, all you're left with is the shock.'

Given Anquetil's accomplishments, both as a man and as a sportsman, understanding him is an ambitious goal. Yet it is certainly possible to describe him and the things he did, the character traits and achievements that made him into a still-iconic figure. First among these is his career as a cyclist. 'He's one of the mythical characters both for cycling, and for France,' says Bernard Hinault, his most worthy successor in French cycling and godfather to Anquetil's son Christopher. 'He was a winner, and I had that in my spirit, so I warmed to him. When I was small, he was for me the champion cyclist. But above all he was a gentleman, as much for his personal qualities as for his sporting achievements. I have always been irritated by the game of comparing champions from different times, but to be compared to him was an honour.'

Irritating as it may be, comparing champions from

different eras is compelling. It's also the only way for fans brought up on one generation to situate their heroes in the context of those who have gone before. In this light, Anquetil still fares well nearly 40 years after he retired. Of course, Hinault's irritation comes from it being an inexact science. (It may also come from the fact that Eddy Merckx always comes out on top.) Yet to the extent that it is possible to be objective, Anquetil is almost invariably placed in the top five cyclists ever. Simply being the first man to win the Tour de France five times and the first to win all three major Tours – France, Italy and Spain – gives some measure of his achievements. He was also only the second rider, after Fausto Coppi, to win the Tours of France and Italy in the same year, a feat subsequently achieved only by Eddy Merckx, Bernard Hinault, Stephen Roche, Miguel Indurain and Marco Pantani. Lance Armstrong never managed it. In fact, he didn't ride the Giro at all until 2009, after his comeback from retirement, and even then it was ridden as a warm-up for the Tour rather than with a real focus on winning (nor did he win the Tour that year either).

In a league table compiled by *L'Équipe* after his death, giving a point for each victory in what it defined as the most important races – the world championships, the three grand Tours, the five one-day monuments (Milan–San Remo, Tour of Flanders, Paris–Roubaix, Liège–Bastogne–Liège and the Tour of Lombardy), the Grand Prix des Nations and the hour record – Anquetil was fourth, one point behind Coppi and two behind Hinault, with Merckx an incredible sixteen points clear. If Armstrong's career had been included in the same table, he would have languished ten points adrift of Anquetil with fewer than half his number of victories.

In a similar table compiled for the Cycling Hall of Fame website using a more complex points system based on the prestige of different races and on placings, not just victories, Anquetil still finished fourth – not bad for a rider often criticised for being little more than a glorified time-triallist and lacking the breadth of achievement of his rivals. This time he was two places ahead of Armstrong and, once again, Coppi, Hinault and Merckx topped the list. Yet the ranking gives no consideration to his victories in time trials – his nine Grand Prix des Nations victories are overlooked, as are his fifteen other major time-trial triumphs, as well as his hour record. Had these been included and given similar weighting to other one-day races, Anquetil would move into a clear second place.

None of these comparisons can accurately weigh the significance of these victories, however. Armstrong's record bears no comparison to that of Merckx, for example, yet his unparalleled Tour de France achievements and his unique story mean he is the first cyclist since the great Belgian to transcend the sport and enter the wider public consciousness. Even on this intangible measure, Anquetil more than holds his own. His famous double victory in the week-long Dauphiné Libéré stage race followed immediately by the 557 kilometres Bordeaux–Paris, the longest one-day race, was voted the greatest sporting achievement of the twentieth century in *L'Équipe*.

Anquetil was also awarded France's highest civilian accolade, the *Légion d'honneur*, from General de Gaulle. De Gaulle, it is reported, was aghast at the initial absence of Anquetil's name from the list, an absence explained to him as being due to the cyclist's outspoken comments about doping. De Gaulle was not impressed: 'Doping? Don't know what you're talking about. Has he made "La Marseillaise" be heard abroad, yes or no?'

When Anquetil received the award, his standing was such that the skier Guy Périllat, world champion and Olympic silver medallist, who was receiving the same accolade that day, was more impressed by being able to rub shoulders with the famous cyclist than with his own medal: 'We received the

Légion d'honneur together from General de Gaulle. Receiving it at the same time as him seemed like a consecration. He had always been a sort of hero in my eyes, someone whom I dreamed of imitating in my discipline.'

Even today, Anquetil's reputation is still common currency in France. The presidential elections in 2007 saw the ruthlessly efficient victory of Nicolas Sarkozy, which prompted the headline '*Sarkozy gagne à l'Anquetil*' ('Sarkozy wins like Anquetil'). Nor is his contemporary relevance limited to the mileage that politicians can make out of being associated with him. His ambivalence towards one-day races was as much to do with the fact that they added little to his contract value as it was that they were subject to the vagaries of fortune and beyond his control. Instead, he focused exclusively on those events that most suited his calculating style and would bring him the greatest rewards in terms of profile and therefore money. Top of the tree, of course, was the Tour de France, victory in which would guarantee his prestige and his income – a single-minded approach echoed and exceeded by Lance Armstrong.

What's more, his trenchant views on doping still have an unfortunate and pronounced resonance in today's cycling. 'I dope because everyone else dopes' is an excuse still widely heard, as is the suggestion that so much is demanded of cyclists that a distinction should be drawn between 'doping' and expertly administered medical assistance designed to protect riders from themselves and the requirements placed on them. Only his frankness in confronting the issue is at odds with those implicated in today's drugs scandals. This reveals some of the crucial aspects of his character, notably his openness and his nonconformity, as Brunel points out: 'After he'd written the articles in which he says, "I dope because everybody dopes," he was interviewed on television later in the winter with the sports minister who told him off and said to him that declarations like that could lead to confusion. Anquetil replied, "You're sports minister, and yet you think I rode Bordeaux–Paris using just sugar." That's Anquetil's nonconformity. You must remember that at the time the cachet of a minister was much more than it is now. People still believed in politicians, in the institutions. But Anquetil was very open when it came to the topics he was prepared to broach in conversation. He was a long way ahead of his time. In fact, in general, racers still have a tendency to hide things, but he was open.'

This candid approach to taboo subjects has led to him being portrayed as a rebel by some people, but even though his comments earned him a suspension – the latter-day equivalent of bringing the sport into disrepute – he himself denied that he wanted to destroy anything, certainly not cycling, which had made him who he was. 'I wouldn't say he was a rebel,' agrees Brunel. 'I'd say that he was completely nonconformist, completely ahead of his time in terms of morality, in terms of freedom. He was very independent intellectually – a free thinker – but not a rebel. Was he provocative? Yes, I think that's it. He made fun of rules, of conventions, of others. He mocked them a bit. I remember one day he drove backwards through Rouen with Pierre Chany. He knew the town, and he took all the one-way streets backwards. Chany asked him why he'd done that, and he said, "So that if they stop me, I'm not in the wrong – going backwards on a one-way street is OK."'

In the court of public opinion, this desire to challenge and poke fun at authority didn't combine well with his reserved nature and timidity. Although France in the 1960s was split in its admiration for Anquetil and his great rival Raymond Poulidor, it was Poulidor, the eternal second, who inspired by far the greatest affection. Anquetil's reserve was taken for hauteur, his disregard for rules as arrogance. Where Anquetil's fans respected his achievements, Poulidor's fans were infatuated with his open nature and his stoic acceptance of the misfortune that inevitably seemed to accompany his defeats.

'I think his problem was that he just wasn't comfortable in a crowd,' says Hinault. 'He didn't like it if people came up to him and jostled him. Poulidor was the opposite. He was happy to sign autographs. "Maître Jacques" not so much. A bit, but not too much. But he wasn't at all like that with his friends. In his circle, he was the kindest of all.'

Brunel agrees that the public got the wrong man: 'Yes, he was a bit reserved. He had those cold, blue eyes. You couldn't slap him on the shoulder. He was a character who inspired a bit of distance, and for that reason he didn't earn the popularity or respect that he should have. People loved Poulidor instead. Yet in terms of personality, there was one who was interesting, engaging, generous, and that was Anquetil. The other one was tight and not someone who sparkled intellectually. Poulidor was intelligent – in terms of racing, in terms of a communion with nature, with his well-being – but he was not the great personality that Anquetil was. Yet the public chose the other one. That's how it was – a misunderstanding by the public. Popularity is the aggregation of a series of misunderstandings.'

Plenty of people did understand him, however, in spite of his taste for provocation, something from which his friends weren't immune. His great Italian time-trial rival Ercole Baldini, the man who bettered Anquetil's first hour record, was no exception. 'Anquetil won the Grand Prix de Lugano seven times, I think,' says Brunel. 'After he'd won it six times, the organiser said to him it would be better if he didn't come back next year, as he was finding it difficult to get sponsors because Anquetil kept winning. Then, in the winter, he changed his mind and said he could come after all, as he was a star, an important rider, but if he were to let Baldini win, it wouldn't be a bad thing. "I've not got anything against you. It's for the good of cycling," the organiser explained.

Anquetil said, "OK, but you have to pay me at the start. I don't want to wait around after to be paid and have to face the journalists. And it's double the normal rate. If not, I won't come." It was all agreed, but when he arrived he went to see Baldini and said, "Listen, don't say anything to the organisers, but if you want, I'll let you win today, but you must give me your appearance money." Baldini agreed and gave him the money up front, so he took all three fees, and he went and won the race. Just for a laugh. It was just a game for him. He got on really well with Baldini. They were very good friends. In fact, Baldini is still a good friend of Jeanine. It wasn't about the money for Anquetil. It was about having fun. He just wanted to have fun.'

ONE

The 'Viking' of Quincampoix

THE SOURCE OF ANQUETIL'S distinctive looks – blond hair, piercing blue eyes – and his associated character traits – reserve, hauteur, even arrogance – have been the subject of much debate. Indeed, their importance seems to have been magnified by his unique personality. Only an explanation based on his origins can account for his individuality, the theory goes – nature rather than nurture. His exceptional physical abilities and his scorn for social norms must be due to genetics rather than upbringing.

The most appealing of these deterministic explanations, and the one to which Anquetil himself was most attached, is that he was originally of Viking stock. He would no doubt have been encouraged in this line of thought by the historical association between Normandy and the Vikings. After all, the Vikings not only pillaged northern France, as they did much of the rest of Europe, but they also settled in the seaward reaches of the Seine valley. In AD 911, the local Frankish king signed a treaty with the invaders ceding much of the land between Rouen and the Channel, and by AD 933, five generations before William the Conqueror, Vikings had definitively colonised most of modern-day Normandy.

To establish a link between the Vikings of that time and

Anquetil's immediate predecessors is beyond the scope of this book, but it's clear that he was passionate about the Normandy landscape in which he was raised. Late in his cycling career, for example, he turned down a lucrative contract to race for an Italian team, as it would have involved him moving away from his beloved Rouen countryside. Even if Anquetil's close friend Richard Marillier says his decisiveness meant he wasn't a typical Norman – 'If there's one person you shouldn't cite as an example of a Norman, it's Jacques Anquetil. "Perhaps yes. Perhaps no," that's a Norman answer. Always hesitant. In rugby, the Norman answer is to kick to touch and see what happens next. He was the opposite. He was a Norman who wasn't a Norman.' – the immediate family tree unearthed by his daughter Sophie for her book about her father *Pour l'amour de Jacques* (*For the Love of Jacques*) confirms a long-standing link to the region.

Going back for several generations, his ancestors all came from within a small radius centred on Rouen. His parents, Ernest and Marie, were from modest stock in neighbouring villages, Ernest originating from Quincampoix – some eight miles north of Rouen – where the family would again settle when Jacques was seven. Underlining the intimacy of family liaisons in that area and at that time, their own union came about as a result of the marriage of Ernest's sister to Marie's brother.

Both Ernest and Marie had had their childhoods curtailed – another common feature of French village life in the early part of the twentieth century. Ernest's early assumption of adult responsibilities resulted from the death of his father in the First World War. Two years after his father's demise, at the age of only eleven, Ernest completed his period of compulsory education and assumed the traditional role of the only man in a house of six (he had one younger and three elder sisters at that time) by becoming an apprentice to a local builder. The extra income was essential to supplement the meagre living afforded to his mother Alexandrine through her daily efforts selling wild produce collected from the local woodlands – mushrooms, berries, asparagus. These were transported by handcart to the market in Rouen, after which Alexandrine still found sufficient energy for her nocturnal activity as a seamstress. An unintentional side effect, however, of Ernest's contribution to the family coffers was to put a definitive end to his own aspirations as a cyclist, already limited by his mother's opposition to the sport: his two elder brothers (both also called Ernest) had died as infants because of chest infections, leading Alexandrine to ban bikes from the house.

As for Marie, she was raised in the state orphanage from the age of two. Her lowly status was perpetuated by her position as a linen maid for the Count of Amiens, until the independence brought about by her marriage to Ernest on 25 May 1929.

Further back in Anquetil's lineage, the same pattern of French provincial peasantry is repeated, the only notable feature being a passion for the name Ernest. Not only were Jacques' father and his two unfortunate siblings called Ernest, Ernest's eldest sister – Jacques' aunt – was called Ernestine, while his grandfather was Ernest Victor Anquetil. This Ernest was a lumberjack, while his wife, Augustine-Alexandrine, was a seamstress.

If you think that this suggests not just a passion but an obsession with Ernest, you'd be right. It stems from the previous generation, that of Jacques' great-grandparents, and reveals a considerable deviation from the conventional genetic heritage discovered so far. Ernest Victor's mother was Melanie, but Ernest Victor was not the son of her husband, Frédéric Anquetil. Although Frédéric is the origin of the name Anquetil in this family, he was in fact only Ernest's adopted father. The story of his biological paternity is much more complex.

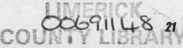

The central character is Melanie Grouh, later to become Melanie Anquetil. The picture painted of her by Sophie is again of someone from lowly stock, earning a living as a maid with a wealthy bourgeois family in Alsace. The location is significant, as is the timing – 1870, the year of the outbreak of the Franco-Prussian War. By the end of the war, Melanie had given birth to a child, her son Ernest, the fruit of a relationship with a German colonel who was killed during the fighting.

How exactly a lowly French servant came to bear a son to a serving officer in the occupying army is unclear, although there are several hypotheses. First, with all being fair in love and war, it would not be unrealistic to assume a degree of coercion. The purported moral rectitude of social superiors has never been a compelling argument even in peace time, let alone during the temptations of war; the concept of *noblesse oblige* was not always interpreted as a responsibility to be benevolent.

Nor, on the other hand, is it difficult to imagine a situation in which the young Melanie relied on – or was compelled to rely on – her feminine charms. There is an obvious reference point in the form of a short story written by Melanie's rather more famous contemporary, Guy de Maupassant. 'Boule de Suif' tells the story of an eclectic mix of ten of Rouen's inhabitants fleeing the invading Prussians in a stagecoach. As well as various representatives of polite society, the group includes the eponymous heroine, a prostitute. After winning the favour of her initially hostile travelling companions thanks to her generosity in sharing her food with them, she is nevertheless subjected to relentless pressure to sleep with a Prussian officer who ends up detaining them. Having acquiesced, against her own better judgement, for the sake of the group and their onward journey, Boule de Suif is then once again ostracised as the voyage resumes and refused a share of the food bought in the interim by her fellow travellers.

Aside from the uncommon similarity in time and place, there is another reason for wanting to link Melanie's story to that of Maupassant. Almost 100 years later, in 1967, Jacques bought his last house, a chateau in the village of La Neuville-Chant-d'Oisel, eight miles to the east of Rouen. The chateau had previously belonged to none other than Maupassant's grandfather, and the writer himself was a frequent visitor, along with contemporaries such as Gustave Flaubert. If nothing else, the coincidental association of one of France's most famous and controversial writers and Anquetil's family life, both past and present, seems fitting. Maupassant was renowned for his merciless commentary on the hypocritical social conduct of his time, as well as for his own decadent behaviour – he died of syphilis.

There is also a third possible explanation for this unlikely liaison, at the same time the most obvious and the most unlikely: that Melanie and the Prussian officer were simply lovers. In fact, the evidence for this is also the most compelling, as Anquetil's daughter Sophie points out in *Pour l'amour de Jacques*:

> The German was called Ernst. It's this certainty, and the fact Melanie chose to name her child Ernest – without even mentioning his own subsequent determination to call all of his children Ernest or Ernestine – that makes me believe that it was a love story. You don't name your child after the man who raped you, even if it were possible to know his identity in a time of war.

Whatever the truth behind the liaison between his great-grandmother and a Prussian officer, this is certainly the most realistic explanation of Jacques Anquetil's distinctive physical characteristics, not to mention those unromantic character traits so mercilessly magnified and dissected by a voracious press and an alienated public.

All of which suggests little credence should be given to the

West Indian 'sage' who first mooted to Anquetil that he was a scion of Erik the Red or Harald Hardrada. Even Anquetil remained sceptical as to the veracity of these claims, although not, it should be said, sufficiently sceptical to stop journalists giving him the rather flattering sobriquet of 'The Viking of Quincampoix'. No doubt this heroic explanation of his glacial blue eyes and his fair hair appealed to him, as surely would the image of Vikings as explorers and adventurers, pushing the boundaries, as he did on a bike and in life with such audacity.

Aside from the historical link between the Vikings and Normandy, the myth has also been perpetuated by etymological study of Anquetil's surname. Apparently, the name 'Anquetil' – not uncommon in Normandy, if the Rouen phone book is anything to go by – derives from an old north European language and is composed of 'Ans', a pagan divinity, and 'Ketell', a cauldron, signifying domesticity. The resulting meaning of 'domestic divinity' seems all the more appropriate given his later unconventional family arrangements.

This is all both laudable and plausible, but what it fails to take into account is that Jacques was not an Anquetil by blood. The name came into the family by adoption, thanks only to the stubborn independence of spirit and disregard for social mores (traits he appears to have passed on to Jacques, adopted ancestor or not) of Frédéric Anquetil, first in marrying a single mother with a child sired by the eternal enemy, and then in adopting her son. It also conveniently overlooks the disagreement as to the origins of the language from which the name is derived. Some say Scandinavian, and thus Viking; others say Germanic.

Back to square one. Yet it's perhaps not surprising that Anquetil warmed more to a spurious Scandinavian explanation for his less publicly acceptable character traits. According to Sophie, he was the only person at home allowed to broach the subject of his half-Prussian grandfather, and when he did it was only in passing. Anquetil no doubt appreciated that in post-war France it was preferable, if only in terms of a career based largely on reputation, to associate himself with distant Viking heritage rather than the alternative of admitting bastardised German ancestry. As so often throughout his life and career, the apparent reality of Anquetil's world – the effort he was making in a race or the amount of food and alcohol he'd consumed beforehand – is at odds with what actually happened. Whether thanks to a Viking cultural heritage, a Prussian bloodline or simply hearty Norman peasant stock, one of the essential elements of Anquetil's character is clear: you were encouraged to see only what he wanted you to see.

TWO

Look, Dad,
No Stabilisers

IF THE IMPACT OF Anquetil's origins on his subsequent life is questionable, and if the reality of some of those origins is spurious, there's no doubting the significance and the earthy reality of his rural upbringing.

Anquetil was born on 8 January 1934 in the clinic in Mont-Saint-Aignan, the town next door to where the Anquetil family had a house in Bois-Guillaume. Then, as now, both towns were suburbs of Rouen, the difference being that the populations have almost tripled since just before the Second World War, as is the case with many attractive locations around larger cities. The social dynamic of Mont-Saint-Aignan has been further modified thanks to a student population of 20,000, while the traditional half-timbered cottages of Bois-Guillaume, in one of which Anquetil lived and which he described as 'the type of house the tourists found attractive but the inhabitants found uncomfortable', have been either replaced or renovated in a fit of suburbanisation and gentrification.

The first seven years of Anquetil's life were spent in a hard-working, relatively countrified but far from isolated household. Ernest, the father, was a builder and Marie, the mother, was also required to work. She recalled with a degree of chagrin the clear-eyed look of reproach in the eyes of her son when she was obliged to restrain him in the house, for want of being able to afford a nanny and for fear that he would be run over on the street outside, while she was out. The hotheadedness and independence that might have led to an early demise certainly brought other troubles. At the age of four, for example, he broke a window pane in a neighbour's house when he wasn't allowed in to see their daughter, having previously warned the neighbour of the outcome of being refused entry. The neighbour's mistake was to scoff at the threat, leaving the young Anquetil, in an early demonstration of the spirit of contradiction that would colour his life, with little choice but to meet the challenge.

Another challenge to which he would eventually rise more successfully than even he could have imagined was that presented by his father the same summer in Bois-Guillaume. Later in his life, Anquetil recalled in his book *En brûlant les étapes* (*Skipping Stages*), co-written with Pierre Joly, the day his father returned home with an air of mystery for which he was not usually renowned:

'Has the boy been good today?' he asked.

'Well, he's only broken one plate and torn one pair of trousers so that counts as one of his better days,' replied his mum.

'Good, he can have his surprise.'

The surprise was in the form of a magnificent red bike. Magnificent in the eyes of a four year old, at least. Less magnificent, from Anquetil's mum's point of view, due to the distinct absence of stabilisers. But Ernest Anquetil wasn't one to wear kid gloves, and the prospect of his son needing such assistance left him cold (he had already announced before his first son's birth that he would be a professional cyclist, and to him you didn't win the Tour de France by starting with stabilisers). Instead, he took Jacques straight outside and enrolled him on what was to become an immediate crash course in keeping his balance. Perhaps some more detailed instructions other than 'hold tight to the handlebar' would have helped to avoid the inevitable – Jacques in a ditch with the bike on top of him. Yet the inevitable happened and, according to Anquetil's own memory, his father didn't try to hide his disappointment: 'You didn't even manage one metre.' The lesson was over, and Ernest returned to the house to tell Marie, in a voice directed more at Jacques than his wife, 'You were right. He's too little. We'll have to put the bike in the cellar . . .'

The threat of the bike being relegated to the cellar so soon after its appearance, combined with the blow inflicted to his pride by the look of disappointment in his father's eyes, was all the motivation the young Anquetil needed to try again. It's not recorded how many times he had to fall off into the ditch at the side of the road before he succeeded unaided. But the following day, while his parents were out – scorning all assistance from friends and neighbours in the process – and after several hours of trying, teach himself he did, even if the only way he could stop was to fall off. At least he was well practised in this particular element of bike riding.

Yet the resulting assertion from his dad that Jacques had cycling in his blood was, according to Anquetil himself, not immediately confirmed. He confessed instead to preferring almost any other juvenile activity and adventure to riding his bike. Nevertheless, according to one of his mother's favourite recollections of her son growing up recorded by Joly, he still demonstrated a certain prowess and a notable determination:

> 'My husband and his brother-in-law decided to cycle to Clères, five miles away. "I'm coming with you," said Jacques. "That would be very nice, but only if you can make it on your own," replied his dad. I suggested a ten-mile round trip at the age of five was madness but was overruled.'

In adulthood, Jacques would accept that he'd been helped up some of the hills en route, but at five the pride that would be a determining factor in so much of his later life made him reject any such suggestion. 'I would have made it myself . . .' was the familiar refrain.

Just as well, then, that the freedom craved by the young Anquetil – and by all accounts desired for their mutual benefit by his parents as well – was only a couple of years away, even if it was the silver lining in a much bigger cloud. In 1939, Ernest was mobilised in the French army to fight against the German invasion, but by 1940 he had managed to avoid capture during the capitulation and had returned home in time for the birth of his second son, Philippe. In 1941, however, it became apparent that the only work available to a builder in occupied Rouen was to assist the Germans with their defence installations. This was a step too far for Ernest, so the family decided to cash in its chips in Bois-Guillaume and move another five miles out of town to a smallholding in the hamlet of Le Bourguet, near Ernest's village of origin, Quincampoix. The plan was to emulate the family's in-laws – Ernest and Marie's sister and brother – and cultivate strawberries for sale at the market in Rouen.

This move to a traditional country cottage, consisting of two rooms and a kitchen, no electricity and a hayloft upstairs, surrounded by its own fields, was the real beginning of Anquetil's love affair with the Normandy countryside. 'What I remember most is the smell of apples and ferns,' he told Joly. (The ferns were used for putting under the strawberry plants to stop the fruit being splashed with mud when it rained.) In fact, he often expressed satisfaction at the prospect of having his own small farm, even if this was with the luxury of hindsight (and, thanks to his considerable wealth, the luxury of luxury). 'As a smallholder, you like your little plot of land in the same way as you do a lifejacket, but also in the same way as a lord does his manor,' he told his daughter Sophie. 'A penniless lord, at any rate. All the same, it didn't dishearten me to think that one day I'd be doing the same kind of thing. Even if things are really tough, you're still your own boss, and that's priceless.'

Whether or not this nominal independence would have overcome his desire for material wealth and social advancement is uncertain. Yet even when he had attained both of these, his passion for his native land didn't abate, eventually leading him to buy Maupassant's chateau on the other side of Rouen and accumulating, at one time, 700 hectares of farm land, not to mention 150 head of cattle.

According to his first wife Jeanine, who now lives in Corsica in a hilltop village nestled between the mountains and the sea, even the self-proclaimed 'Island of Beauty' wouldn't have been enough to tempt him away: 'I don't think he'd have wanted to leave Normandy, even to live here. Maybe he could have managed six months here and six months in Normandy, but I'm not certain.' And this in spite of a taste for warm climes and island life acquired on numerous holidays to the Caribbean.

All of which confirms that while life in Quincampoix may not have been the 'Cider with Anquetil' idyll it could have been in another era – the vicissitudes of making a living from the land and the presence of German soldiers, not to mention unexploded shells and bombs, precludes such a rosy picture – it certainly afforded a lifestyle that suited an energetic young boy. Not that there wasn't still plenty of trouble to be had and mischief to be made. Throwing bullets collected from the surrounding woods into a fire to hear them explode was a favourite pastime, as was disobeying parental instruction and rigging a home-made raft – constructed from half an aircraft fuel tank, no less – for mucking about with on the local pond. Then there was the prank of putting stones in the church lock and watching the unfortunate curate unwittingly undermine his own authority by swearing blue murder as he tried to open the door (no doubt providing plenty of amusement for the seemingly angelic young Anquetil when at choir practice).

All this took place when there was time in and around completing the day's tasks, of course. The list of jobs for the seven year old included gathering grass for the rabbits, digging over the garden, spreading the fertiliser and laying the table. Even if he admitted to having more often than not accomplished his part in the Anquetil family division of labour while daydreaming of pilfering wild birds' eggs or setting traps for rabbits, he also later acknowledged the importance of such jobs in having prepared him for the rigours of a career as a professional cyclist. 'My muscles were kept busy,' he wrote.

Of course, the image of French or Italian peasants dreaming of escaping a life of agricultural drudgery is part of the myth of cycling and also one of its greatest clichés. But, as with most clichés, it is founded on a degree of historical truth. Anquetil is simply one of the most famous examples, though there are others. In fact, large parts of the professional peloton in the 1950s and '60s were made up of journeymen riders, invaluable teammates to the stars, who preferred the considerable grind and occasional glamour of a career on the roads of France to the even more considerable grind and guaranteed absence of glamour of life in its fields.

According to his daughter Sophie, Anquetil himself said:

> 'I don't think I'd have done what I did had my home life been more comfortable. You have to be hungry to want to overcome all the challenges involved in professional cycling. Nowadays, we're not disposed to make these types of sacrifices. But, if you make a comparison, it's still easier to become rich by pedalling like a maniac for a period of your life than spending decades at a work bench or in a factory.'

Philippe Brunel told me that Anquetil said the same thing to him: 'He always said this was an important aspect of his character. He said it was bending over picking strawberries when he was young that accustomed his back to such hard labour and discomfort, and that, relatively speaking, being on a bike was easy. All thanks to the strawberries. I think it's true.'

Guy Ignolin, who was something of a deluxe teammate for Anquetil for several seasons in the famous St Raphaël team, also agrees. He won three stages of the Tour de France during his career, as well as taking a second place in the French national championships, just ahead of Anquetil. He was also, like Anquetil and so many others, from a modest background. 'We were, above all, manual people,' he said. 'Most of us had stopped school by the age of 14 or 15. In general, those who succeeded on the bike when Jacques and I were riding were those who were used to a "hard" life, who had been used to working manually from a young age.'

In addition to an early inoculation against hard work, another activity common to many cyclists at the time was a considerable journey to and from school, almost always accomplished on foot. The obvious contemporary comparison is with the continued success of Ethiopian and Kenyan runners, inured to both hardship and long distances. According to Ignolin, Anquetil was no exception: 'Jacques used to tell me, "When I went to school, I ran there every day." He even used to say he'd run across the fields sometimes, as it was shorter than going by the road. And I did the same. I ran to and from school four times a day – in the morning to go to school, at midday to come home for lunch, back to school in the afternoon and then home in the evening, although I may have taken a bit more time over this, as it normally involved coming home with the other kids who lived nearby. Still, it was maybe four miles per day . . . It meant we were more resistant, certainly when it came to long distances.'

Anquetil himself said that one of his most potent early memories was the sound of his boots clip-clopping on the road as he ran to and fro. Writing towards the end of his career in *En brûlant les étapes*, he added:

> I don't believe you're born a champion, but I think a certain way of life helps to develop such talents as you have. The heart is a muscle like any other and can be strengthened in the same way. I had the chance to do just that. At 32, I'm already an ancestor, a man from the time before mopeds – thank the Lord.

Precisely because he was from a time before mopeds, his only hope of being able to join his friends from the village on their weekly Thursday afternoon pilgrimage to the cinemas of Rouen ('Ah! The cinema, the Westerns, the adventure!') was to obtain a new bike – his second bike, rescued from a state of decrepitude by his dad, now being too small. He had hoped that he might receive one as a present to coincide with his First Communion, but the more significant coincidence was with a bad year for the strawberries, an unfortunate combination of frost followed by heat wave. The resulting poor harvest precluded expenditure on luxury items such as new bikes, so Anquetil showed some of the determination to have his own way that would strike fear into his rivals in later life. He proposed that his father dismiss one of his harvesters and allow him to take her place; the money he would earn could then be used to pay for his new bike. His father, well versed in the difficulties and strenuousness of harvesting strawberries, initially demurred, not believing, in spite of his upbringing, that Jacques would cut the mustard. Eventually, however, he acquiesced, and by matching the requirement to fill 50 panniers a day the 11-year-old Jacques soon had enough money to afford his first proper bike: a sky-blue Stella that was the envy of his friends, even though it was not yet a proper racing bike.

When not adding to this training of heart and muscles by requiring him to pick strawberries, Anquetil's father Ernest also encouraged him to train his stomach, or at least to develop the constitution that would one day earn him a place in the pantheon of bon viveurs. 'When Jacques started to watch what he ate and drank, having mineral water instead of cider, his dad said, "You'll never make it as a cyclist if you can't drink a bit of cider,"' Jeanine remembers. 'He was told, "You have to drink cider." He was brought up like that.'

According to Anquetil's own version in *En brûlant les étapes*, the cider-related story happened slightly differently – by his account, his father woke him up by popping cider corks in his ear at 2 a.m. on the eve of a race, teasing him about the fact he liked it but couldn't drink it. Whichever is true, this example of the behaviour of Ernest reveals that not all of the hard edge to Anquetil's young life can be seen in a positive light. The 'tough love' that Anquetil said he at times perceived as vexatious but which generally helped to toughen his character was occasionally the precursor of a deep and sometimes violent rage in his father. At various points, and with varying degrees of provocation, he is said to have threatened to knife Jacques' legs so as to prevent him from ever riding his bike again and to burn the car he'd won in one of his first races.

Even this wasn't enough to make him lose his affection for his father, however. Sophie recalls her father telling her about her grandfather:

> 'You couldn't doubt the affection he had for my brother and me. It warmed the heart, but it never got in the way of what had to be done. That's to say, working the land. If you really had flu, you were smothered with tenderness, but if you feigned an aching head, you'd most likely find it on the floor.'

'There was no lack of love in his family,' maintains Maurice Dieulois, one of Anquetil's closest friends from his youth. 'He had a huge admiration for his father, though he was a tough chap, the dad. He was a builder, which was hard work at the time and involved lots of physical work, and Jacques admired his father for being capable of it. He loved his parents lots, and they loved him, too.'

'He held his father in very high esteem, and he didn't drink that much,' says Jeanine, before adding, 'Jacques loved his parents, but there were times it was too much for his dad, because he would have liked to have been a cyclist himself, but instead had to become the head of his family at only 11 years old.' Eventually, it also became too much for Jacques' mother, who moved to a rented apartment in Paris, although not while the children were still dependent on her.

This may not have been the way they would have chosen to demonstrate it, but the purchasing power that allowed Marie this freedom to move to Paris indicates the extent to which the family had risen above the level of subsistence farmers. The progress had been gradual, first with the expansion of the smallholding and then the taking on of labourers to help in the harvest. It had culminated in Ernest managing to replace his handcart with a truck on which to transport the strawberries to market. But, in Normandy at least, strawberry fields were not destined to last for ever. The only strawberry cultivators left in Normandy now are of the pick-your-own variety, according to Dieulois.

With progress up the social ladder and ensuring material comfort taking their natural place as the family's prime motivators, Anquetil's parents decided he should continue this trend. The way he would do this, at the ripe old age of thirteen and three-quarters, was to attend technical college in the southern Rouen suburb of Sotteville. With the growing number of factories in greater Rouen and a decent practical qualification, there should be little to stop him ending up with a good job, went the parental logic. After all, he had been an able performer at school, regularly at the top of the class, and he demonstrated an enthusiasm for arithmetic that would hint at the meticulous way in which he would later be able to calculate the amount of time he could give to various rivals in races and yet still beat them by the finish.

According to his daughter Sophie, this thoroughness manifested itself in another way, too, and offered another portent for his career as a cyclist. In fact, show me the schoolchild and I will show you the man: never one to do more work than was necessary, Anquetil could not see the point in scoring sixteen out of twenty when ten would suffice to keep him ahead. What's more, she says her father, in typically individual fashion, would spend the first few weeks of each new school year learning his textbooks off by heart and completing all the exercises in them. 'Once I'd done that, I'd nothing else to do for the whole year,' he told her. Employing an appropriate cycling analogy, he added, 'I just took it easy at the back of the bunch. I could follow everything, as the work had already been done, so I had nothing to worry about.' Although later criticised for his similarly singular preparation for big races, the effect was much the same: Anquetil could afford to take it easy at the back of the bunch and follow everyone, as the work had already been done.

The upshot was that although technical college would mean he was deprived of his immediate proximity to nature and potentially his inheritance as a smallholder – and the opportunity to be his own boss – by all accounts Anquetil wasn't unduly perturbed at the prospect of leaving home and, later on, of working in a factory. 'I didn't have a definite plan. I didn't find technical college unpleasant, and besides, as soon as classes finished I was out in the countryside again,' he told Sophie. As with most 14 year olds, he was more interested in chasing girls and messing about with his friends than worrying about what he'd later become. In fact, it was the friends he made at Sotteville technical college, rather than the lessons he learned there, who would make the most important contribution to his subsequent career.

THREE

The Apprentice – Part I

IT'S ALL VERY WELL saying that genetics and upbringing are integral to the development of a champion, but the list of key ingredients is incomplete if you don't also take into account chance or fate. Anquetil was widely considered to be a lucky rider during his 17-year professional career. He had a couple of serious illnesses during this time – enough to end the careers of lesser riders. But in spite of the inevitable falls and crashes associated with such a long time involved in such a dangerous sport, he never once broke a bone.

Yet the biggest slice of luck to come Anquetil's way arrived in 1947, before his career had even started. It came in the form of a chance encounter with a friend who would stay close to him throughout his life. That friend was Maurice Dieulois: 'We met for the first time at technical college – Lycée Marcel Sembat in Sotteville. In fact, we met a couple of weeks before school started, when there was an introductory day to explain the courses available to us, and it just happened that Jacques and I were sat together in the hall. We hadn't known each other previously, and we didn't know anybody else at the school. I was all set to train as a car mechanic – I was reasonably interested in that sort of thing. Jacques was undecided. The teachers explained the courses, what was involved, and I changed my mind and decided metalworking sounded more appealing. Jacques said that it didn't sound bad, so we both ended up choosing metalworking together. All a bit by chance, really.'

Another stroke of chance came on the first day of term two weeks later. 'After we'd met and got on during this introductory day, we met again in the schoolyard,' recalls Dieulois. 'The teachers called the metalworkers' class together, so we went in and sat next to each other – the benches had two places each. As the days and weeks passed, we became good friends.'

The crucial aspect of this blossoming friendship was not that the young Anquetil – he would not be 14 until the following January – now had a friend to help offset the effects of his naturally reserved character, not to say timidity, nor that he had settled on becoming a metalworker. More important was that Dieulois was a cyclist – a racing cyclist.

'As a result of my family background, I was passionate about the bike,' says Dieulois. 'My father had been a cyclist and was also director of the AC Sottevillais, the local club. He rode in the late 1920s, or thereabouts, and had a good career as an amateur – mainly regional but some national races. I spent all my childhood surrounded by bikes. On Sundays, we went to watch races or to club meets. I knew all the riders.'

Although the bike had been significant in Anquetil's life up to that point, it had only been so as a result of it being an object of considerable value that he had to work hard to be able to afford and because it was of great practical importance. 'I didn't like it or dislike it, my bike,' he told his daughter. 'It meant a lot to me, because it was useful, but there was no hint of a calling to be a professional cyclist.'

For obvious reasons, Dieulois's relationship with his bike was much more affectionate: 'I had a bike, which I used to get to school, and Jacques had a bike, too. He lodged in Sotteville during the week, going home on Thursdays and Saturdays, and the bike was for the journey. But for me the bike was already more than just for that. It was also for going out on rides, and the more we became friends the more we started to go out on our bikes together.'

Before the seed of competitive cycling and the possibility of it becoming a profession began to germinate, however, there was the small matter of some adolescent fun and games to be enjoyed. In Anquetil's own book, his school friends recall this as 'the time of friendships, of getting into trouble [though the French phrase they used can also mean sowing wild oats] and of Jacques dreaming only of doing the things others wouldn't dare'.

'He came from the country, we were from the town and we thought we were a bit better than the country boys,' remembers Dieulois. 'He was a bit reserved, but he was quickly at ease and happy to be with his group of friends. Pretty soon he liked to make it clear that he was capable of doing what others could do. Rising to a challenge wasn't just a trait that would come to the fore when he was on the bike. If a friend was doing something, he'd have to do it, too. I remember one example. We often went with friends to the riverside after school to mess about among the barges. They were tied up to the quay with metal ropes, and we would challenge each other to climb up the ropes, hand over hand, without falling into the river. I saw him fall in once – he was up to his waist in the water. But he had to make it, so he went back and did it all the way the next time – that was his character.'

Not that swimming was a problem for Anquetil. One of his more audacious stunts was to swim under the boats travelling along the river, in spite of the proximity of their propellers. Unsurprisingly, he was described by another friend as a 'hell of a swimmer'.

When cycling did enter into this *Boy's Own* world of

adventures and escapades, it was still just another form of mucking about with mates. 'Our first rides together were just rides in the woods, as you would now do on a mountain bike,' says Dieulois. Collectively and affectionately known as the 'Cyclo-cross of Saint Catherine's hill', after their preferred destination, another friend told Anquetil's co-author Joly how Anquetil used to hate the fact that they would play these games on bikes with fixed wheels: 'They're crap. You have to pedal all the time.' But it didn't stop him persisting until he was the only one still racing. The same was apparently true of the slalom races through the trees. Even if they all ended up in an inevitable tangle of legs and bikes, Anquetil always managed to last longer than the rest.

When there was a more serious sporting element to Anquetil's activities – such as during college PE classes – he demonstrated the same degree of aptitude and talent, even if it didn't involve two wheels. 'His first competitions were running races when he was at school,' explains Dieulois. 'The gym teacher took us running in the woods next to the school, and Jacques showed his athletic qualities there – he had a good heart and good legs. He was a good runner; in fact, he even won an inter-school cross-country race at Bihorel, a suburb of Rouen. He used to say, "If I'd never met you, perhaps I'd have persevered with cross country instead of the bike."' In the wider context of the history of cycling, the importance of the coincidental meeting of Anquetil and Dieulois in a Rouen schoolyard sometime previously is clear.

It took a while, however, for his talent on a bike to show itself. Once again, it was Dieulois who initiated the process. 'We started going out for good rides, doing some proper training. Physically, he wasn't very strong to start with. When he arrived at school at the age of 13, he wasn't very athletic, and he had pretty chubby cheeks. I was ahead of him physically at that age, even though he grew taller than me later on.'

Within a couple of years, however, the boys were managing regular rides to the sea at Dieppe, some 30 miles away, allowing Anquetil to demonstrate another of the attributes that would serve him so well later in his career. 'He didn't have great kit, and he had quite a heavy bike,' Dieulois remembers. 'What he did have, though, was great tenacity, never wanting to be dropped.'

On the rough and sometimes steep lanes of the Normandy countryside around Rouen, it would indeed have taken considerable willpower to keep up with ostensibly superior companions, especially given unfavourable material and an age disadvantage that manifested itself in physical inferiority. I went for a ride with the heirs to Dieulois and Anquetil at the AC Sottevillais and discovered this much for myself – and also that I didn't have his excuses. I'd like to say that my struggles were a result of riding with younger and fitter guides riding on their better bikes, but, apart from the fitter bit, the reverse was the case. From personal experience, therefore, I can vouch for the fact that just the climb from Rouen to Quincampoix is hard work – gaining over 300 feet in altitude – and this is far from the toughest climb in the area. In fact, the Seine and its tributaries have carved steep-sided valleys into the surrounding plateau, creating a punishing series of short but often steep climbs, interspersed with the winding undulations of the plateau itself. One of these climbs, leading to the village of La Neuville-Chant-d'Oisel, where Anquetil bought his chateau and where his second companion Dominique still lives, has been renamed 'La Côte Jacques Anquetil', complete with pictures of the man himself and distance-to-go signs. Nearby, there is also a Côte des Deux Amants (Hill of the Two Lovers); given his later personal life, it might have been more appropriate simply to rededicate this in his memory. Add to this a network of small lanes running through the agreeable pastoral landscape, with few cars even today, and it's clear Anquetil had plenty of scope for effective training rides throughout his life.

By the last year of his schooling in 1950, Dieulois was already taking advantage of this blessed geography by participating in the club runs of AC Sottevillais: 'André Boucher was in charge, and I was already under his wing doing gym work in the winter. In this respect, Boucher was ahead of his time – as he was with encouraging us to do mountain-bike-style riding in the woods. When it wasn't a training ride too tough for me, I went out with him and the other riders.'

This soon led to racing: 'I was 16 and a half when I got my first licence and started to race. It was at this time that Jacques started to become more interested. He came to see me race, and we talked about these races in class up until we left school in July 1950. So that's how he got to know the people in the club and how I came to introduce him to André Boucher.'

A more detailed account in *En brûlant les étapes* has it that Dieulois finally threw down the gauntlet to Anquetil to join him on a club training ride after being exasperated once too often by his friend's deconstruction of his races and how he made it all sound so easy – too easy. Even though this was Anquetil's first ride of anything like the distance and intensity involved – eighty miles at a typical club average of maybe twenty miles per hour – it took four of them working together to drop him in the last two miles. It was this impressive performance that inspired Dieulois to make the crucial introduction to Boucher.

It was too late in the summer of 1950, however, for Anquetil to consider racing that year. Instead, the plan was to begin at the start of the 1951 season. This would provide plenty of time for the pre-season training invaluable to even the most gifted athletes. It would also provide Boucher with all the time he needed to assess the potential of the young Anquetil, which in reality was very little time indeed. The ease of his pedalling, the speed with which he could regain a group after a puncture and his tenacity was all Boucher needed to see. 'I had in my hands a natural-born cyclist, whose legs went round like clockwork,' he told Joly. As a result, he made Anquetil the same offer he'd made to Dieulois the previous year: the provision of two bikes (one for training and one for racing), a year's free supply of tyres, free maintenance of the bikes for the year and a performance bonus. 'You were paid so much per kilometre for races won or those in which you finished in the top three,' recalls Dieulois. 'It was X centimes multiplied by X kilometres.'

Needless to say, this appealed to the hard-headed Norman peasant in Anquetil and his appreciation of the value of money, a trait Dieulois acknowledges: 'Yes, he was motivated by a desire to improve his social standing. His parents were working class, and they didn't earn the moon, just enough to get by. Jacques quickly understood that the bike meant both the chance for a bit of freedom and to lift himself up the ladder. Even at amateur races, there were important prizes. In fact, when he was still a young amateur, at the age of 17 or 18, he kept a little notebook in which he noted down all the prize money he'd won. He'd cut out the results from the Sunday papers and stick them next to the tally of his winnings.'

This reveals the state of Anquetil's motivation when he was faced at the beginning of 1951 with the choice between pursuing a career as a metalworker, for which attendance at Lycée Marcel Sembat had been intended to prepare him, or the altogether more alluring world of professional cycling, for which the *lycée* had also provided an unexpected opportunity.

Not that he was particularly averse to metalworking per se, and he had certainly shown some aptitude for it while a student. 'He did fine at school, because he was a bright kid,' says Dieulois. 'But he just did what he had to. He wasn't motivated to do more than that. Having said that, being at technical school, we had to do practical classes and make things, and at the end of the school year there was a show of our work. When he brought his parents, he was very proud to be able to show them what he'd made with his own hands. We'd worked for a year on the machine – we'd used hand tools more in the first year – and he was proud to have turned something as a metal worker.'

Nevertheless, this doesn't convince Dieulois that his friend would have been happy to stay a metalworker for long in the event of his sporting ambitions, either as a cyclist or as a runner, having been curtailed: 'I think he'd have tried to find something else to do to advance economically or socially. He would have struggled to have worked as a metalworker in a factory or workshop.'

This identification by Dieulois of what amounts to a restless thirst for success is another of the list of key ingredients in the stereotypical sporting champion that can be ticked off in Anquetil's make-up. There may have been an unbridgeable gap in the physical abilities of the two young men that was the essential reason for Anquetil's eventual rise to the very top of world sport while Dieulois was left only with fond memories of his brief period as a promising amateur. But the fact that Dieulois exhibits not a hint of bitterness or envy at his friend's success, after having been something of a hero for the young Anquetil (six months his junior, a significant difference at the age of fourteen) and the catalyst for his future fame and fortune, implies a fundamental difference in character. When I met Dieulois, he was the picture of contentment in his modest but respectable detached house in a quiet Parisian outer-suburb near to where he worked for 40 years until his retirement. He was happy to reminisce about his old friend and happy to indulge his grandson Benjamin's desire to show me his small collection of Anquetil memorabilia. While

Benjamin was out riding his bike around the garden, in full cycling garb, it was not without a degree of pride that Mme Dieulois said Anquetil was something of a favourite uncle for her grandson, even though he died more than ten years before Benjamin was born. Yet for all Anquetil's apparent modesty with regard to his own achievements and his loyalty to his friends, it's difficult to imagine a similar picture had the roles been reversed.

All of which makes it seem less surprising that Anquetil in fact gave up his first job as a metalworker after only six weeks. (He maintains he was proud to have worked for three months at the Julin workshop in Sotteville, from 31 January to 1 March 1951.) The straw that broke the camel's back was not the prospect of the career extending ahead of him, nor the relatively meagre pay of 64 francs per hour (this was before the conversion of 100 'old' francs into 1 'new' franc by de Gaulle in 1960, equating to about 6.5p per hour or around 60p per day). Instead, it was being deprived of Thursday afternoons off for training.

Dieulois recalls the fateful decision: 'André Boucher required us to train with him on Thursday afternoons, so you needed time off to do this. I had a boss – I was also working as a metalworker to start with – who let me free. But when Jacques worked with Julin, next door to my parents – he came to eat at their house at lunchtime – he couldn't get the time off. André Boucher had already seen he could be good, and he said you need to come training. So, he left, and with M Boucher had to persuade his parents to take him on and let him have the afternoon free, because it was his parents who decided the work that needed doing. I remember that it was M Farcy, who was the club president, and Boucher who went to see Jacques' parents to say, "He absolutely needs his Thursdays to train." I don't remember exactly what his father said, but he accepted, and that's how Jacques went back to his parents to work on the strawberries.'

FOUR

The Apprentice – Part II

IN SPITE OF ALL the upheaval and risk, Anquetil wasn't unduly concerned by the prospect of abandoning his first career: 'I had my club jersey, and at night I dreamed about my first winner's bouquet and also, to be quite honest, about the "Miss . . ." who would hand it out.' In his own book, he admits that he wasn't always a winner, at least at that stage of his life, when it came to girls.

This youthful, somewhat naive assessment of the possible glamour associated with cycling captures one of the sport's most powerful appeals. Anquetil's teammate Guy Ignolin was a member of the supporting cast rather than one of the leading lights. He was someone who would never earn enough from cycling to not have to work after he retired from the sport. Yet even for him there was more than just the reflected glory of being alongside a star and a deferral of the need to get a proper job. Now retired after a second career as the owner of a bar, he remembers the hard work and the hours spent travelling but says to paint a picture of a gruelling and unglamorous treadmill is not always accurate: 'Apart from one Tour of Spain, where the hotels were a bit iffy, there was nothing to complain about, certainly when I was with Jacques. In fact, we mostly stayed in nice establishments that I couldn't have afforded to stay in otherwise.'

Brian Robinson, Anquetil's English contemporary, has similarly fond memories: 'We went on a tour of criteriums in Spain. I don't know what year it was, but there was [Federico] Bahamontes, Darrigade, Anquetil and me – just the four of us. It was early days in Spain then, and we were riding around football fields against a load of locals. It was a lot of fun. We took it as a holiday, actually, as it was so easy, and we stayed in the best hotels. It was great – best week's holiday I've had. Certainly, Anquetil would have champagne breakfasts and that sort of thing. What else happened, we don't know, but Jeanine was there . . .

'We used to ride for no more than an hour round those football stadiums. It was no effort at all really. Just a question of nudging them out of the way, if you like. You'd get the occasional one who got really fired up – "I want to beat Anquetil" – so then you had to group together and tame them, you know, but the programme was always designed in favour of the stars.'

Back among the strawberries, Anquetil's aspirations may not yet have been so grand, but the cycling bug had certainly caught hold. His mother told Joly he would be glued to the radio for the final part of each stage while the Tour was on, although he always caught up on the work not completed in the interim. This contrasts to some extent with Anquetil's oft repeated insistence that he had no real passion for racing his bike – that he was not one of those people who derived pleasure simply from riding. Indeed, before he took up cycling in earnest with AC Sottevillais, his daughter records how he used to tell her that he mocked his friends mercilessly for their affection for a sport that thus far had brought them no greater reward than 'chocolate medals'. Asked by Sophie if he hadn't loved the sport that made him who he was, his answer was equivocal:

'Not for one second and entirely, for my whole life. The bike
is a terrible thing that drives you to make excessive efforts,
inhuman efforts. It takes a racing cyclist to understand
what it means to hurt yourself on a bike. Apart from that,
everything else about cycling is wonderful: the friendships,
the tactics, the ambience, the glory.'

The glory for himself, for his friends and family, and for
France was not disagreeable either, he added.

But he also went on to add that had he had the good fortune
at 20 to have been the beneficiary of a rich American uncle
who had left him a vast estate, or had he won the jackpot on
the lottery, he would have given up cycling there and then.
Or, says his daughter, he at least said he would.

There was no American uncle, however, so sooner or later
Anquetil had to embark on his first season as a bike racer. The
first race was on 8 April 1951 in Le Havre and was hardly
a portent of things to come. In fact, it's not without some
amusement that Dieulois recalls his friend's debut outing:
'His first race was in Le Havre, and I won it. Jacques finished
in the peloton, and I won the sprint to take an early lead in the
season-long *maillot des jeunes*, a points competition organised
by the local *Paris-Normandie* newspaper. But he was really
miffed after the finish. There was no photo finish in those
days, of course, just a judge who read out the numbers as
the riders passed, but he had no luck and the judge missed
him, and his number wasn't called out as he crossed the line.
He wasn't a happy chap.'

Legend has it that Anquetil had promised himself only three
races to achieve a victory before giving up cycling. Whether
or not this is true, it took him until his fourth attempt – the
70-mile Grand Prix Maurice Latour on 3 May – to bring home
the winner's bouquet, following a fourth place and a third
in the intervening races. As well as winning a racing frame,
Anquetil succeeded in getting his name in the paper, not just
in the results, but also in the write-up, even though he was

rather damned with faint praise: 'Everything considered, apart from young Anquetil, we find it difficult to see who deserves special mention.' The desire to receive a kiss from a local beauty queen was less immediately realised, however. Instead, his prize was presented by the august figure of Mme Maurice Latour, the decidedly middle-aged wife of the former champion rider and cycle-shop owner in Rouen in whose honour the race was staged.

By the end of his first year, Anquetil would have racked up enough victories – most of them on his own, several minutes ahead of the field – to have become a first-category rider had he not been under 18. (It should be noted that although his opponents were restricted by category, they were not restricted by age, so his direct rivals were often older, in theory stronger and in practice more experienced.) There are two that stand out. First was his victory in the Normandy team time-trial championships in July 1951 with, among others, Dieulois. 'We set off as five, and the time was given to the first three to finish,' recalls Dieulois. 'We were up against the big clubs, such as Caen, Le Havre, Cherbourg, and we were young, nobody knew us, so we weren't favourites. But to general surprise, we won it, against all categories, and it made quite an impression on the press.' The team beat AS Cherbourg into second place by nearly two minutes, with Etoile Sportive Caennais third.

In *Paris-Normandie*, under the full-page headline 'Triumph of Youth in Caen', it read, 'Three kids: Anquetil, Dieulois and Levasseur (58 years old in total) win the title of Normandy team time-trial champions for AC Sottevillais.' If their combined ages adding up to only 58 isn't impressive enough, it should be noted that Levasseur was 24, meaning Dieulois and Anquetil were both just 17 at the time – and this in a race open to all categories.

The next staging post was in Anquetil's first official individual time trial, held as the conclusion of the season-long *maillot des jeunes* competition. As a result of his leading the competition after the penultimate leg, he set off last of the top fifteen riders in the standings, preceded by four minutes by Dieulois. One version of the story has it that Anquetil was vexed by the prospect of overtaking his teammate and friend, and slowed down for five or six miles so as to remain behind him. Eventually, however, he had little choice but to pass him, going on to win both the race and the overall competition.

Dieulois demurs when asked about Anquetil's reticence, but is happy to acknowledge his superiority: 'It was his first open time trial – he'd won one at the club over a much shorter distance – but he dominated the race. I don't know by how much he won, but he won easily.' In fact, he covered the 51-mile course at an average of more than 25.25 miles per hour. After the race, local journalists were already making comparisons with Fausto Coppi, still the sport's undisputed star, and Anquetil himself was intrigued by the legendary 'Il Campionissimo'. However, when he was told by the assembled hacks that Coppi was famous for observing a strict diet, among other things, Anquetil was decidedly nonplussed. 'That's a shame, as I do like chips so much.' Even if chips are hardly haute cuisine, the seeds of his later reputation as a legendary gourmand and bon viveur, not to say provocateur, when it came to demonstrating what he could consume not just prior to but also during races were thus sown.

'That was typical Jacques,' acknowledges Dieulois. 'If he saw a racer he wanted to impress or intimidate, above all when it was someone who made a lot of fuss about the virtues of being serious and not eating or drinking too much, Jacques would always exaggerate. He showed that he could both eat and drink, and then win a race the next day – that he had a stomach that allowed him to do that sort of thing.

'But all this came with age. It was much simpler when we were younger. With Jacques, we both liked the bike, but at a certain point we both liked to switch off and enjoy going out and doing other things, to enjoy being young. We had fun, meeting up with friends and going out to the cinema, or going to the local bar and playing cards or dice and then eating together. We drank a bit and said "I can drink a bit more than you", like all young people do. But this was in the winter during the off-season. When training started again on 1 January, we were serious.'

Serious for Jacques didn't mean giving up his culinary preferences, nor resisting the temptation to stay up late, but it did mean regular gym attendance. There was, however, an ulterior motive for this apparently uncharacteristic keenness: the frequent attendance at the same gym of his current squeeze. It's not without an awareness of the irony of the situation that Anquetil recalled with pride in *En brûlant les étapes* a medal given to him by Boucher in acknowledgement of his exemplary attendance record. '[I was] the only bloke on the pull in the whole of France who got a medal for his persistence,' he wrote.

The success of the unlikely combination of strawberry picking, relaxation in the off-season and serious training – whatever the motivation – was clear for all to see. 'You rapidly knew he'd be good,' Dieulois recalls. 'Not when he won the first race, perhaps, but after he'd won several, and he'd won them solo. He always arrived on his own – he was a cut above. He'd become thinner in the cheeks, but he had grown as well. He'd grown bigger than me. He'd really changed from being an adolescent to a young man.' Indeed, his first racing licence, signed at the very end of 1950 in anticipation of the season to come, has him down as measuring 1.71 metres and weighing 63.5 kilograms (nearly ten stones for not much more than five feet seven inches) – hardly the same physique as his dad (built like a brick privy, by all accounts) but a long way from the frail, skinny youth we are sometimes led to imagine.

This new physical maturity, combined with the experience accrued in his first year of cycling, paid considerable dividends in his second season in 1952. 'He quickly understood that the best way to earn a living from cycling was to win,' is how Dieulois puts it. He also recalls that Anquetil's dad frequently reminded his son that 'all I know about cycling is the winner's bouquet'.

First, on 26 May, came the championship of Normandy and an early lesson in the sometimes harsh realities of being a marked man. Surrounded by five members of the Caen team, Anquetil was some five and a half minutes down on the lead group with just under fifty miles of the race remaining. On seeing his trainer Boucher at the roadside, he decided this was the moment to abandon. Needless to say, this was not part of the Boucher master plan, and Anquetil was given the requisite extra encouragement to continue: 'You've no right to abandon.' According to Joly, Anquetil then added to the impression that he was about to abandon by loosening his toe-straps. In doing so, he also loosened the noose placed around his neck by the Caen team and, catching them unawares, set off in pursuit of the leaders. He not only succeeded in making up the deficit but then went straight past to win, on his own, by three minutes.

Boucher told Joly in *En brûlant les étapes*:

> 'For me, Anquetil the champion was born then, after 18 months of apprenticeship. On his own, in less than forty miles, he made up eight and a half minutes. At only 18 and a half years old, Jacques Anquetil had become amateur champion of Normandy and had qualified for the French national championships that would be held on 12 July in Carcassonne. It was the beginning of an exceptional career.'

The rest of the year was certainly pretty exceptional. He won the 51-and-a-half-mile Grand Prix de France time trial, effectively an amateur Grand Prix des Nations, by an astonishing 12 minutes (after which his height and weight were recorded as 1.73 metres and 68 kilograms – nearly an inch taller and more than half a stone heavier than 18 months previously). Then, after finishing third overall in the qualifying races for the forthcoming Olympic Games, his first appearance at a national level, he became the youngest-ever French national champion by winning in Carcassonne, beating one of the favourites for the Olympic crown on the way. This victory was not without another crucial intervention from Boucher, however, to galvanise Anquetil and to help compensate for his apparent willingness to accept seemingly imminent defeat, an attitude that would blight his later pursuit of one-day races. Boucher, prevented from following the race, had to hide himself at the roadside at the crucial point in order to be able to leap out and tell his pupil to give it his all – an instruction executed with Anquetil's customary efficiency.

Apart from the privilege of wearing the tricolour jersey of national champion, his victory in Carcassonne also propelled Anquetil into the French team for the Olympic Games in Helsinki. He'd gone from young strawberry picker, having scarcely left his native Normandy other than to see relatives near the Belgian border, to international athlete in the space of a year and a half. Although caught up in some selectorial politics as a result of not being from a fashionable club, he was far from overawed by the experience. He was, however, disappointed by his 12th place in the Olympic road race on 3 August, despite being the best-placed French rider and winning a bronze medal in the team competition. This reveals how quickly his own expectations had developed to match his new status. After all, by the end of the year, at the amateur world championships, he would be rubbing shoulders with Rik Van Looy and Charly Gaul, other future stars of cycling's golden era.

After the successes of 1952, Anquetil decided there was little more on offer to him as an amateur, so for the 1953 season he took out a licence as an independent, the now defunct category intended to provide a bridge between amateur and full-professional status. The principal aim of this move, it should be no surprise, was to earn more money. It would also provide an entry into local professional races, although this is something Anquetil rather uncharacteristically deferred, under Boucher's watchful eye, until the August of that year. In the meantime, he won the Normandy championship for independents before finally taking the plunge with the professionals at the Tour de la Manche, a local three-day stage race designed for those with aspirations of greater things.

Against the massed ranks of such serious rivals, Anquetil wasted no time in demonstrating his extraordinary abilities. On the very first stage, he finished second, on his own and only 24 seconds adrift, to none other than a young Jean Stablinski – the same Stablinski who would not only become an inseparable friend and invaluable teammate but also a multiple Tour de France stage winner and world champion. No disgrace there, then, but even better was to come the next day in the 24-mile time-trial stage. Anquetil won by nearly two minutes, putting two minutes fifty seconds into Stablinski and taking the leader's jersey in the process. (Later in his career, Stablinski would proudly declare that he was ageing well: 'Anquetil still only takes a minute out of me every ten kilometres.')

This effrontery was all the excuse the professionals needed to gang up on Anquetil during the last stage the next day. For the 115 miles to Cherbourg, he was subjected to the kind of working over only experienced once in a career before you either capitulate or assert your dominance. It was a close-run thing. 'I've never been a drama queen, but if I'd made a fuss to the press, I would have had the crowd in tears. I had to put up with everything,' Anquetil later wrote. By 'everything' he meant illicit assistance between ostensibly rival teams, being cut up by other riders, delays in receiving assistance and eventually being forced off into a ditch.

Cue an unlikely hero – an unheralded independent from Nantes called Maurice Pelé, whom Anquetil had unwittingly brought down with him as he fell. The result was what he would later describe as the only present anyone ever gave him during a race. 'It breaks my heart to see what they're doing to you, so I'm going to help,' said Pelé. Between them, they caught up with the bunch and overall victory was assured, much to the consternation of Antonin Magne, *directeur sportif* of the second-placed rider, Attilio Redolfi. (This was the same Magne who would later perform this very role for Raymond Poulidor at the height of his rivalry with Anquetil.)

'So, Attilio, you're losing to debutants now?' Magne said. Redolfi's response was measured: 'Mr Magne, I would suggest you get in touch with this boy's father in order to sign him up, for what this young Anquetil has done is quite something. We were all working together, trying to bring him back on the first stage, but we couldn't get close.'

Greatness was beckoning, but it took one more feat and one more example of Anquetil's growing awareness of his own value before the 19 year old could really make the breakthrough. The first was his victory in the time trial that concluded the season-long *maillot des as*, another competition organised by *Paris-Normandie*. He won by nearly nine minutes and covered the 76.8-mile course at an average of almost 26.3 miles per hour, prompting one commentator to suggest that such a speed was only possible because the Norman kilometre was in fact only made up of nine hundred metres. The second was his invitation to appear in one of France's most prestigious criteriums, the Circuit de l'Aulne at Châteaulin. Prevented, he maintained, from beating that year's Tour de France winner Louison Bobet only by being held back in the final sprint, the race was more significant for Anquetil's successful negotiations for appearance money. Offered 15,000 francs, he insisted on, and received, 25,000 francs, the equivalent of £25, more than twice as much in one night as he would have received in one month working as an apprentice metalworker. Both on a sporting and a financial level, Anquetil had clearly made the right career choice.

FIVE

A Star is Born

THE GRAND PRIX DES NATIONS is a race that must now be talked about in the past tense. Yet for all cyclists active while the race was still being held, a victory in this end-of-season time trial was likely to be a highlight of their career. For 72 years, from its inception in 1932 (like the Tour de France and so many other races, the brainchild of a journalist), the Grand Prix des Nations was both the most prestigious time trial in the world and a classic race in its own right. It was variously considered an unofficial world championship and the concluding round of the year-long World Cup, all the other events in which were prestigious road races. The list of previous winners justifies this elevated standing, including, among others, Coppi, Hinault, Merckx, Chris Boardman and, in 2001, Lance Armstrong.

In spite of this honourable roll call, worthy of comparison with any other bike race, the Grand Prix began to decline in stature in the 1990s with the introduction first of a dedicated world time-trial championship and then an Olympic road time-trial event. Its demise was cemented by the arrival of the UCI ProTour in 2005.

In 1953, however, the race was still very much an important part of the here and now, not just for cycling, but also for the French national consciousness. Every year, crowds lined the

82.5-mile course from the centre of Paris out into the rolling countryside to the south and west of the capital. The victors of the previous two races were Tour de France winners and global cycling stars Louison Bobet and Hugo Koblet. Little wonder the young Anquetil confessed to nerves before the event, as he explained in *En brûlant les étapes*:

> 'I couldn't stop thinking about it. Although by nature relaxed, I couldn't get to sleep. I reread the list of winners: [Maurice] Archambaud, Magne, Coppi, Koblet, Bobet . . . I tried to reassure myself, to rid myself of a curious feeling: fear.'

Anquetil's anxieties can hardly have been eased by the speed of his rise from regional obscurity to the verge of international stardom. His first race against the professionals had been less than two months previously, and already Francis Pélissier, the *directeur sportif* of his new team, was proclaiming him as a potential winner: 'Winning a race with somebody like Coppi is child's play. Real sport is trying to win with an unknown. This time I'm going to make a kid win the Grand Prix des Nations.'

Although seemingly rash and clearly designed to make life easy for headline-seeking journalists, Pélissier's statement was taken seriously, and for good reason. For a start, he was one-third of the famous Pélissier brothers, all of whom had been professional cyclists. Henri, the eldest, won the Tour de France in 1923, and Charles, the youngest, remains to this day joint holder, with Eddy Merckx and Freddy Maertens, of the record number of stage wins in any one Tour after his eight victories in 1930. Then there was the fact that Francis was no mean cyclist himself, twice winning the Bordeaux–Paris one-day event. More important still, since his retirement as a cyclist he had based his considerable reputation as a team manager on his ability to discover new talent.

It was this eye for a new star that led to Pélissier stealing a march on a host of rival managers and persuading Anquetil to sign up for his La Perle team in time for the Grand Prix des Nations. Anquetil ended up with a lucrative two-month contract worth a total of 100,000 francs (£100), apparently the same deal as Pélissier had previously arranged with 1951 Grand Prix des Nations winner Hugo Koblet, who was at the very peak of his earning powers at the time, having just won the Tour de France. This transition from regional independent to highly paid professional was not without its hiccups, however.

The crux of the matter was that having made Anquetil such a mouth-watering proposal, Pélissier insisted it was only valid if he sign there and then. After an attempt at prevarication, Anquetil acquiesced, but in doing so he almost ended his relationship with his coach at AC Sottevillais, André Boucher.

Unknown to Anquetil, Boucher had been planning for Anquetil to turn professional the following year under what he considered to be the more avuncular tutelage of Antonin Magne. The populist, anti-conformist Pélissier was something of an anathema to him. Magne, on the other hand, was a former double Tour de France winner (not to mention three-times winner of the Grand Prix des Nations) and was behind the success of Louison Bobet. Boucher considered him wise to the apparent perils of pushing Anquetil too far too soon. Softly, softly, catchy monkey was the Magne creed, and he shared with Boucher a reputation of being something of a disciplinarian when it came to the behaviour expected of his riders.

(It should be noted that this offers the intriguing possibility of Anquetil riding for the man who was to become mentor to his great rival Raymond Poulidor, though the likely success of this relationship is questioned by British rider Vin Denson, a teammate of Anquetil's in the mid-1960s: 'Magne would never let his riders drink wine in the evenings during a stage race, and he was always at the table taking their pulses. The morale of the riders was in their boots. With [Raphaël] Géminiani – Anquetil's *directeur sportif* – and Anquetil, assuming we hadn't done anything silly during the race, we'd always be given wine. We needed it to relax after all the effort.')

There might also be another reason for the falling out. According to one of Anquetil's French biographers, Jean-Paul Ollivier in *Jacques Anquetil: la véridique histoire* (*The True Story of Jacques Anquetil*), Anquetil had already decided to enter himself for the Grand Prix des Nations prior to Pélissier's offer. To make it worth his while, he had also asked his club to guarantee him the £200 prize money should he win, but they refused. This apparently left Anquetil with less reluctance to distance himself from his erstwhile mentor.

Whatever the reason, Boucher judged the situation sufficiently serious to threaten legal action to have Anquetil's contract with Pélissier overturned on the grounds that, being under 21, he was still a minor. Yet Anquetil somehow managed to persuade Boucher to put this disappointment behind him in time to help him prepare for the race. Although contracted to Pélissier, Anquetil insisted, even at the tender age of 19, on ignoring his training advice and on doing things his own way (a method to which Boucher had contributed greatly). This involved reconnoitring the course several times with Boucher, noting where he needed to make the greatest effort, where he needed to take care and even sending himself postcards with snippets of useful information. There were also the inevitable sessions behind Boucher's Derny (a motorised bicycle), Anquetil's preferred method of training.

Come the day of the race, however, conditions were far from propitious for a bike race, let alone the appearance of a young phenomenon. The morning of 27 September was grey, with rain in the air, and the wind was gusty and occasionally strong. 'On the start line, I watched the wind blow the spectators' hair on end like in horror movies,' Anquetil recalled.

Whether due to the wind or nerves, he also confessed to setting off like a rocket, ignoring the carefully planned schedule. In spite of a puncture after less than three miles, and the subsequent use of a heavier spare bike for some considerable distance, this rapid start benefited Anquetil, who was leading at the first time check after thirteen miles, fifty-six seconds up on the Italian rider Agostino Coletto. Far from beginning to slow, he soon caught the riders who had set off four and eight minutes before him, and even though he was temporarily disconcerted by being re-overtaken by one of these riders – Gilbert Desmet, a Belgian who felt entirely at home on the cobbles of Rambouillet – he went on to increase his lead all the way to the finish in Paris. In fact, by the time he'd made it back to the Parc des Princes, his winning margin had increased to nearly seven minutes over the second-placed rider, Roger Creton. Ken Joy, all-conquering British Best All-Rounder champion, was beaten by nearly 20 minutes. What's more, although the conditions were far from ideal, Anquetil had come within thirty-five seconds of the record set two years previously by Koblet.

The reaction was unanimously favourable. The headlines included every shade of congratulation, from the accurate, if tame, 'The New French Hope' to the more poetic 'The Angel of the Nations'. Even in the insular world of British cycling, the magazine *Cycling*, the predecessor to today's *Cycling Weekly*, was impressed, in spite of the capitulation of the British contingent. 'British Hopes Fail in Grand Prix des Nations' was the headline, though this was closely followed by 'Great Ride by 19-Year-Old Frenchman Anquetil'. The report also demonstrated a quite surprising degree of magnanimity, given what had hitherto been assumed to be an innate British superiority in races against the clock:

> The dashing of our hopes of success in a classic event in the
> Continental calendar should not in any way detract from the
> merit of the great winning ride by the 19-year-old French
> independent Jacques Anquetil. Anquetil, a slim, pale but
> beautifully proportioned rider, showed a delightful, strong
> and supple action.

Back in France, Pélissier himself fanned the flames: 'Now
we're going to make them suffer. You've seen nothing yet. This
is just the beginning.' And *L'Équipe* was sufficiently moved to
write, 'Sensational! J. ANQUETIL, 19-year-old "independent",
dominates from start to finish.' It also included a front-page
editorial by the newspaper's founder, not to mention Tour
de France director, Jacques Goddet, entitled 'When the Child
Champion was Born'. 'The triumphant explosion of the son
of a strawberry grower into the world of professional cycling
is certainly one of the most remarkable achievements in the
history of French cycling,' he wrote in typically flamboyant
style, adding, 'The kid from Normandy, with the angelic face,
follows Pindar's maxim: become what you are.'

What Anquetil had become, among other things, was
nothing short of a media phenomenon. In the days following
his victory, he received visits from dozens of journalists –
eleven in one day – all intent on finding out the 'real story'
of this unheralded star. In what was rapidly becoming typical
Anquetil fashion, however, the 'real story' was as much
about what the papers wanted as it was about the truth of
his background. Although he was now wealthier than his
parents had ever been and had no further need to work
on the land, pictures of him in scruffy clothes pushing a
wheelbarrow full of strawberries were too tempting to resist.
Although his parents had been wealthy enough for their son
to go to technical college, the modesty of their surroundings
was emphasised with scant regard for the accuracy of the
picture painted. 'Slave to the Land' screamed one headline
the following day.

The impact was pronounced, and nowhere more so than in the even more modest house shared by Raymond Poulidor and his parents and brothers. In fact, unlike Ernest and Marie Anquetil, Poulidor's parents didn't even have the luxury of owning their own land. There was no chance of Poulidor forsaking his 15-hour days in the fields to attend technical college. Pierre Chany, one of Anquetil's closest friends, and one of the most renowned cycling journalists of all time, emphasised the disparity in their upbringing in *Pierre Chany, L'homme aux 50 Tours de France* (*Pierre Chany, the Man of 50 Tours de France*), a series of interviews recorded by Christophe Penot, another journalist:

> At 18, Anquetil was champion of France and went off to the Olympic Games. At 19, he won the Grand Prix des Nations. The first time Poulidor caught a train was when he was 20 to join the army. He came from Masbaraud-Merignat, where his parents were sharecroppers. He spent his whole childhood in clogs. It takes a while to make up for that.

To Poulidor, cycling was the only possible route out of a life of agricultural drudgery, which no doubt goes a long way to explaining his unexpected reaction to this first stunning victory of his long-time rival. Still living in his native Limousin, the region around Limoges, although in considerably more comfortable surroundings than those of his upbringing, Poulidor readily admits that Anquetil became something of an idol for him from that day on. 'Yes, it's true,' he recalls with a smile that belies the acrimony that would colour much of their later relationship, at least while both were still racing. 'When he won the Grand Prix des Nations, he was 19, and I was only just 17. When he won, he was a kid. It was extraordinary, winning a time trial like that. When you look at the photos, the position he had on the bike . . . When you see him in his cycling shorts, with those little legs, there is nothing of an athlete about him. Except he was made to ride a bike.'

If this seems unlikely, Guy Ignolin, Anquetil's future teammate, was equally impressed: 'I remember reading in the papers when he won the first Grand Prix des Nations. It really struck me this young kid winning, and it was held over 140 kilometres at the time. Then he won again in 1954. He was a phenomenon.'

The level of interest and expectation rose another notch three weeks after his victory in Paris when he won again, this time at the Grand Prix de Lugano in Switzerland. It had taken a considerable press campaign to persuade the organisers to invite him to their race, but once there he managed to beat both the conditions – torrential rain, always Anquetil's worst enemy – and his rivals. Although both Coppi and his great Italian rival Gino Bartali had to scratch from the race, those still present included the respected Italian Pasquale Fornara, who finished second, beaten by one minute twenty-nine seconds. Ferdi Kübler, winner of the Tour de France in 1950 and world champion the following year, could only manage third.

This success led to the silencing of the few remaining doubters of Anquetil's qualities and also to two significant invitations. The first was to participate in another high-profile time trial, the two-man Baracchi Trophy in Italy. The second was to meet, en route, the greatest living cyclist of the time, the legendary Il Campionissimo, Fausto Coppi.

The trip was organised by a mutual acquaintance in Caen and, inevitably, by two journalists from the *Paris-Normandie* paper who had followed Anquetil from the start of his career and who were now keen to take advantage of the coverage likely to be afforded by a meeting between the ageing champion and the new star. Anquetil, already conscious of the oxygen of publicity, was also a genuine fan of Coppi and was only too happy to meet his hero. 'For me, Fausto Coppi was something of a god,' he wrote. 'Subconsciously, and no doubt naively, I thought I'd be able to lift a corner of the veil hiding so many stunning victories and perhaps snatch a few of their secrets.'

However, according to Anquetil's own account, few secrets were revealed. He was rather taken aback by the austerity of the room in which they met while Coppi was having a massage – bare-walled and like a monk's chamber. He was also rather perturbed by the presence of Biagio Cavanna, Coppi's blind masseur, who had previously performed the same role for such Italian greats as Costante Girardengo, Learco Guerra and Alfredo Binda, and who submitted Anquetil to an impromptu examination by touch. In spite of his heart racing, Cavanna was impressed, especially by his stomach, and declared him the morphological double of Coppi.

Coppi, for his part, was glowing in his assessment of Anquetil's achievements to date: 'His performances are all the more impressive and convincing for the fact that Jacques isn't yet 20. They are indisputably the sign of a great talent. I've always thought such talent reveals itself young.'

He was also dismissive about concerns that Anquetil had been overdoing the publicity and the celebrations engendered by his victories: 'Jacques had no choice, as everyone wanted to get to know him. What's more, you recover quickly at his age. A few mistakes like this aren't too serious. I for one didn't always behave as I should have when I was 20.'

To make the point that he was now a reformed character, Coppi went on to stress the benefits of not eating too much, 'unlike Louison Bobet'. Writing his account of their meeting some 13 years later, Anquetil couldn't help but emphasise the irony of this comment by highlighting it with an exclamation mark. After all, it was Bobet about whom his former lieutenant and friend Raphaël Géminiani would write, 'Louison would think for a whole week about drinking a beer. His resolve would finally snap, but after he'd drunk it he would chastise himself for two weeks for having done so.' It was also about Bobet that the journalist Pierre Chany wrote in *Sport Vedette* magazine:

> One of Anquetil's finest successes has been to give Louison a complex. Louison eats grilled meat; Jacques prefers moules marinière, which are advised against in every book on sports nutrition. Bobet drinks mineral water; Anquetil opens bottles of champagne. Bobet sleeps for ten hours; Anquetil goes for a drive in the middle of the night and still turns up at a criterium the next morning as fresh as a daisy. He maintains that there's nothing better to calm a cyclist's nerves than a quick spin at 80 miles per hour!

It's no surprise, then, that Anquetil couldn't bring himself to promise to follow Coppi's advice. The only pearl of wisdom Anquetil vowed to take to heart after his interview with the great man was the need to find a manager – someone to help him negotiate the Machiavellian world of professional cycling. Even then he managed to resist Cavanna's attempts to seduce him. The rigours of Cavanna's approach were too much for him: 'I didn't dare tell him that I was going to try and get by without too much rigour and with my own ideas about sensible behaviour. He wouldn't have understood. He didn't know that the group discipline of Boucher's training methods was already intolerable and that I had to escape to go to the cinema.'

Even if Anquetil then lost to Coppi and his partner, amateur world champion Riccardo Filippi, in the Baracchi Trophy, the visit and the race served to increase his stock still further, especially when Anquetil's own partner, experienced French rider Antonin Rolland, said he had been crucified by him and had been incapable of leading for the last 20 miles. Still more publicity was to come during a second 'pilgrimage', Anquetil this time taking his mother, aunt and uncle to Lourdes. 'Such a nice young man' was the tone of many articles, even if he did crash the car he was driving, a Simca Chatelaine estate, won at the Grand Prix des Nations. (Looking like a French version of an Austin Cambridge and with a top speed just touching 80 miles per hour, not to mention taking 25 seconds to reach 60 miles per hour in spite of its go-faster white-wall tyres, it perhaps didn't quite live up to the demands Anquetil seems likely to have made of it.) An exploratory trip up some of the neighbouring Pyrenean *cols*, including the Tourmalet, Aspin and Peyresourde, accompanied, when asked why he was there, by the sound bite 'Because I'll soon have to come and suffer here', was the icing on the cake for the hacks.

Although outwardly phlegmatic, the consequences of this youthful, meteoric rise to a level of popularity and notoriety more normally associated with film stars must have been pronounced, as Anquetil's daughter Sophie suggests in her book about her father:

> What's it like for a 19-year-old kid who yesterday was picking strawberries to be on the front page of all the newspapers? To be congratulated by the president, to have the whole of France at his feet? To earn in one race what your parents can't earn in a year? What impact does that have on you? Surely something changes inside?

In spite of frequent interrogations, Sophie never managed to elicit a direct response, though she does reveal what would turn out to be his exceptionally far-sighted assessment of the situation:

> 'I understood straight away that I was becoming a hero for others, and I also understood immediately that if I couldn't take myself for such, I'd no business telling others not to think like that. It has irresistible advantages that you just can't refuse. Which? Well, if you keep a cool head, you can, in your own personal life, build the life you want and of which you are the master.'

SIX

Wounded Pride

YOU'D BE FORGIVEN FOR thinking that the combination of a precocious talent like Anquetil and a crafty old manager such as Francis Pélissier would be a match made in heaven. After all, it was Pélissier who'd surely endeared himself to Anquetil's commercial instincts by beating his rivals to the punch and putting his money where his mouth was. Anquetil had then returned the favour with his exceptional rides in the Grand Prix des Nations and the Grand Prix de Lugano. What's more, both men had shown themselves to be aware of the importance of publicity, both for themselves and for the team that paid their wages.

But you'd be wrong. Anquetil's first full season as a professional had hardly begun before the first cracks started to show in their relationship, and once again it was Anquetil's uninhibited lifestyle and his insistence on doing things his own way that was the cause. Or at least that's the way Pélissier perceived the proliferation of civic receptions and late nights that filled Anquetil's social calendar at the end of 1953 and the beginning of 1954. Anquetil himself did not deny his hectic lifestyle but resented the implication that it was of his own choosing. 'What stupidity!' he replied. 'I'm only 20, and I've just started out as a cyclist. I was invited to lots of things by lots of people who had good reason to invite me. What would people have said if I'd started saying no to them all? The answer would have been that success was making me big-headed. So I went along with it. But I can assure you that most of the time it wasn't much fun. Instead of having to stay up late listening to pleasantries, I would have preferred to spend my evenings with my friends.' Perhaps invitations to open the dancing with 'Miss Calvados' and her ilk helped soothe his disappointment.

Pélissier's assessment of Anquetil's motive proved more accurate when it came to his increasingly provocative approach to diet and training. Nowhere was this made clearer than when he arrived at the La Perle winter training camp in the village of Les Issambres on the Côte d'Azur. According to Pierre Chany's contemporary report in *Cyclisme Magazine*, Anquetil arrived at 9 a.m. after having driven across France through the night. While the other riders already there, including such luminaries as Raphaël Géminiani and Louison Bobet, were preparing their daily training ride, Anquetil set about sating the appetite provoked by his long journey. Nothing unusual there, you might think, except that he boldly walked into the bar run by former professional cyclist Apo Lazaridès and ordered not breakfast but a seafood selection, langoustine and a carafe of dry white wine. Lazaridès, who'd recognised the precocious athlete, was beside himself. 'Watching the kid tuck into his langoustine with mayonnaise, I understood that even though he's only just entered the world of professional cycling, the exit isn't far away,' he said to Géminiani and Bobet that evening. (It must be pointed out that Lazaridès' reaction should be seen in the context of him being the man who reputedly stopped while leading on his own during an ascent of the Col d'Izoard in the Tour a few years previously for fear of being attacked by bears, so desolate did the country seem to him. It seems the difference in the constitutions of the two men was pronounced.)

This was like a red rag to a bull for Pélissier. Although not averse to a good photo opportunity or even a good wind-up (and having apparently been capable of similar excesses, being described in a documentary of the time as a man capable of drinking a pint and a half of rum in the evening and winning Paris–Tours the next day), such a blatant disregard for the basic tenets of the profession of cycling in one so young – look after your body, sleep lots and well, no rich foods and certainly don't eat to excess – was taken as an affront to his position as *directeur sportif*. None of this worried Anquetil, however. Even though Pélissier took it upon himself to lay out a long list of suggested amendments to his training regime, Jean-Paul Ollivier records the cool response:

> 'Mr Pélissier, you've been a champion cyclist, you've won very important races, you're an important *directeur sportif*, but training methods have changed. Those I've been using have served me well, so don't waste your time. When it comes to my preparation, I will continue as normal.'

Such brazen self-confidence was in marked contrast to his relative humility in front of the challenges that awaited him in his first full season. The first big test was the prestigious week-long Paris–Nice stage race (or Paris–Côte d'Azur as it was called that year), curtain raiser for the whole season. 'I've been designated team leader, but I've never ridden more than 125 miles in a race before,' Anquetil said. 'What will experienced riders with plenty of victories to their names, such as Maurice Diot and André Darrigade, say? I have to say, I'm a bit scared of such a test, especially if the weather is bad. And I don't want to abandon. I hate to do that.'

He had no need to fear not finishing the race. In fact, he ended up seventh overall and managed to win the time-trial stage, beating the Belgian Raymond Impanis, the eventual overall winner, into second place – not bad for a 20 year old.

The only disappointment was the absence of Coppi, who'd had to retire from the event, and the loss of an opportunity to make a direct comparison. Less promising was his defeat in the hill-climb time trial up Mont Faron, where he was nearly caught by Bobet, who started two minutes later. It may have been a time trial, but the steep gradient was clearly not to Anquetil's liking.

A series of respectable performances on the road (which Anquetil nevertheless described as disappointing, as he felt he was capable of victory on at least two occasions) then paved the way for an aggressive performance in the Tour de l'Ouest in August, which cemented his place in the French squad for the world championships in Solingen in Germany. Equally significant, however, was the absence of a stage victory or overall success to reflect his aggressive approach, absences that would end up colouring Anquetil's assessment of the merits of such an ostentatious expenditure of energy. In Germany, he performed creditably in his first professional world race championships with a fine fifth-place finish, in appalling conditions, three minutes behind the winner Bobet and just beaten in the sprint for fourth. Bobet's victory underlined his current pre-eminence in the world of cycling and confirmed the beginning of the end of Coppi's reign (Coppi cracked on the last lap of a seven-and-a-half-hour rain-drenched epic, to be overtaken by Anquetil).

Another impressive showing in the Critérium des As, run behind motorbikes at the horse-racing circuit in Longchamps, saw him lose by just three seconds to Bobet. This was no mean feat: Bobet was fresh from his second-consecutive Tour de France victory and it included victory over his La Perle teammate Koblet.

All of this relative success – very impressive for such a young and inexperienced rider but still clearly in the realms of 'potential greatness' rather than 'current star' – went some way to smoothing the relationship between Anquetil and Pélissier. At least, there had been no further causes for upset. All that was to change, however, at the end-of-season time trials, where it was hoped that Anquetil was about to fulfil Pélissier's assertion that last year was just the beginning.

First up was the Grand Prix Martini in Geneva, where Anquetil could only manage a disappointing third place, two minutes seventeen seconds down on local favourite Koblet and also behind Pasquale Fornara, whom he'd beaten the previous year at Lugano. This was all the excuse Pélissier needed to renew his attacks on Anquetil's attitude and approach to training, especially combined with the rumours of too much of the good life and not enough training, which were proof that the press could be a double-edged tool.

If this and his impending military service ('What would I be like after 30 months in the army?') weren't sufficient to dampen his enthusiasm, his reception at the La Perle headquarters the week before the Grand Prix des Nations surely were. Anquetil recalls an unsettling atmosphere as soon as he arrived: 'The mechanics wouldn't look me straight in the eyes, and people were speaking quietly in my presence as they do when they're near someone who's unwell.' Things took a turn for the worse when he discovered that it wouldn't be Pélissier in the following car but Roger Jacquot the mechanic. Pélissier would be following Koblet.

Anquetil recalled his anger at the time in *En brûlant les étapes*:

> Pélissier didn't have a reputation for following those who came second. I went mad. I went into his office without knocking. 'What's up, kid?'
> 'Nothing, other than the fact you've no faith in me!'
> 'But I do, I do . . . But I've got to follow one of you, and as I've two stars . . .'

Anquetil also explained that the consequences of Pélissier's decision were not merely psychological. Pélissier had a wealth of experience, manifested in a thousand and one tricks of the trade to help his racers and almost as many means by which to encourage commissaries to turn a blind eye to these nefarious manoeuvres. The previous year, Anquetil had noted how Pélissier had arranged for an 'unofficial' car to drive almost on the wrong side of the road some 100 yards ahead of him so as to slow down traffic from the opposite direction and thus reduce the eddying wind that can disrupt a rider's rhythm. Then there was the 'feeding-zone trick' that Anquetil would now have to try and encourage his new entourage (Jacquot and Anquetil's own indispensable corner man from AC Sottevillais, Sadi Duponchel) to adopt. This involved the rider quite legitimately holding onto the team car to receive food and drink. The difference with Pélissier was that he had refined the process to such an extent that not only did he make it seem quite normal for the rider to hold on for the entire 500-metre zone (ostensibly while Pélissier looked for something vital for the rider that he appeared to have misplaced) but he drove at speeds of up to 50 miles per hour while this happened. Anquetil described the impact of not only being deprived of this support but of seeing it go to his principal rival as being like he'd been spat at.

The blow to his morale was as nothing compared with the blow to his pride, however. This, of course, provided the perfect antidote to any lack of motivation from which he might previously have been suffering. Depending on which report you read, a night out in Paris or a 100-mile training ride in torrential rain (or possibly both) saw him arrive at the start line in determined mood. His principal determination was not to win the race, however, but to beat Koblet, with whom he had no particular grudge, in order to prove Pélissier wrong. He went as far as instructing Duponchel and Jacquot to base all his time checks on Koblet.

The immediate result of this approach seemed promising – ten seconds up at the first checkpoint, twenty-five seconds after twenty-five of the eighty miles. By halfway, notwithstanding a rear puncture and two bike changes, Anquetil was more than four minutes clear of Koblet. But he was more than two minutes down on the Frenchman Isaac Vitré and the Belgian Jean Brankart. Another puncture and another two bike changes (a spare bike being used while the flat tyre on the original was replaced) left a deficit of forty-five seconds to Brankart with only fifteen miles remaining. Yet all was not lost. In Anquetil's own words, he didn't know what came over him: 'Throughout the last few miles, I was no longer human. I had become a machine, a runaway robot. The crowds were screaming, and I returned to the attack. It's difficult to explain, that incredible feeling, that liberating resentment.'

In the end, he made up the time on Brankart to beat him into second place by a meagre 21 seconds, and he also managed to beat the course record – held previously by Koblet. To rub salt into Pélissier's wound, Anquetil ignored him at the finish – instead shaking hands with Boucher, who was sitting next to the *directeur sportif* of the La Perle team, before combing his hair and walking off – and then delivered his winner's bouquet that evening to Mme Pélissier at the couple's bar in Mantes-la-Jolie, en route from Paris to Rouen. 'He's a peculiar kid. He never raises his voice, and you can never tell whether he's happy or not,' she later said.

History would also serve its judgement on Pélissier's fateful choice of rider when it became clear that Koblet would never again reach the heights scaled in his record-breaking year of 1951, when he not only won the Grand Prix des Nations but also the Tour de France. That this failure was put down to his inability to resist the distractions available to a handsome young cycling champion was an irony surely not lost on either Anquetil or Pélissier.

Perhaps the most revealing aspect of this whole episode, however, was Anquetil's enormous pride, a pride which, if wounded, would so often serve to inspire him to his greatest feats. No one characterised this better than Jean Bobet, former professional cyclist turned journalist and brother of Louison, who described it as a spirit of contradiction: 'Take the picture of a professional cyclist as it should be: careful, meticulous, serious. Erase it all and say, "Jacques Anquetil is the contrary of all that." Truth be told, he's always contrary to someone or something.'

SEVEN

Mission: Impossible

IN THE CONTEXT OF the usual progression in the career of a top professional athlete, the next 30 months of Anquetil's life should be classed as peculiar at best. They began on 22 September 1954, just after his second-straight victory in the Grand Prix des Nations, with his arrival at the Richepanse barracks in Rouen and the start of his compulsory national service. As for all young Frenchmen of the time, two and a half years of military life lay ahead of him. Anquetil's stint in the army, however, would end up bearing little resemblance to that of most of his compatriots.

For a start, and by his own admission, Anquetil was not exactly a model soldier. 'I was sometimes candid, never disciplined, but always sincere,' he wrote in *En brûlant les étapes*. This in itself would surely not have set him apart from many other young Frenchmen, but, of course, Anquetil was accompanied in his military career by something that did define him in a unique way: his reputation. A reputation, it should be said, that his potential superior officers would have at best perceived with ambivalence, thanks to his much publicised exploits – not all of them on the bike. Nevertheless, Anquetil managed to turn this ambivalence to his own advantage in inimitable fashion: 'I arrived, preceded by my reputation and by 30 bottles of champagne. The lieutenant advised me to leave the former in the changing-rooms and bring the latter on patrol.' Not without reason, perhaps, would Anquetil later be referred to as 'the James Bond of cycling'.

Another benefit of his standing as a sporting superstar was that he was soon transferred from the barracks in Rouen to those of the Centre Sportif des Forces Armées in Joinville in the east of France. This immediately went some way to assuaging his concerns about the impact the military would have on his career, as he would later write: 'I met the runner Pierre Poulingue, who kindly told me, "Don't worry, you're allowed to train." I started to live again as if he'd suggested we bunk off, something we also did, by the way. In fact, I had a sufficiently good understanding of the layout of the town to have no need for an officer's pass.'

It soon became clear that Anquetil would be allowed to do much more than just train. Indeed, he was shown such leniency with regards to mundane military obligations that in both 1955 and 1956 his results reveal that he was allowed to ride an almost complete racing calendar. This meant that while the army could bathe in the reflected glory of his achievements in time trials, he could continue his apprenticeship in the wider world of professional cycling.

In 1955, for example, he started the season at the criterium in Oran in Algeria, a long way from his erstwhile colleagues in Rouen. This was followed by his induction to the one-day races that dominate the spring, the highlight being his 14th place in Paris–Roubaix in spite of suffering a broken chain. Shortly after came the Tour of the South-east Provinces, where Anquetil was given a platform for testing himself both in the mountains and in particular against one of his fiercest later rivals, Charly Gaul. Gaul, one of the finest climbers cycling has ever known, won the hilly event, but not before Anquetil had shown his resilience by coming back from a heavy time loss the previous day and beating him in a sprint to win a stage. Antonin Magne felt the experience was decisive in forming Anquetil's character. 'I saw Anquetil pull himself together, I felt the way he wanted to redress his wounded pride and I saw him win the next day in Gap in front of Gaul, even though there were not insignificant mountains in the stage,' he told *L'Équipe*. 'That day, Anquetil really pleased me. I felt he had the temperament of a fighter.'

Then came an experience of a different sort in the Dauphiné Libéré, the traditional warm-up race for the Tour de France. Anquetil finished 15th overall, more than an hour down on Bobet, the overall winner. Even in the time-trial stage, he could only finish third, but while the results were not to his liking, the experience gained in the vicissitudes of professional cycling was instructive. His La Perle team was on the verge of bankruptcy, and Francis Pélissier's idiosyncrasies had become exaggerated by a heart illness the previous winter, leading to a lack of morale and a lack of practical support. The team provided no massages throughout the race, and Pélissier's descriptions of the stages to come amounted to nothing more detailed than 'see you in Saint-Étienne'.

In spite of this setback, by the end of the year Anquetil had had the opportunity to become national pursuit champion, to finish sixth in the world championship road race, to beat the newly crowned world champion, Stan Ockers (along with such luminaries as Brankart, Fornara, Koblet and Kübler), in the Grand Prix Martini in Geneva and to become only the second man to win three-straight Grands Prix des Nations. As if to emphasise that it was business as usual, this victory was greeted with a headline in *L'Équipe* that read 'No Surprises in the 21st Edition of the Grand Prix des Nations'. Such was his dominance, in fact, that Jacques Goddet was moved to write that Anquetil won with miraculous ease: 'It was enchanting – the rare pleasure of being able to watch a difficult task being accomplished by an artist.'

Another commentator, Maurice Vidal, writing in *Miroir du Cyclisme*, agreed:

> The style of Jacques Anquetil is astonishingly perfect. It could even be said that it's too perfect. In fact, efficiency in cycling is often achieved at the expense of the beauty of the effort . . . Anquetil's beauty is in his attitude. To watch him turn the pedals is a pure artistic pleasure. Whether he's chasing a record, a rival on the track, the clock in the Grand Prix des Nations or surmounting a col, he maintains the same feline allure.

The next year, 1956, proceeded in a similar vein, and his results were similarly mixed. At the beginning of the season, he crashed out of Paris–Nice, the press again making no allowances for his ostensible position as a conscript in the army by questioning a seemingly fragile morale. Victory overall in the Three Days of Antwerp gave him his first significant road-race win since the Tour de la Manche when he was still an independent. He followed this by demonstrating his growing versatility as a rider in retaining his national pursuit title and finishing second in the world pursuit championships to the Italian specialist Guido Messina. Further victories in the Grand Prix Martini and the Grand Prix des Nations – a record fourth in a row – went some way to repaying, through the resultant publicity, the faith placed in him by the army.

After all, the indulgences required for Anquetil to race so much certainly needed repaying. As well as the dispensations required to race in serious, prestigious bike races, there was also the permission to participate frequently in the lucrative series of criterium races that were as much to do with riders earning considerable fees in appearance money as they were with the prestige afforded to the victor. The number of these participations can be deduced from his recorded successes: in 1955, Anquetil won two and finished in the top five in another four criteriums; in 1956, he won seven and was on the podium in another five. He must have ridden a good deal more to have had this level of success. Then there was the track. Anquetil had by then become a regular, normally in the company of André Darrigade, at the Vélodrome d'Hiver, the famous Parisian track of the time, known universally as the Vél d'Hiv. His contracts for such events were reported at 30,000 francs (£30) per appearance.

There was even time for Private Anquetil to fan the flames of his growing rivalry with Louison Bobet. The first incident came within a few weeks of Anquetil entering the army, at the Baracchi Trophy time trial, ridden in pairs, at the end of the 1954 season. Perhaps because he was still a relatively new recruit, Anquetil was only given permission to race at the last minute. Chastened by his experience getting to the start line in Lugano a couple of weeks before at similarly short notice (the private plane he was being flown in had to make an emergency landing in a field due to fog, and he had to complete his journey by train – he still won the race comfortably, of course), he decided to drive to Italy. It took him all night and, as Albert Baker d'Isy noted in *L'Équipe*, was far from the best preparation: 'At 8.10 a.m., with a start time of 9.27 a.m., Anquetil, who'd only just arrived, was still eating his breakfast, hardly ideal for a quick start.' Although Baker d'Isy added that Anquetil performed well, the French pairing lost by one minute twenty-six seconds to the Italian duo of Coppi and Filippi, and Bobet was furious.

The extent of the burgeoning bad blood between the pair was made clearer in the following year's French national road-race championship. Involved in the decisive breakaway, powered by Bobet, who was seeking to add a French crown to his Tour de France and world championship titles, Anquetil dropped back to help Darrigade catch up. Darrigade then beat Bobet in the sprint for the title, which prompted him to thank Anquetil publicly: 'I understand that Anquetil turned down Bobet's invitation to collaborate with him to stop me from rejoining them. We were already good friends, but right now I can't thank him enough. He's more than a friend. He's become a brother of the road.'

This unfettered freedom to race while in the army, and at a crucial stage in his development as a rider (he was still only 20 when he was conscripted), clearly had a beneficial impact on his later career. It was also in marked contrast to the man who would later be touted as his main adversary and greatest rival, Raymond Poulidor.

Poulidor's upbringing and subsequent experiences as a cyclist have inured him to the vicissitudes of life. At home in his native Limousin, in a smart detached house in the small town of Saint-Léonard-de-Noblat that backs onto rue Raymond Poulidor, and still inundated with requests for his presence at various events, Poulidor has long since accepted and made the most of the cards that fate dealt him. It's with no bitterness then, simply with a desire for people to understand the differences between them, that he recalls his own military experiences: 'I say it in my book: when I went into the army in 1956, I was 20. In 1956, I could have been like Anquetil, winning important races, but I was in a small, local club, so I hadn't turned professional. The result was that I did my two and a half years of national service split between Germany and Algeria [Anquetil spent just four months in Algeria]. When I came back, I was nearly 23 and weighed 85 kilograms, even though I had been careful not to go to the bars too often. It was only once I was back from the army and my parents had moved farms to somewhere where the soil was better and we could use horses rather than cows for work on the farm that I could try my hand at racing seriously, and even then I did another year as an independent before turning professional in 1960, straight away getting good results. I could very well have done in 1956 what I did in 1960 and 1961 – that's to say, at Anquetil's age.'

There is some evidence to bear out this assertion. 'In 1956, when I was still an amateur and before I'd joined the army, I won a race eight minutes ahead of a professional racer who'd just ridden the Tour,' Poulidor recalls. Then there is the comparison between his and Anquetil's performances in another local race. In 1955, while in the army, Anquetil won the Bol d'or des Monédières. The following year, Poulidor, when a year younger than Anquetil had been and when still an amateur, came sixth behind Bobet, whom he'd dropped on a climb part way through the race. After the race, Bobet said, 'Who is this rider who's applauded more than me and that everyone calls Pouliche?' The nickname 'Poupou' would not be adopted until later.

This contrast with Poulidor's life in the army and the delay it caused in his development as a cyclist is highlighted by the culmination of Anquetil's career to that point – breaking the world hour record, a feat accomplished while still on national service. With the ease of his transition to the track and his successes as a pursuiter, momentum had been building throughout 1955 for Anquetil to make an attempt on the hour record. This momentum came to a head, after his third-straight win in the Grand Prix des Nations, with the reluctance of the army to accord even to Anquetil the two weeks deemed necessary for preparation, arousing the ire of French journalist and writer Antoine Blondin, again in *L'Équipe*. 'It's not a question of giving Anquetil permission, but a mission,' he thundered. After suggesting the army was now demonstrating itself to be as far behind the times in sport as it was in war – a sore point after the tribulations of the recent past – and then proposing they portray Anquetil's attempt as punishment ('sentence him to two weeks of Vigorelli [the track where the attempt would be made]'), the powers that be finally acquiesced. Another contributing factor to this decision may well have been Anquetil's decision to offer his earnings to an army charity.

Thus Anquetil set off for Milan and his first tilt at the

record at the end of October 1955. To cut a long story short, on Saturday, 22 October, in front of 10,000 overtly sceptical Italian fans, he failed by a considerable distance, posting 45.175 kilometres compared with Coppi's record of 45.848 kilometres. This was not only a long way off the existing record but was also worse than the performances of the three record holders before Coppi (Maurice Archambaud rode 45.767 kilometres in 1937, Frans Slaats had posted 45.485 kilometres the same year and Maurice Richard had covered 45.325 kilometres a year earlier).

The reasons for his failure, it seems, were legion, and everyone with any claim to have an opinion was encouraged to express it. Pélissier, apparently, 'knew he was bound to make a mistake, and if not would invent an excuse. Also, he was badly advised, and if he'd received good advice, he wouldn't have listened.' Maurice Richard said Anquetil's preparation hadn't been specific or serious enough, while the journalist Pierre Chany captured the prevailing mood: 'There were so many mistakes it would have been a miracle if he had broken the record. The conditions were against him, he'd ridden little since he'd arrived in Milan and he had become bored by the sterile discussions of his advisers.'

There was also the vexed issue of the markers used to determine the inner limit of the velodrome to ensure each lap was the required minimum distance. These had already caused controversy when Coppi set his record, with his predecessor Archambaud claiming that he had fewer than the required number (14 per bend instead of 28). Indeed, by some accounts, this led to Coppi's record being reduced by 73 metres from 45.871 kilometres to 45.798 kilometres, though neither of these corroborates the official UCI figure, and that which Anquetil set out to break, of 45.848 kilometres.

Whatever the situation in 1955, the markers were an important element in Anquetil's subsequent failure on his next attempt on 25 June 1956 (this had to be brought forward from the traditional end-of-season period, as even Anquetil was obliged to spend some of his military career in Algeria, and this was fast approaching). Initially, demonstrating the optimism that he often displayed when facing such considerable challenges, he had refused to be too concerned about the fact there were still 28 bags on the bends of the track and that these bags were filled with sand rather than foam. However, after a promising first half-hour, when he had been over three laps up on Coppi's schedule – putting him on target for 46.3 kilometres – and had managed to beat, by two seconds, Archambaud's record for the time taken to cover twenty kilometres, things started to go wrong. As fatigue set in, Anquetil started to clip the sandbags with his pedals and began to appreciate the importance of their make-up and their number. 'It wasn't cycling; it was bowling,' he would later write. 'I tried to get back on track, but I knew it was a lost cause.'

His assessment proved accurate. He rapidly lost ground and eventually stopped after covering 41.326 kilometres in 54 minutes 36 seconds – 'Way off the mark,' as he put it. While the crowd were chanting the name of Coppi, Anquetil had to be carried from his bike, unable to straighten his legs. 'I was like one of those little toy knights that children throw away once they've lost interest in the horse they're supposed to ride on.' With hindsight, it wasn't just his over-enthusiasm and the sandbags that got the better of him. André Boucher, with whom he'd been training, had wanted to postpone the attempt, as wind conditions were unfavourable, finally agreeing to a start only at 7.30 p.m., while his indispensable corner man Sadi Duponchel was unconvinced about Anquetil's choice of bike.

It was Duponchel, however, who had the presence of mind to goad a spent Anquetil into a final attempt: 'Kid, tell me we're not going to give up at that.' Anquetil's reply was revealing of the effort he'd just made: 'OK, I promise you that straight away, as tomorrow I know I won't want to.'

It was also Duponchel with whom Anquetil indulged in one of the most unlikely preparations for any serious athletic effort in the history of human sporting endeavour, let alone the agonising pursuit of the world hour record. Frustrated by the constant media attention in Milan and finding himself in the unusual position of sleeping badly, Anquetil and Duponchel took themselves off to a nightclub on the banks of Lake Como and danced until the small hours. According to Anquetil, the sleep of the unjust that subsequently overcame him and the relaxed state of mind that ensued more than compensated for the energy expended.

In the meantime, while Anquetil was letting his hair down, two Italian mechanics had been commissioned to make a replica of the bike used by Coppi in his successful attempt. This was apparently a work of art in itself, enamelled in an extraordinary green colour and containing mica windows in the pedals to reveal the bearings turning. More importantly, it also featured a longer wheelbase than Anquetil's pursuit bike, invaluable for alleviating the lower back and buttock discomfort he had experienced last time.

It was therefore with renewed morale and renewed machinery that Anquetil embarked on his third effort on 29 June. The rest of the setting that greeted Anquetil and the fifteen thousand spectators looked familiar to those who had been present four days previously: two flags placed twenty-six metres apart as the reference point for each lap; Captain Gueguen from Anquetil's regiment stationed to ring a bell to indicate Coppi's lap times; Daniel Dousset, his manager, on the back straight with a spare bike; Boucher in the stands; and Duponchel as the roving corner man. 'I put great store on his familiar voice to either restrain my ardour or keep me going,' Anquetil said. The one significant difference was in the markers. These had been reduced in number from 28 to 14, as had been the case for Coppi, and the sandbags had also been replaced by bags filled with foam.

Against such an auspicious backdrop, Anquetil was finally able to live up to expectations. Managing to resist the temptation to set off too fast, as he had done previously, Anquetil completed each lap exactly on the bell and in accordance with his schedule: the first 20 laps at 31 seconds each; the next 27 laps at 31.2 seconds; then 37 more between 30.4 seconds and 30.8 seconds. Anquetil's own recollection best sums up the finale: 'Sadi shouted, "It's in the bag, kid. It's in the bag." The stands were silent. On the 84th lap, Boucher shouted, "Give it everything." The bike sped like a champagne cork, and I made up seventy-five metres in one lap. "Forza Jacqué!" came roaring from the stands. It felt as though I could ride for a lot longer than an hour. The last lap was covered in 29.2 seconds. I'd ridden 46.159 kilometres.' He had beaten Coppi by the not insignificant margin of 311 metres.

After the achievement came the plaudits: 'Ah, the crowd. Those who were whistling me four days ago were kissing my bike, my jersey, wanting to touch me like they must do on the days of religious processions.' Even in the immediate aftermath, however, and running high on adrenalin and surrounded by this tumult, Anquetil still found it difficult to show his emotions. When Captain Gueguen congratulated him on realising a remarkable feat, Anquetil's response was, 'Yes, the crowd seems happy.'

According to Dieulois, it was always thus: 'He was always a quiet boy, never exuberant, never showing off his emotions by waving his arms or shouting when he won. He was always quite reserved, but at the same time very satisfied with what he'd achieved or managed to accomplish, even if it was without showing it.'

And surely breaking the record of his idol at the still tender age of 22 would have given him great satisfaction.

One report suggested the merit of his achievement was as much in having the courage to be the first to challenge such a benchmark as in the actual distance ridden. Chris Boardman, who himself set three hour records, agrees: 'The first big challenge with the hour record is to be prepared to consider it. There is no second place, and people forget that. The marks he set demonstrate for me just how similar human beings are when it comes down to it. The differences come from how they apply themselves (which is why I fared well in the Tour de France prologues – I specialised when no one else did). I would guess if you evened out training, knowledge and equipment, we would have all been in a very tight grouping. Who knows who would have come out on top?' In mid-1956, it was Anquetil who reigned supreme, a fact that was not lost on the military. He was received at the barracks with a guard of honour and promotion to the rank of corporal. Mission: accomplished.

EIGHT

Chercher la Femme . . .

ARMY LIFE, THEN, WAS not the obstacle it might have been to the development of Anquetil's career as a cyclist. Yet although he had enjoyed more or less free rein to ride when and where he wanted, and although he spent only four months in Algeria – rather than the year or more experienced by most on national service – Anquetil began his return to civilian life as if he'd just spent the last two and a half years having been sent to Coventry. In less than a year, he'd found time to begin a secret affair with his doctor's wife, rebuff the attempts to seduce him into marriage by a ballet dancer from the Opéra d'Algers and still have his best season yet as a cyclist: he rode and won his first Tour de France, won Paris–Nice for the first time, won his fifth consecutive Grand Prix des Nations and, just to demonstrate his extraordinary versatility, became the first rider to win the Paris Six Day in the same year as the Tour.

It all began on 1 March 1957, the day of his release from the army, which had just concluded with his stint in Algeria. His first race was Genoa–Nice, to be staged the next day. More significant than an impressive second place – he was beaten by Bobet in the sprint – was the fact that this took him to the Côte d'Azur at the same time as a certain Jeanine Boëda.

Jeanine – universally known as Nanou – was a mother of

two and married to Anquetil's doctor. As a result, Jeanine and Anquetil had already known each other for several years before their fateful encounter by the Mediterranean; in fact, since he had first been introduced to Dr Boëda, although there is some uncertainty about the exact date. In his daughter's book, Anquetil is supposed to have been introduced to Dr Boëda by his friend Sadi Duponchel as early as 1951, although Jeanine told me she met Anquetil for the first time only in 1954. It's possible, of course, that the two men had merely been professional acquaintances for the first three years of their relationship and only later did this extend into a personal sphere. Nevertheless, it's difficult to imagine Anquetil would have been quite as gauche in 1954 as Jeanine would later describe, suggesting that their first encounter may have been a year or two earlier, before Jacques had been exposed to the high society to which his prodigious early victories and burgeoning wealth would open the door.

Whatever the precise timetable, between his introduction to the doctor and the spring of 1957 he had become an increasingly regular guest at the doctor's house in the Rouen suburb of Petit-Quevilly, Dr Boëda expressing both a personal and a professional interest in the young man and in his career. Like so many champion cyclists – consider Coppi's thighs, Indurain's enormous lungs and Armstrong's extraordinary ability to cope with lactic acid – Anquetil was in some ways a freak of nature, later being recorded as having the largest heart in French sport. Jeanine, however, found nothing interesting or appealing in the timid young man incapable of stringing more than three words together the first time he ate with them: 'I remember the first time my husband brought him home for dinner with us. He was on the edge of his seat. You'd almost have thought he'd never seen a knife and fork before in his life. It was only because the kids admired him and played with him that he relaxed a bit. I didn't find such a bumpkin attractive in the slightest.'

On the other hand, Anquetil, according to his daughter, was immediately smitten – Jeanine was, after all, a dead ringer for Martine Carol (the French screen goddess of the time, whose own personal life was almost as turbulent as Jeanine's would become, involving as it did four husbands, drugs, an attempted suicide and an early death), and she was also a daughter of a respectable Rouen family. The result was the embodiment of all that which was still unattainable to Anquetil. Sophie recorded his thoughts in *Pour l'amour de Jacques*:

> 'Even though she knocked me out, there was no more to it than that. I may well have been a champion cyclist, but I knew there was still a long way to go if I wanted a woman like that. What's more, she was the wife of my friend, so even though I fell in love with her straight away, I stopped thinking about it just as quickly.'

The flame appears to have been rekindled pretty quickly in the spring of 1957, however. No sooner had he arrived on the Côte d'Azur than the two had met, and by the end of the next day had begun the affair that would lead to them living together for the next 25 years.

According to Jeanine, the initial meeting was coincidental – she was simply on holiday, staying with friends in Villefranche-sur-Mer near to Nice, with her children, Annie and Alain, but without her husband. Even the meeting after the race the following evening that would spark their affair was only brought about by the insistence of her children to see Anquetil after the finish. She invited him to dinner, and he said yes but then backtracked. In spite of this hesitancy, they ended up dining together anyway, along with a mutual friend. 'It's then that Jacques came to my room, on 2 March 1957,' Jeanine remembers.

Piecing together other elements of the story, though, it would not be unreasonable to assume that their combined presence on the Côte d'Azur in early 1957 had a degree of planning. For a start, Anquetil's own carefully calculating nature had already manifested itself in his dominance in time trials and would later be so noticeable as to earn him the nickname of 'Maître Jacques' (Master Jacques). Although derived from the French title awarded to lawyers, and indicating the degree of respect he inspired in cycling fans, rather than affection, this also captured perfectly his desire to be in control of every situation (whether as owner of a smallholding or one of the most dominant sports stars of his generation). Nowhere would this be more clearly demonstrated than in his later family arrangements, and there seems little reason to imagine he wouldn't have employed the same approach when pursuing Jeanine.

He would surely also have been aware that Jeanine had begun to warm to him prior to his departure for Algeria: 'At the start, he seemed to mess up my life. My husband and kids were too attached to him. But, little by little, I began to follow his career, to look forward to his visits, to enjoy the time he spent with us, laughing, drawing up plans for winter holidays we'd spend together. Thus went our lives until the spring of 1957, when what was bound to happen, happened.'

The impact was immediate and pronounced: 'By the morning, I knew I would love Jacques for ever. But everything else was terrible: to live with Jacques, to never leave him, to be by his side for every second of every day as I wanted, and as Jacques wanted, I knew I'd have to leave my kids, as I knew my husband would never let them go . . . and I knew I couldn't have any more kids . . . but Jacques didn't care. He wanted me!'

It's at best an unfortunate irony, then, that it was Anquetil's affection for Annie and Alain that had finally won Jeanine round from her initial distaste when she was preparing herself for what she assumed would be the inevitable consequence of their affair: the eventual loss of her children. 'It was because he loved the kids,' she recalls. 'My husband was very intellectual, and he only saw the children on Sundays, whereas Jacques had a real fondness for them, and they were very much attracted to him. That was the first thing that seduced me. And then he was also a faithful friend, honest, straight, and above all kind and fun to be with.'

Fifty years later, sitting at home in Corsica while her great-granddaughter (Sophie's daughter) has an afternoon nap – her living room dominated by an imposing portrait of her former husband – it's difficult to know whether the round-the-clock babysitting service she still provides as an indefatigable 79 year old is evidence of her own affection for children or her continuing attachment to Jacques. Sophie is not her only grandchild (there's also Steve, son of Alain and Dominique), but it is clearly Annie's daughter and her children who represent the strongest link to Jacques and are the reason Jeanine settled in Corsica some ten years ago. Annie also lives within a five-minute drive, yet it's her love for Jacques – 'I still miss him terribly, every day' – manifested in her desire to be near Sophie's family, that shines through.

Certainly, even at an early stage in their affair, when their relationship was still a closely guarded secret, Jeanine demonstrated an extraordinary willingness to accommodate her lover. It was to Jeanine, in fact, that Anquetil entrusted the thankless task of conveying to another former lover his subsequent loss of interest.

The woman in question was Paule Voland, a ballet dancer with the Opéra d'Algers. According to an article in the French weekly tabloid *France Dimanche* (a slightly upmarket version of the *News of the World* but nevertheless including such headlines as 'Her Husband Changed into a Woman', 'The Most Virile Men are the Most Faithful' and 'What Women

Really Want to Say to Men but Don't Dare . . .'), Anquetil was reported to have begun a relationship with her while in Algeria with the army.

Under the title 'The Mysterious Love of Jacques Anquetil' – and under the pretext of having overheard Voland whisper to a friend that they planned to marry – the paper boldly trumpeted that the whole of France now knew the identity of the future Mrs Anquetil thanks to this 'soap opera' being played out between a 'big star' and a 'pretty dancer'. According to the article, the couple met through Charly Bonardi, at the time president of the Algerian Cycling Union. His wife, who went by the stage name of Mona Gaillard, was the mistress of the opera's ballet troupe. It was she who took Anquetil under her wing and 'introduced him to l'Opéra and to the pretty dancers'. The paper also reported that it was she who euphemistically 'helped him discover all the secrets of life behind the curtain' – the implications of what this might have meant for a famous young bachelor surrounded by a gaggle of attractive young women are clear.

The attraction – whether in a general sense or in the specific form of Paule Voland (22 years old, daughter of a civil servant and first in her class at the Algiers conservatoire – it's a surprise there are no 'vital' statistics) – certainly appears to have been sufficient to motivate Anquetil to take even greater liberties with his role as a soldier. The paper had him bunking off from barracks every night in a Peugeot 203 bought for the sole purpose of conveying himself the 30 miles from Boufarik, where he was stationed, to the capital. Never mind the curfew or the road blocks – circumvented by distributing pictures and autographs – or the fact that he was supposed to have an armed guard with him whenever he went out training. (Tensions were high in Algeria when Anquetil was there, as the armed struggle for independence had begun in 1954 and had been escalating since 1955 when the Front de Libération Nationale killed 123 civilians in the town of Philippeville

– now Skikda – while thousands more had died during the reprisals by the French army.)

According to *France Dimanche*, the relationship even continued once Anquetil had returned to France at the end of his national service – by which time he had already begun his affair with Jeanine: 'She went out with him and introduced him to her parents. He took her to France to see Paris.' They were reportedly pictured hand in hand, and had apparently been to meet Anquetil's parents as well. On 2 June 1957, with the blessing of the opera's director, Voland terminated her contract, 'renouncing a career that she considered incompatible with the duties of marriage'. She announced that their wedding was planned for shortly after the world championships at the end of the summer and recounted how Anquetil phoned her every night from the Tour de France.

Then, the bolt from the blue: at the end of the Tour, Anquetil denied all knowledge of any marriage proposals. In spite of Voland purportedly receiving a telegram telling her not to worry, he would no longer return her calls. But he would speak to a *France Dimanche* reporter: 'There's no question of me getting married, either to Paule Voland or to anyone else. Of course I went out with Paule Voland, but if we've got to talk about getting married every time I go out with a woman, we've got a lot to talk about. People tell me of a telegram. I can assure you it wasn't me who sent it, though I'd like to know who did pull that trick. No, right now I've other fish to fry. I'm getting ready for the world championships.'

In Sophie's book, the story is corroborated by Jeanine, who recalled meeting Voland – describing her as a superb young woman – in Rouen, although she insisted Anquetil had made no promises and that there had been nothing more than a brief flirtation between them:

'There she was in Rouen, not hiding the fact she wanted him
to marry her. She couldn't forget him, she loved him, she knew
he loved her, she was ready to offer herself there and then
. . . But she was out of luck. Jacques and I were already in
love. The situation helped us to relax a bit.'

In fact, the meeting between Jeanine and Voland was far
from coincidental: 'Jacques fobbed her off on me: "Take care
of her, Nanou. Tell her whatever you like, show her Rouen,
take her to the shops but most of all make sure she gets back
on the train."'

Of course, in typical Anquetil fashion, the backdrop for
all this activity in his personal life was his best season yet
as a bike rider. With hindsight, it almost seems as if he
was combining the two on purpose, though he'd not yet
experienced the full extent of the rancour he would incur
later for his continued 'lack of professionalism' to goad him
into such intentional excesses.

It also proves beyond doubt that, although he was in the
peculiar position of having the media scrutinise his every
move, he didn't miss out on some of the joys of being a
young man. Many people have suggested that Anquetil's
later behaviour was the result of him being deprived of his
youth or a chance to enjoy it – or both. His journalist friend
Pierre Chany wrote:

After the 1953 Grand Prix des Nations, he no longer belonged
to himself. When he retired, he gave the impression he'd
been everywhere and done everything. In fact, he was
still a kid who knew little about life. When he retired, he
uncovered another world.

Philippe Brunel, successor to Chany as chief cycling writer
at *L'Équipe* and friend of Maître Jacques towards the end
of his life, told me Anquetil had been forced to live his life
backwards. The implication is that the excesses of youth
simply came at the end of his life after an enforced period

of early maturity. 'He made a bit of a pig's ear of things emotionally, but you mustn't misunderstand it,' Brunel told me. 'He hadn't lived before, so when he got to the end of his career he was a man who hadn't had adventures. Nothing much had happened in his life. He very quickly became a star and was in the limelight, so he couldn't do anything without people knowing about it. Anquetil in reality hadn't lived, so when he finished his career he suddenly wanted to make up for lost time, emotionally and sentimentally. He lived life the wrong way round.'

Yet it was a fact of life in the 1950s that adult responsibilities were often assumed at a much younger age, as had been the case with his father a generation earlier. What's more, Anquetil's awareness of and insistence on his own commercial value so early in his career suggests he was far from a callow youth. Even if living life as a national hero may have been unusual, Anquetil doesn't seem to have let that get in the way of him making the most of his bachelorhood. Indeed, if any excuse needs to be made for his later family arrangements, it would seem to be more a case, as with his contract negotiations, of too much, too soon, rather than of having lost out. Certainly, he himself acknowledges his enjoyment of being young, free and single. Writing in 1966 in his book *En brûlant les étapes* – in a chapter entitled 'First Tour de France, First Victory: Thanks to Darrigade' – Anquetil describes his friendship with his former teammate: 'I'd known him since 1953, and he was my best mate. We'd chased after innumerable victories together, and also innumerable girls, with varying fortunes . . .' If his quotations at the end of his affair with Voland are anything to go by, it must have been Darrigade whose success rate with the girls was lower than his success rate on the bike. Maybe this, and the fact Darrigade could apparently eat more than Anquetil – clearly no mean feat – was the reason for their friendship.

This first victory in the Tour was just the highlight of a remarkable season. Following his second place to Bobet in Genoa–Nice, Anquetil returned to the capital of the Riviera in the leader's jersey of Paris–Nice for his first overall victory in the race, thanks to his time-trial win on the roller-coaster stage from Alès to Uzès (this in spite of requiring one month and one thousand two hundred kilometres of training to lose the extra ten kilograms that was his leaving present from the army). This immediately propelled him into the position of favourite for the Tour, yet he couldn't even be certain of being selected. At that time, the Tour was run on a national team basis, and while Anquetil's star was certainly rising, French national team selector Marcel Bidot had the unenviable task of trying to fit a quart into a pint pot. Alongside Anquetil, he also had to consider three-times winner Bobet and his successor in 1956, Roger Walkowiak, as well as that year's runner-up, Gilbert Bauvin. He also had to consider how best to make whoever he selected function effectively together, rather than be riven by the rivalries that so often plague teams with too many stars.

To illustrate the complicated politics involved in the selection process, Darrigade, for example, said he would ride only for Anquetil. This was the best support Anquetil could have asked for. Darrigade might have had no chance of winning overall, but his popularity, his willingness to work for the team and his ability to win stages (three in 1957, twenty-two in his career) meant that not selecting him would cause a furore almost as big as if Anquetil were not selected. Darrigade was essential to Anquetil in another way, too. It was he who persuaded Jacques it was high time he rode the Tour: 'The Tour de France is marvellous, Jacques, an experience you'll never forget. You should waste no more time.' Anquetil needed little encouragement. Moreover, in a clear attempt to further unnerve the ever-serious Bobet – his most realistic rival for team leadership – Anquetil responded to Darrigade's urgings by saying that he would take a suit to be able to go out and about in the evenings to escape the hotels he'd be living in for three weeks. In an event as arduous as the Tour de France, such decadence was hitherto unheard of.

With what turned out to be impeccable timing for Anquetil, Bidot had his mind made up for him by Bobet while he was attempting to become the first Frenchman – and only fourth foreigner – to win the Giro d'Italia. Part way through the race and sitting pretty in the pink jersey of overall leader, Bobet announced, live on the radio, that he had decided against participating in the Tour: 'I'm leaving it for the youngsters. Let them take the responsibility of winning.' Whether motivated by his anticipated victory in the Giro or by concerns that his efforts in Italy would cause him to lose form in the Tour is uncertain, but his decision backfired disastrously. First, his confidence in his position in the Giro proved unfounded, and he ended up losing by a meagre 17 seconds to the Italian Gastone Nencini. (His defeat was hastened by provoking the ire of another rival, Charly Gaul, by attacking him while he was answering a call of nature, a move that inspired Gaul, a former butcher, to threaten to turn him into sausage meat and become a deluxe, if unofficial, teammate for Nencini.) More importantly, perhaps, it forced Bidot's hand, leaving him no option but to build his Tour team around a nucleus of promising young riders, of whom Anquetil was the youngest and most promising. According to Pierre Chany, Anquetil and Darrigade had both been out of the reckoning five minutes before Bobet's announcement.

Anquetil needed no second invitation, however, and took advantage of the absence of a nominated leader to win his first Tour. Although the overall margin of victory suggests otherwise – he beat Marcel Janssens into second place by nearly 15 minutes – success didn't come quite as easily as it might have appeared. He won the third stage into Rouen, giving his bouquet to Jeanine, and took the yellow jersey for two days after the stage to Charleroi, yet he was in danger of approaching the Alps with a serious deficit. It was Darrigade, earning the homage Anquetil paid to him in his book, who stressed the dangers of not paying attention in the race. On several occasions, breaks with contenders for overall victory had stolen a march on Anquetil, obliging him to make considerable efforts to reduce the deficit. On one descent in the Ardennes, he missed a bend and had to ride across a field, preceding Lance Armstrong's famous cyclo-cross escapade in the 2003 Tour by nearly 50 years. Darrigade told him he'd no hope of winning the Tour if he was 15 minutes down by the time they reached the mountains: 'You have to do something special beforehand.'

Suitably inspired, or perhaps chastened would be a better word, Anquetil attacked in the feeding zone on the last stage before the Alps and made up 11 minutes on his most serious rivals en route to winning the stage into Thonon-les-Bains. He finished close enough to the front on the next stage into the Alpine town of Briançon to regain the yellow jersey, having been fortified both on the rest day and in his passage over the fearsome Col du Galibier by a draught of champagne (the first courtesy of team sponsor Félix Potin, the second received from a supporter in the crowd). By doing so, he won further approving comments from his friend and mentor: 'I didn't think you'd be such a good climber. You may not be Charly Gaul, but there isn't a bloke born who'll beat you by five minutes.'

Even several further moments of inattention – notably on a transitional stage to the Pyrenees when seven riders from the top ten overall broke away while Anquetil was dawdling at the back of the bunch, requiring Darrigade to lead him in a fearsome pursuit that he later described as the greatest achievement of his career – and what Bidot described as a 'serious rough patch' in the Col d'Aubisque in the Pyrenees, couldn't prevent Anquetil from extending his lead all the way to Paris, winning the two remaining time trials on the way. In doing so, he became, at 23, the youngest Tour de France winner since the war and at the time the fifth youngest ever. (Only Felice Gimondi and Laurent Fignon have won at a younger age since, while the 'surprise' 2007 winner, Alberto 'Kid' Contador, was 24.)

The celebrations in Paris included a rapturous reception from the crowds and a telegram from the president. The enthusiasm was exaggerated by the success of the entire French team. In addition to overall victory, it had accumulated 21 days in yellow, the team prize and 12 stage victories. To emphasise Anquetil's unique stature, hinted at by newspaper headlines such as 'Anquetil Wins His First Tour de France' and 'He Came, He Saw, He Conquered', Darrigade couldn't help pointing out that the beaten rivals didn't just extend to those who'd been in the race. Clearly thinking of Bobet, he said, 'Jacques was simply the strongest. It seems those who stayed away made the right decision.' Anquetil himself later referred to Bobet's decision, telling *L'Équipe*, 'It was a brazen challenge. The best way possible to ensure we stuck together as a team.'

After a whirlwind tour of the lucrative post-Tour criteriums, Anquetil again won the Grand Prix Martini and the Grand Prix des Nations (beating Ercole Baldini, the man who broke his hour record, into second both times) before being reunited with Darrigade – along with Italian rider Fernando Terruzzi – for his first appearance at the Paris Six Day, which they of course won. Jean-Paul Ollivier reported Anquetil's response when asked about his preparations for coping with the lack of sleep inevitable in such a race: 'I've been to the circus in Rouen and several times to the cinema. These past few weeks, I've quite often not been in bed before midnight, which is as good a preparation as any. It certainly meant I could have some fun with my friends.'

The acclamation of the notoriously hard-to-please Parisian crowd was nothing short of remarkable. Little did Anquetil know, however, that this was as good as it was going to get for some considerable time.

NINE

Femme Fatale?

EVENTUALLY, THE CLANDESTINE NATURE of Anquetil's affair with Jeanine became too much of a burden. Although the peripatetic life led by Anquetil and the apparent ease with which Jeanine could find time away from her husband meant the practicalities were not insurmountable – a skiing holiday in the Alps provided ample opportunity for them to be together, for example – the emotional pressures on the couple meant that things soon came to a head. It was Jeanine who precipitated the next stage of their relationship in early 1958 by revealing all to her husband, whose response was to cut all ties with his former friend and insist she stayed with him. With Anquetil ensconced in an early season training camp on the Côte d'Azur and her husband showing no inclination to give her a divorce, Jeanine found herself on the edge of the abyss.

According to Sophie, Jeanine was so traumatised by the dilemma of her situation – choosing between Jacques and her children – that she swallowed a whole packet of sleeping tablets and switched on the gas. Only the timely intervention of a servant prevented anything more serious than ten days' recuperation in hospital and being whisked off to stay with family friends.

Down by the Mediterranean, Anquetil's distraction was

clear for all to see: his legendary appetite was diminished, his training performances were well below par, and his habitual ability to sleep like a log was compromised. Finally, his anxieties got the better of him, and he returned to Normandy in an attempt to discover Jeanine's whereabouts and take her away with him. The scene when he found her address and knocked on the door adds even more potency to the Anquetil legend: it was Jeanine herself who answered, clad only in slippers and a nightie (or a dressing gown, depending on which source you believe), and the couple immediately fled into the night in the back of a van borrowed from the *Paris-Normandie* newspaper. Within a couple of hours, the lovers were shopping for new clothes for Jeanine in the chic boutiques of the rue du Faubourg Saint-Honoré in Paris.

The thrilling nature of their flight is still evident in her eyes when Jeanine recalls the events of that fateful night: 'Oh yes, it was an adventure all right, because when I left I was a doctor's wife, I had two children and a fine house, and I left in slippers and a dressing gown. I left without so much as a penny, and Jacques had only just won his first Tour when I left. I didn't know if he was going to make a career out of cycling. We didn't know. It really was jumping into the unknown.'

The picture of Jeanine swapping her well-heeled but conventional lifestyle for something infinitely and immediately more exciting inadvertently gives further credibility to the maxim that life imitates art. In particular, it reinforces the curious correlation between Anquetil's life and the Normandy society so powerfully portrayed by his famous literary predecessors from Rouen. This time it was not Maupassant's Boule de Suif, however, but Madame Bovary, Flaubert's most famous creation, who was being invoked. Bored, frustrated and perhaps unappreciated, Jeanine had emulated her fictional double and jumped wholeheartedly at the opportunity for freedom and fulfilment that life with Anquetil seemed set to provide.

Yet while part of the allure for Jeanine was this sense of romantic adventure, she maintains Anquetil was the exact opposite. Although happy to enjoy the high life afforded by his successes as a cyclist, these luxuries accrued thanks to his calculating approach to making the most out of his chosen profession. Not for him the whimsical notion of fulfilling a dream. 'Oh no, he wasn't an adventurer at all,' she remembers. 'He knew exactly where he was going. When he was younger, he'd told me he would earn a living from the bike. As soon as he saw he could be a champion, he set about riding his bike in the same way as a director goes about running a company. This meant he pushed himself to the limits to get the best out of himself – even his teammates acknowledged that he would suffer more than they would [Jeanine repeats this several times, for emphasis]. That was Jacques – he knew nothing would be able to stop him from achieving success. And if he couldn't have been a cyclist, he'd have done something else. He wasn't the reckless type who'd just say let's give it a go and see. He was much more considered.'

Perhaps for this reason he felt able to reassure Jeanine, even as they were driving to Paris, that though she was choosing him over her children she would end up with both in the end. On the other hand, perhaps his words were no more than the seductive platitudes voiced by a lover keen to reassure his quarry that she had made the right decision. Certainly, Jeanine's explanation of Anquetil's reasoning is itself unclear – or at least her memory of it is: 'I knew I'd get them back. I knew they'd come back to me later. He loved kids so much. The proof is that when he knew he wanted to marry me, even though I knew I couldn't have any more children and that that was his thing – he said, "Yes, but after my career I'll have a child, because I want a child of my own. We'll see about that later – not while I'm racing – because otherwise, by the time I've retired, it will be six or seven, and I won't have seen it grow up." That was his love for kids, and he loved mine as if they were his own.'

Rather confusingly, then, Jeanine appears to see this willingness to postpone his desire to perpetuate his lineage – at best a delaying tactic for not facing up to the reality of their situation, at worst a declaration of guaranteed infidelity – as proof of his love for her (even though he would have to use a surrogate mother to satisfy his needs) and confirmation that her children would return. Equally confusing is how such an obsession with becoming a blood father sits with her assertion that he loved her children as though they were his own.

Whatever the motivation, in the end, of course, he would prove to be right, no doubt judging correctly that the appeal of the glamour associated with cycling (not to mention a much-missed mother) would prove more alluring than the best a remote, intellectual father figure could offer, however well intentioned. Initially, the children were conferred exclusively to the care of Dr Boëda, who also had Jeanine's parents staying with him. 'They were with my ex-husband and my parents,' she remembers. 'My parents had stayed at the house to start with, so he used that as a reason that I shouldn't see my children. Then he showed my parents the door, so the children were left with my ex-husband and his new wife, who didn't care for them that much, and eventually the children couldn't put up with this stepmother who kept them away from their father any more.'

First of all, the children visited Anquetil and their mother as a result of the limited access Jeanine had subsequently been allowed: 'The children were already quite big – they were seven or eight years old – so even though they stayed with their father, they had but one dream, which was to come to the house and go to races with Jacques. They had an admiration for Jacques that was overwhelming. As soon as I had them, I took them everywhere. We took them to Italy once when Jacques was racing there, and I had to go to court because we took them one day early. I was acquitted, of course, because taking them only one day early . . .' The result, according to Sophie, was that within two years of Jeanine's departure the children started to ignore the strictures placed on them and made their own way to see their mother and Anquetil.

Back in 1958, however, there were no children to be cared for, and the two lovers concentrated their attention on each other, as Jeanine recalls: 'The happiness I felt to be by his side night and day, the freedom to belong to each other as we wanted, was so powerful that I even managed to forget, for an instant, the enormous loss of my children.' Anquetil endeavoured to repay the compliment by saying his motivation was to be 'worthy' of Jeanine. This romantic aspiration went so far as to drive him to make his first serious attempt to win Paris–Roubaix, then as now the most prestigious of the one-day classic races.

Jeanine even suggested there was a precedent for such devotion in his pursuit of victory from their youth: 'Do you know he won his first race for me when he was eight? He was still scared of monsters at night but could already turn the pedals of his bike like a madman. For me, he beat the son of the butcher by the width of his tyre.' For the romantic at heart, it may come as a disappointment to discover that this story is unlikely to be true, or at best to be apocryphal. Although Jeanine and Anquetil were both born in Mont-Saint-Aignan, by the age of eight Jacques had already been living in Quincampoix for a year. Even if he had taken his bike with him on a return visit to friends or family (although these were in Bois-Guillaume rather than Mont-Saint-Aignan), it's still difficult to see what the then fifteen-year-old daughter of a respectable family would have been doing watching an eight-year-old strawberry grower's son beating the butcher's boy on his bike. Perhaps the answer is provided by the fact that the paper that carried this story was sufficiently interested in the romantic to overlook such tedious factual discrepancies; after all, it also said that Jeanine was 26, while Jacques by this time was 24. In reality, Jeanine was nearly seven years his senior.

Unfortunately, the romance of the story came to an end with a bump – several thousand bumps, more like – on the notorious cobbles en route to Roubaix on 13 April (unlucky for some). Having decided to counter the acknowledged expertise in this kind of event of several of his rivals – notably Van Looy, Léon Van Daele, even Bobet – by employing the unlikely tactic of a long break, Anquetil and three companions (he'd dropped the rest) were still ahead of the main bunch with only fifteen kilometres remaining. Disaster struck, however, when Anquetil punctured, obliging him to make a solo burst to regain the lead group. Even though he succeeded in this objective in only five kilometres, the effort proved futile, as the main bunch also caught the leaders with only four kilometres remaining, leading to a mass sprint, won by Van Daele. Anquetil ended up 14th.

This admittedly unfortunate series of events, depriving Anquetil of his only real chance of success – breaking away on his own before the velodrome – immediately led to assertions that the puncture had robbed him of certain victory. For anybody other than Anquetil, this would be impossible to claim. For a start, his breakaway companions remained to be beaten – even if he was the strongest, this was far from guaranteed (although he maintained he was certain to have beaten them in the sprint). Then there was the fact that the lead held by the front four with fifteen kilometres to go had already been cut to one minute fifteen seconds. Given that Anquetil and his companions had been away for the best part of 200 kilometres and that the bunch behind was still made up of 70 riders, such a margin looks uncomfortably small.

Yet Anquetil built a reputation on achieving that which others maintained was impossible, and he certainly believed it was simply bad luck that had deprived him of victory. Bad luck, of course, was not an excuse Anquetil was accustomed to having to make. Demonstrating once again his desire for mastery of his surroundings, he declared, with a distinct hint of bitterness, 'One-day races are a lottery. I'm not interested in them any more.'

In doing so, he immediately exacerbated his increasingly strained relationship with the public. Although a degree of sympathy for his plight was felt, his reaction had in effect cast aspersions on a significant part of cycling's reputation. Although Anquetil didn't seem to want to admit it, there was more to the sport than stage races and time trials. One-day races were an integral part of its appeal, so for Anquetil to imply that 60 years of cycling heritage and legend – including everybody who'd been anybody as a cyclist, from Maurice Garin to Coppi, and from Magne to Bobet – was based solely on good fortune did not go down well. What had started as a fairy tale, with a homage befitting his stature in *L'Équipe* on the day of the race – 'For the first time in his career, Anquetil is starting a classic race with the declared intention of winning. Until now, Jacques has always achieved his goals. It's one of the most remarkable aspects of his career.' – had turned into a public-relations disaster. Worse was to come.

Before the 1958 Tour de France had even started, Anquetil had been obliged to mount another political campaign to determine the make-up of the team. This time, as defending champion, his presence was not in question. Instead, it was a question of who would join him – and whom he would accept as teammates. The debate centred on Bobet, of course, and Raphaël Géminiani, Bobet's right-hand man, previously a Tour runner-up in 1951. Anquetil could countenance one or the other but not both: 'They know each other too well. I don't want them to truss me up like a turkey.'

Eventually, Bobet agreed to the sacrifice of his former lieutenant, and what had seemed likely to be a two-way battle for overall victory between Anquetil, aided by Bobet, and Charly Gaul became a three-way tussle, with an enraged Géminiani banished to the Centre-Midi regional team. (He was so contemptuous of French national team *directeur sportif* Marcel Bidot that he paraded a donkey around at the start of the Tour and said he'd named the beast Marcel, as it too was stubborn and stupid.)

Keeping his promise to attack, Géminiani stole a ten-minute advantage over Anquetil on the stage to Saint-Brieuc before Anquetil suffered another setback in the first time-trial stage, losing his speciality by seven seconds to Gaul. In practice, such a small deficit was little more than a blow to his pride, although the extent to which Anquetil's pride was wounded should not be underestimated. Before the race had begun, Anquetil had complained to journalists that the time-trial stage up Mont Ventoux should not have been called a time trial: 'It's not the time I'll lose to Gaul that worries me – three or four [minutes] at the most. It's the fact that people will say he's beaten me at my own game, and I don't like that.'

The Pyrenees passed without great incident, the next significant event coming on the 17th stage, the day of the time trial up the fearsome Mont Ventoux (1,610 metres of altitude gained over 22 kilometres of climbing at an average of 7.1 per cent, with a steepest section of 11 per cent). Here, Gaul beat Anquetil by just over the predicted four minutes, while Géminiani put on the yellow jersey, a position he was to cement on the next stage to Gap thanks to Gaul suffering a mechanical problem, reputedly the victim of sabotage.

All of this, however, was merely the appetiser for one of the most remarkable days in the history of the Tour. The situation at the beginning of stage 20, from Briançon to

Aix-les-Bains, was the following: Géminiani was the race leader; Anquetil was in third place, seven minutes fifty-seven seconds behind; and Gaul was more than fifteen minutes adrift. With only the final time trial remaining as an alternative option for effecting any significant changes to this position, this last serious mountainous stage – two hundred and nineteen kilometres over five mountain passes through the Chartreuse – would prove crucial. Both Anquetil and Gaul had no option but to attack to reduce their deficit. Gaul initiated the fight at the start of the second climb of the day, the Col de Luitel (exactly as he had predicted, down to the very hairpin). In spite of the freezing rain that was Anquetil's greatest dislike – and an ill-advised decision to wear a light silk jersey rather than a heavier woollen one – he was still within two minutes of Gaul, and ahead of Géminiani, at the foot of the next climb, the Col de Porte. Here, however, the wheels began to fall off. Anquetil's own recollection is stark: 'From the first hairpins of the Col de Porte, I thought I'd gone mad. I was diminished by 60 per cent. Why? I wish I knew. It was as if my lungs were stuffed with cotton wool. I was suffocating. Standing on the pedals, I must have looked like a fish out of water. The last thrashing about before . . . Before what?'

Before the chest infection from which he was suffering would eventually knock him out of the race. But not before he'd lost an incredible 22 minutes to Gaul in the space of a mere 60 kilometres. (Although he was the only one with such a legitimate medical excuse, Anquetil was not the only one to suffer at the hands of Gaul and the weather that day: Géminiani lost 15 minutes and with it the yellow jersey and any hope of overall victory.) And not before he'd once again demonstrated his exceptional courage by completing the following day's stage, even though he knew any chance of winning had disappeared, even though he was motivated only by the contribution he could make to the team prize (worth around £3,000) and even though he was coughing up blood.

By the end of this next stage, the situation had deteriorated further. Although still entertaining thoughts of starting the next day, the reality of his imminent abandon became apparent when he was taken to hospital in Besançon with a temperature of 40.6 °C and X-rays revealed the extent of his infection. He later wrote:

> Never had I felt so lonely. My morale was at rock bottom. I imagined it was the end of my career as a cyclist. I congratulated myself for having taken out insurance for just such an eventuality. I pictured myself an invalid at 24, shuffling around the village trying to be useful, doing the easy jobs normally given to old folk.

That night, he had a nightmare about a phantom cyclist made up of raindrops. Every time Anquetil approached him, he would melt away, only to reappear several hundred yards further down the road. 'He had, of course, the sad face and modest smile of Charly Gaul.'

While Anquetil was lying in his hospital bed contemplating the possible end of his career, Gaul won the final time trial to secure overall victory. As if losing his Tour de France crown and fearing for his health and his future as a professional cyclist weren't enough, Anquetil had to face up to two more slights. On the one hand, he was almost entirely ignored when it came to invitations to the lucrative round of post-Tour criteriums (although it seems unlikely that he would have been able to participate); on the other, the public criticism of his lifestyle and his subsequent failings as a cyclist reached a crescendo.

'We told you so,' his critics cried. 'A champion can't live such a lifestyle with impunity.' His response was immediate and dismissive: 'Do people still hold that against me? It started when I was 19, when I won the Grand Prix des

Nations. No sooner had I bought a car than people were telling me I was getting too big for my boots. I went to receptions hosted by friends and people said I was out partying all the time.'

Not that Anquetil helped himself; he couldn't resist provoking his assailants: 'Here's the routine I'd advise for the evening before a race: a pheasant with chestnuts, a bottle of champagne and a woman.' Even though he was quite capable of such excesses, the reality of Anquetil's preparation was somewhat different. Just because he had a singular approach to training didn't mean he didn't train hard, which just added to the sense of injustice he felt at the way he was portrayed. Training hard usually meant long, sustained sessions at high speed – two or two and a half hours at fifty-five or sixty kilometres per hour, depending on the route – behind either Boucher on his Derny or Jeanine at the wheel of their car. The routes were planned carefully so that this speed had to be maintained even on the hills – Anquetil's task was simply not to be dropped, regardless of the terrain. Sometimes, for variety, he'd ride in front of the car but at a similar sustained rate, checking his time for each milestone passed.

The intensity of these rides should not be underestimated. Anquetil's friend and teammate Jean Stablinski recalled in a special edition of *Cycle Sport* magazine published in 2004 how he once accompanied Anquetil on one of these outings and wanted to stop after only 20 miles. Anquetil himself said he lost three kilos in weight during each serious session on the bike. All of which appears to have been sufficient to compensate for the relative lack of distance covered: he reckoned 3,000 kilometres would be enough to get to peak condition, though the season normally started with him having covered around half that. Then there's the meticulous way he'd prepare for time trials or important stages, memorising the route so carefully as to be able to know in advance which gears he'd use in any given corner.

Géminiani was later moved to describe his preparation for time trials as an art form.

Of course, all of this should also be seen in the context of the difference in approach to training between then and now. Anquetil, for example, wrote about his distrust of the newfangled idea of interval training: 'It makes me laugh. In fact, if I've understood it correctly, the idea is to emulate in training those conditions found during a race. But, by definition, each race is different from the one before and the one after, so it seems to be a red herring.'

Brian Robinson, Anquetil's English contemporary, confirms that the approach was not widely adopted: 'I came out of one Tour – Bobet was still there, so it was maybe 1958 – and I did the post-Tour race nearest to Bobet's home. I'd had a week off after the Tour, and I stayed at the St Raphaël training camp. The trainer there was an old six-day man. He said, "You've got loads of miles in your legs. You don't need any more miles. Go 30 kilometres out, and when you come back sprint for every kilometre sign." Which I did, and I was absolutely flying the following Sunday at this Bobet race, and I took every bloody prime there was. But he tapped me on the shoulder on the next-to-last lap and said, 'It's me who wins today."'

Robinson also points out that the racing calendar was so heavy in his and Anquetil's day – as much as 235 days every year – that training was often secondary to racing. '[Rik] Van Steenbergen never trained,' he recalls. 'He just raced. There's a race every day in Belgium, so he'd do his 100-kilometres training in a race. He'd have his car at the side of the road, then he'd wheel himself off, put on his tracksuit and head off back home. That was his training. He never actually trained as such. I can quite see his point, as that's what kills you in the end.'

In contrast, prior to the 2007 Tour de France, one of the big favourites, Alexandre Vinokourov, anticipated racing a mere 30 days. Even in 2003, when he wasn't a nominated leader for the Tour and was therefore constrained to race a full calendar in the run-up to the event, he raced for only 60 days before it started.

Nevertheless, the gap between perception and reality continued to grow in the aftermath of the Tour, with particular emphasis placed on the impact Jeanine was having on Anquetil's career. Her high public profile, her film-star looks and her proximity to Jacques certainly made her an easy target. This was further aggravated by Anquetil's insistence on having her close to him at all times, breaking the strict rule in professional cycling in the late 1950s of keeping women at arm's length. Sophie wrote:

> My father knew the taboo like the others. Except he wasn't like the others, and with regards to Nanou he wanted her by his side 24 hours a day. So Nanou didn't leave him. She was there at the start, at the finish, at the hotel. She drove his car through the night. She passed on his requests to organisers, to soigneurs, to the whole entourage. She even collected his prize winnings from the post-Tour crits [criteriums]. She was his mistress, his mother, his wife, his nurse, his manager, his driver.

This is borne out by Jeanine's own recollections: 'He couldn't do without me. He wanted me to be there all the time, so I drove, carried his suitcases, arranged his hotels. I drove 100,000 kilometres per year. That's without counting the month of July for the Tour and without counting the winter – December, January – when we were on the coast and didn't drive much. In the round of the criteriums after the Tours, I wasn't one of those women who just turned up for a week. I did the whole thing, and I did all the bookings for other riders as well. And in addition to the money I collected for Jacques, I also sometimes found myself with the money for his teammates, and even for some of his rivals and friends

– Altig, [François] Mahé . . . and many others. I had money in all my pockets, in my bag, in my hands, everywhere. Once showered and dressed, the guys would come and find me and say, "Have you got my dosh?" I was their cycling sister, and they were all very kind to me.'

The press was less sympathetic. Following the dictum established after Coppi's affair with a married woman – the infamous 'White Lady' – the papers operated under the principle of 'If a champion loses a race, look for his white lady'. In an unflattering play on words, Jeanine even became Bidot's 'bête noire', in reference to her assumed role in the national team manager's failure to find a French winner for the first time in five years.

Even those papers that purported to be more understanding were unequivocal in their assessment of Jeanine's impact on Anquetil's performance. In a *France Dimanche* article published immediately after the end of the Tour, entitled 'I didn't Lose the Tour because of the Woman I Love', the paper still felt obliged to emphasise his distraction: 'He stayed with her, hand in hand, right until the start. A few moments before the flag dropped, he kissed her passionately. When he got on his bike, his eyes were full of a very different passion from that for victory.' As if the point wasn't clear enough, the paper ran a picture of him lying with a transistor radio on his bed after a Tour stage. According to the caption, he was not listening to Tour summaries, but to love songs . . .

The couple, of course, denied all the suggestions that he was suffering from being in love, even though his dad enjoyed repeating the phrase 'Where there's love, there's no cycling'. 'Me, harm his career? But it's the complete opposite,' Jeanine told the paper. 'At the start, he let his training go a bit, but it didn't last. I quickly got things in order. He's just a kid. I have to dress him, watch over his diet, his training.' (She later told me a similar story: 'He didn't like training, so he had to do it quickly. He did three hours of training behind the car – one hundred and twenty kilometres – flat out. Then he was content. If I wasn't in the car, he didn't do his training. I was his trainer.' This claim is also given credence by Guy Ignolin when I asked him about Anquetil's apparent appetite for life rather than training: 'He was often behind Jeanine in the Mercedes for training. He didn't like training, but Jeanine forced him. He didn't like it.')

Still recovering from his chest infection, Anquetil gave Jeanine his wholehearted support: 'What would I do without her? She's the only one who can keep my life in order. Before knowing Jeanine, my life was crazy. I only followed a diet when I felt like it. I trained more or less seriously. I went out all the time, and I went to bed at the time when most people were getting up. Now, all that's finished. Jeanine has completely changed my life. She's given me my second wind. She knew how to take over from my life as a bachelor. She's straight away shared my life as a rider. It's quite simple – I'm not only her husband, but also her champion. What's more, she's been a nurse, and it's essential for a racer that his partner knows how to provide comfort in the challenges that he faces, as much morally as physically.'

Jeanine managed to provide sufficient comfort for him to overcome what he would later describe as the lowest point of his career, even threatening to give up cycling if he couldn't finish his first race back, a low-key criterium in Belgium (he did, just). Then, demonstrating his remarkable powers of recuperation, he finished the season with a bang, winning all three major end-of-season time trials: the Grand Prix des Nations (in another new record, his fourth in six years), the Grand Prix de Lugano and the Grand Prix Martini.

His fortunes were still on the up at the end of the year when Dr Boëda granted Jeanine a divorce. *France Dimanche* celebrated, with no hint of irony and with a back page devoted entirely to the happy couple, under the headline

'Ignoring the Scandal and Gossip, Following His Heart, Jacques Anquetil is Set to Marry the Woman Who Helped Him to Remain a Champion'.

'Everything is ready,' Jacques told the paper. 'Even the house on the banks of the Seine in Saint-Adrien near Rouen. Jeanine is restoring the pontoon so I can go fishing in peace and quiet.'

The wedding took place on 22 December 1958 in a ceremony conducted by Anquetil's friend Maurice Martel, president of the French Skiing Federation, organiser of skiing races for holidaying cyclists and mayor of the ski resort of Saint Gervais in the Alps. The wedding invitation showed Jeanine and Jacques in classic pose: on a bicycle made for two.

TEN

Italian Job

IF 1958 HAD BEEN Anquetil's *année terrible*, in spite of the happy ending provided by his marriage, 1959 didn't turn out much better. He started in upbeat mode by declaring his intention, in a bid to restore some lustre to his tarnished reputation, to up the stakes and target both the Tour de France and the Giro d'Italia. There's no doubt that becoming only the second rider in history – after Fausto Coppi, of course – to accomplish such a double would have had the desired effect. However, right from the beginning of the season, it soon became clear that if competing with a sporting legacy such as Coppi's wasn't enough, he would have another serious rival to contend with.

The emergence of Roger Rivière onto the global stage had been almost as startling as that of Anquetil himself. In the UK, *Cycling* was moved to write that 'his rise to immortality is one of the most rapid ever'. Two years younger than Anquetil, Rivière announced his potential in 1957 at the age of twenty-one by becoming world pursuit champion (the closest Anquetil would come to this title was his second place the previous year) and then by breaking the world hour record that had been taken from Anquetil by Italian rider Ercole Baldini. As if this wasn't enough, he repeated both achievements the following year, in the process becoming the first man to ride five kilometres on the track in less than six minutes and also the first to ride more than forty-seven kilometres in an hour. In fact, his new mark of 47.347 kilometres was not only more than a kilometre further than Anquetil had managed scarcely two years previously, it was also accomplished in spite of a puncture in the last quarter of an hour.

By 1959, Rivière was intent on proving that he was not just an exceptional track rider but was also capable of greatness on the roads, though this did not stop him from taking on and beating Anquetil 3–2 in an omnium (a competition made up of a variety of races) at the Vél d'Hiv at the beginning of the season. The first real confrontation on the roads came during Paris–Nice (or Paris–Nice–Rome as it was that year), where, as a result of the heavy marking to which they were both subjected, the two men were obliged to battle vicariously through the intermediary of their teammates. In this respect, round one went to Anquetil, who enjoyed victory by proxy thanks to the overall success of Jean Graczyk. The extent to which Graczyk owed his victory to Anquetil became clear at the finish in Rome, where he presented his cup to his team leader. Gérard Saint, Rivière's teammate, came third, and Anquetil had the added satisfaction of beating Rivière in the time trial.

Rivière didn't have to wait long for his revenge, though, which came in the form of victory in the Mont Faron hill climb, even if Anquetil wasn't present. Aside from managing to win a race in which Anquetil had never threatened victory, he also demonstrated that his talents against the clock lay not just on the flat but also on more challenging terrain. All this provided journalists with the ammunition they'd been waiting for to talk up the rivalry between the pair. Pierre Chany, one of Anquetil's closest friends, was no different. According to an interview recorded with Christophe Penot for his book *Pierre Chany, L'homme aux 50 Tours de France*, he had already been encouraged by Robert Pons, Anquetil's *soigneur* at the time, to goad Anquetil into a reaction with an article about this rivalry. (The goading was required in Pons' view because of the potentially deleterious influence of Jeanine.) Chany obliged in an article lauding Rivière's new records under a headline that concluded '. . . While at the Same Time Anquetil Eats Moules à la Crème'. Anquetil's reaction to this intentional slight reveals much about his character, though the conclusions that can be drawn depend on which account you believe.

When I asked Jeanine about the episode, she recalled it with evident fondness: 'Yes, he fell out with Pierre Chany, who was a close friend. It was in Italy, and I arrived one day, and he just wouldn't look at Pierre. I said, "Jacques, aren't you going to say hello to Pierre?" And he said, "No, he doesn't tell the truth. His articles are good, but he doesn't tell the truth." So I said, "OK," and went to ask Pierre what he'd done. He said, "I've no idea," so they didn't speak to each other for three weeks. After three weeks, I told Jacques to tell us why he was sulking and wouldn't talk to Pierre, so he said, "It's because in the paper he wrote that while Poulidor [*sic*] and the others are out on their bikes, Anquetil is eating moules à la crème, and it wasn't moules à la crème it was moules marinière." We had a good giggle about it with Pierre afterwards, but Jacques told him, "You're a journalist. You've got to get things right."'

Sophie also records the incident in *Pour l'amour de Jacques*. The only difference is the timetable – three weeks has become three months – and the explanation for Anquetil giving Chany the cold shoulder is the same: that he didn't like his apparent excesses being exaggerated unnecessarily. Certainly, Jeanine was keen I didn't fall into the same trap. 'No, you mustn't exaggerate these things,' she told me. 'When there was an important race, he stuck to his job. Merckx said the same thing. One day, they asked Eddy about Jacques, and he said, "Hang on a minute. When there's a big race, he's a pro." He liked seafood and shellfish and grilled meat, and I don't see any harm in that. But he didn't like rich sauces, and he wasn't a cake eater like Coppi.'

This justification comes in spite of the fact Jeanine is happy to recount that Anquetil was ready to wind up the press and his opponents – precisely by exaggerating – when he wanted to: 'He didn't usually smoke except on rest days in the Tour or the Giro, but when I was there and he knew journalists were coming he'd pinch one of my cigarettes and smoke in front of them to say to people, "Look at me. I couldn't give a monkey's. I'll smoke if I want to."'

Aside from this inconsistency in his dealings with the press, there is another problem with Jeanine and Sophie's take on the story, and that is that Chany's own recollection of events is considerably less flattering. For a start, according to his account in *Pierre Chany, L'homme aux 50 Tours de France*, the dispute lasted not three weeks or three months but two and a half years. In fact, although their paths crossed innumerable times in the interim, it took being sat together at a meal organised by another rider – Jean Graczyk – for 'the boil to be lanced', as Chany put it. What's more, again according to Chany, the discrepancy over the type of mussels Anquetil had eaten was not the reason for the dispute but simply an excuse for it – a means by which Anquetil could smooth their eventual reconciliation without him having seemed to have backed down.

Certainly, there is good evidence that Anquetil was not as fastidious about his consumption of sauces as Jeanine suggests. The magazine *Cycling* saw fit to list what he ate on a visit to the UK that afforded the opportunity for a profile: 'For the record, before his races at Herne Hill, Jacques ate hors d'oeuvres (sausages, meat, salad), sweetbreads in *cream sauce* with *creamed* spinach [my emphasis] and fresh fruit, and he drank spa water and coffee.' Of course, the fact that he once ate a rich sauce doesn't mean Jeanine wasn't correct in her general assertion. But it does suggest Chany's assessment that there was more to their dispute than a simple factual inaccuracy may be more precise. In which case, something often portrayed as only a minor spat in an otherwise long and intimate friendship in fact reveals the jealousy with which Anquetil guarded his reputation and the grudges he could hold against those accused of traducing it.

Whichever, it's also clear the gauntlet had well and truly been thrown down, both in the press and on the bike, between Anquetil and Rivière. (Before their dispute grew quite so out of hand, Anquetil's *soigneur* Pons told Chany that his article had had the desired effect in geeing him up.) However, before battle could be joined in earnest on the roads of that year's Tour de France, Anquetil had the small matter of his first participation in the Giro d'Italia to attend to. Although always in the shadow of the Tour de France, victory in the Giro would be no mean feat. Not only did the list of previous winners read like a who's who of Italian cyclists, from Alfredo Binda to Coppi via Bartali and Fiorenzo Magni, only three foreign riders had managed to add their name to the role of honour. This was in part because the focus for a lot of non-Italian riders, then as now, was on the Tour de France. Yet the bigger factor was that the peculiarities of the Italian race – that's to say Italian expectation of an Italian winner in an event organised by Italians and with the rules enforced by Italians – meant that it was exceptionally difficult for a foreigner to beat an Italian rider on his home ground.

Just how difficult is revealed by the recollections of Guy Ignolin, Anquetil's teammate in the 1964 race. 'Ah, the Giro is a bit "special",' Ignolin recalls. 'I remember one year when I was riding with Jacques, Arnaldo Pambianco, a former winner, asked if he could go ahead to kiss his wife and baby when going through a town. All the roads were lined with crowds; in fact, there were so many people it was like the Alpe d'Huez. I warned Jacques that it might not be a good idea, but he said Pambianco would stop – it would be OK. So, Pambianco went ahead, and we never saw him stop. He got a lead of nearly four minutes. He knew that the roads of the town weren't wide avenues, that they were a bit winding and that because of the crowds nobody could see him if he had a lead of 300 metres . . . It was a struggle for the whole stage to try and catch him, and it was Jacques who took charge. That was Jacques.'

Another of Ignolin's memories is equally revealing and suggests that the 'beat the foreigner' mentality was as much institutionalised as it was opportunistic: 'During one Giro, somewhere on the return to Turin after having crossed into France, there was a break with 15 riders ahead. We'd all been flat out, then there was a fall, or something, and there was a break, and all the Italians flew the coop. Jacques was in the break as well. All the cars with the Italian *directeurs sportifs* had gone past, but when our *directeur sportif* Géminiani wanted to pass in his car the police bikes wouldn't let him. He tried to overtake on the right, so they went right; he went to the left, so they went left. There were no neutral support vehicles at the time, and they wanted to stop him being able to help Anquetil if he punctured.

'After a while, Géminiani got fed up and pushed them with his car, and off they went into the ditch. Police bikes from in front had seen what had happened, and they stopped the car, and the riders got off and got their truncheons out. There's a photo from *Miroir Sprint* – it's a shame I didn't keep it – in which you can see the back door of the car, and you can see a foot coming out, and there's a cop receiving a boot in the chin. It was Louis de Bruyckere, the mechanic. The cops had opened the door and had begun to lay into him, and he was trying to kick them off. Eventually, the race director caught up and started haranguing Géminiani, so he said, "If it's like that, we're all off. It's over. No more Giro. We're off." After that, the break was neutralised, everybody waited until the bunch caught up and we all set off again together.' (Extreme as all this may seem, the story is corroborated, with only a few minor differences, by Géminiani in his book *Les années Anquetil*.)

As a Frenchman, none of whose compatriots had ever won the Giro (the closest any had come was Bobet's defeat in 1957 by 17 seconds), Anquetil was no doubt acutely aware of what to expect, even if he had yet to face up to the reality. In 1959, he would also have been aware that along with the host of Italian hopefuls waiting to chance their arm against him he would have to confront his nemesis from the previous year's Tour de France. Not only had Charly Gaul inflicted such a painful defeat on him in the Chartreuse, he had also already won the Giro in 1956.

Justifiably, then, Anquetil gauged his efforts according to his position relative to Gaul. After having taken the first pink jersey of his career on the short time trial on the second stage, he was happy to relinquish the responsibility of leading a few days later in order to concentrate on Gaul. The race would come down, he assumed, to the final time trial and the passage through the Dolomites. In this context, the unexpected bonus of picking up more than two and a half minutes on Gaul on an earlier mountain stage, when he managed to drop his rival on a descent, with Gaul once more claiming to have been the victim of sabotage, gave him great encouragement and a lead of one minute forty-eight seconds. With the time trial and the mountains to come, Anquetil's calculating mind explained the equation to the assembled media: 'I need another four minutes after the time trial to have a sufficient cushion before the mountains.'

Unfortunately, his victory in the time trial only gave him half the advantage he anticipated needing. In spite of winning the 51-kilometre stage at an astonishing average speed of 47.713

kilometres per hour (faster, it should be noted, than Rivière's hour record), he had the unlikely disadvantage of setting off one minute thirty seconds behind the Luxembourger. By 20 kilometres, Anquetil had caught Gaul, putting him well on course for the required margin of victory. However, far from disheartening his rival as would normally be the case, Anquetil's appearance galvanised him. Over the next thirty-one kilometres, Gaul managed the remarkable feat of remaining within three hundred metres of Anquetil – hence the relatively small gap at the finish of only two minutes one second.

As with the Tour the previous year, the denouement would take place on the final mountain stage, which covered more than 300 kilometres from Aosta to Courmayeur. Gaul waited until the last climb – the Col du Petit-Saint-Bernard – to attack, as he'd said he would. He also said he would take five minutes out of Anquetil, but this proved to be an underestimate. By the top of the climb, his lead was more than six minutes, and by the end of the stage he'd beaten Anquetil by nearly ten minutes. Although so often dismissive of his rivals, Anquetil was gracious in defeat: 'My consolation is to have no excuses. I didn't have the chance to eat anything in the climb, and I could say I "bonked". I punctured three times, and that could have happened to Gaul instead. But, above all, I couldn't keep up – all the rest is just supposition. Beaten fair and square, I'm glad it was by six minutes.' With a final dig at an erstwhile rival, he added, 'It would have been a lot harder to bear if I'd lost the Giro by a few seconds, as happened to Bobet in 1957.'

Back in France, his sights were once again set on Rivière, his most serious current rival, and the Tour de France. This in no way facilitated the task faced by Marcel Bidot in his attempts to bring together an effective team consisting not just of Anquetil and Rivière but also Bobet and Géminiani. The situation was exacerbated by the fact Rivière now rode in the same team as Géminiani, who had become a kind of mentor to him. What's more, Bobet's grudge against his former *soigneur* – now employed by Rivière – meant a special meeting had to be called between the four major players to try and call a truce. This was achieved with more or less success, as Anquetil made clear: 'For the rest of the year, I race against Roger. Today, we're asked to be teammates. The organisers and Marcel Bidot are insisting on it, but I will still race against him.'

Against such a backdrop, it's hardly surprising that the 1959 Tour did little to add to the reputation of any of these four assumed star players. Bobet abandoned at the top of the Col de l'Iseran, never to return to the race. Géminiani was not the force of the previous year and failed in his plan to help Rivière to overall victory. Rivière and Anquetil, meanwhile, neutralised each other to such good effect that although they were separated by less than three minutes with only the Alps remaining, they had let Spanish climber Federico Bahamontes and French national champion Henry Anglade (riding for the Centre-Midi regional team) gain a lead of nearly ten and five minutes respectively. Realising they were by now both beaten by Bahamontes, Anquetil and Rivière were forced to confront the reality that Anglade could still win overall and steal all their limelight. Worse, in fact, than the loss of the limelight would have been the negative impact on their respective earning power on the post-Tour criterium circuit. According to Chany, in an article explaining the convoluted selection politics for the French team, Anquetil's defeat in the Giro meant his standing was more precarious than it had been. This would have been exacerbated as a result of the shift in the balance of power between the managers of the respective riders that would have been caused by an Anglade victory. Anquetil and Rivière were signed up with the hitherto undisputed number-one manager Daniel Dousset. Anglade was attached to his rival Roger Piel, whose stock would rise considerably if he represented a Tour de France winner. Then there's Pierre Chany's assertion in his book *La fabuleuse histoire du Tour de France* of pressure from a representative of the producers of Fausto Coppi bikes, who sought to take advantage of Anquetil and Rivière's rivalry to persuade them to help Bahamontes win, as he was riding one of their machines.

Ignoble as it may seem, all this was sufficient motivation for Anquetil and Rivière to set aside even their own rivalry for the status of top dog and to work together to contrive a way to help a Spaniard maintain his lead over a fellow Frenchman. According to contemporary accounts, this contrivance manifested itself most clearly on the stage to Aosta. Bahamontes, always a timid descender, lost time on the long, rainy descent of the Col de l'Iseran to a powerful group containing Anglade, Anquetil and Rivière. With the Col du Petit-Saint-Bernard still to come, as well as another long time trial, there was still a chance that all three of these riders could challenge Bahamontes. The most likely beneficiary, however, was clearly Anglade, so while he was labouring at the front of the group to try to increase his advantage over the Spaniard, Anquetil and Rivière sat at the back and refused to contribute to the pacemaking. Thus demoralised, the lead group's attempts to stay clear foundered, and Bahamontes managed to rejoin – and with him went Anglade's chance of overall victory.

Anquetil and Rivière's combination as allies of circumstance had worked, and their personal balance sheet was sufficiently even to deny either man the opportunity to claim victory over the other. (It seems appropriate to describe it this way, as they were more concerned about losing to each other than their own performances.) Rivière beat Anquetil in the two long time trials, but Anquetil finished third overall to Rivière's fourth, even if only by twelve seconds. The public, however, was not impressed. The whole French national team was whistled and booed when the Tour finished at the Parc des Princes in Paris. The impact on Anquetil was pronounced, though perhaps not in the way that those in the crowd had hoped. Far from repenting of his actions, Anquetil effectively sought to immortalise them in the name he gave to the boat he bought to keep at his house on the Seine: *Sifflets 59* (*Whistles of 59*).

The year ended with Anquetil taking a leaf out of Bobet's book and spurning the Grand Prix des Nations. The way was open for Rivière to win the race for the first time, but, unlike for Bobet, Anquetil's decision did not backfire on him. Rivière lost to the Italian Aldo Moser, whom Anquetil beat in both the Grand Prix Martini and the Grand Prix de Lugano. It was with renewed confidence, then, that Anquetil decided to play double or quits the following year and omit the Tour de France from his 1960 schedule altogether. If Rivière couldn't win the Grand Prix des Nations in his absence, there was a good chance he might fail in his attempts to win the Tour. Meanwhile, Anquetil was intent on getting back to winning ways by focusing exclusively on the Giro (a focus that may have been magnified after the untimely death at the beginning of 1960 of Coppi, at the age of only 40, from malaria contracted on a trip made with Anquetil to Upper Volta, now Burkina Faso).

After a quiet early season, notable mainly for a surprise pursuit victory over Rivière, Anquetil started the Giro in assertive form. Although only second, by seven seconds, in the first time trial, Anquetil had taken advantage of a small breakaway to become overall leader by the end of the third stage. Although happy to once again let his lead slip mid-race, this time Anquetil made sure that he made no mistakes when regaining it in the last long time trial. Once again setting off behind Gaul, Anquetil reckoned to have upped his speed by five kilometres per hour when he caught him to ensure that there would be no repeat of the previous year's performance by the Luxembourger. His margin at the end of the stage was more than six minutes (Baldini was second on the stage, nearly one and a half minutes down), leading Anquetil to declare it was as though he hadn't felt the pedals: 'I wanted my revenge, and I've had it.' In *L'Équipe*, the stage was reported as 'without a doubt one of Anquetil's masterpieces'.

The impact of this victory was pronounced. Italian three-time Giro winner Fiorenzo Magni conceded the unique pressures placed on foreign riders in the Giro when he told *Paris-Soir* magazine that Anquetil was a class above the rest: 'He's the strongest of the lot. His class, his form, his tactical intelligence, the fact he doesn't leave it to anyone else to control things – all these mark him out as the big winner of this Giro. All the coalitions that could be arranged to help Nencini win would be pointless. It's the Frenchman who lays down the law and is the real boss of the peloton.'

There were only two hurdles to surmount before he could become the first Frenchman to win the Giro. The first was a literal hurdle in the form of the mighty Passo di Gavia. This unmade goat track, climbing to 2,621 metres with pitches up to 22 per cent gradient, was being used in the Giro for the first time. With the last spring snows still clinging to the mountainsides – indeed the top had to be dug out through the drifts – the stony, muddy track, scarcely three metres wide and without so much as a fence at the side to protect the riders from the precipitous drop, was a formidable obstacle. Contemporary film footage of the climb shows riders, including Anquetil, struggling just to keep going, while a report in *L'Équipe* declared it a miracle that there were no deaths.

The second was the reaction of the Italian crowds to a potential French victory. Their only hope lay with Gastone Nencini, winner in 1957 and now three minutes and two seconds behind the race leader. Their plan was simple, and every bit in accordance with the attitude described earlier by Ignolin: push Nencini up the climb of the Gavia. If in doing so they could obstruct Anquetil, then so much the better. By the top of the climb, Nencini, renowned as a dare-devil descender, led Anquetil by 15 seconds. In spite of this slender lead, Nencini managed to pull away from Anquetil all the way to the finish in Bormio.

Anquetil's own account, given to *L'Aurore* newspaper immediately after he'd finished the stage, explains what happened (and reveals the intensity of his efforts):

Anquetil: 'Give me a drink.'

L'Aurore (giving him a drink): 'Was it hard?'

Anquetil: 'Yes, very hard. I dropped Nencini twice on the climb, but twice he came back to me, pushed by dozens of arms. There were hundreds of them waiting to push him . . . When I saw what was happening, I was mad with rage. I started pushing some of the fans back down the hill . . . It's terrible in Italy . . . I'd have had to fight non-stop.'

L'Aurore: 'You couldn't catch him again on the descent even though he was only 15 seconds up on you at the top?'

Anquetil: 'No . . . though I took some risks. I thought I was about to die 100 times. And then I punctured again.'

L'Aurore: 'Again?'

Anquetil: 'Yes, once on the climb and once on the descent, because of the mud. I had to change my bike three times.'

In spite of all this, Anquetil had managed to keep a lead of 28 seconds over Nencini. The race finished in Milan the very next day, and Anquetil secured his first overall victory in the Giro by the same margin. 'Jacques Anquetil has made history,' trumpeted *L'Équipe*. He had also made a clear statement to his rivals back at home about his intent to regain his position as undisputed number one. Sticking to his word to skip the Tour, Anquetil concluded a triumphant homecoming by ensuring the ball was now very much back in the court of Roger Rivière.

ELEVEN

The Beginning of an Era

AS BEFITS A MAN with a reputation for being able to work out his victories to the smallest comfortable margin – often only a matter of seconds – Anquetil's calculated risk in leaving Rivière to contest the 1960 Tour de France paid off, though hardly in a way that he would have wished. Initially, everything was going well for Rivière. Winner of the time-trial stage in Brussels, he soon overcame his only rival for leadership within the French national team – the previous year's second-placed rider, Henry Anglade – thanks to a breakaway on the stage to Lorient in Brittany that gave him his first Tour de France victory in a road-race stage. It also revealed the naked ambition of which Anquetil was perhaps well to be wary, as the attack, provoked by Rivière with only Nencini, Hans Junkermann and Jan Adriaenssens capable of following, spelled the end of Anglade's time in the yellow jersey. In only one hundred and twelve kilometres, the Rivière-inspired group of four managed to take fourteen minutes and forty seconds out of the peloton.

Further evidence of Rivière's form and ability came in the Pyrenees when he won the stage into Pau, and by the rest day in Millau after stage thirteen he was only one minute and thirty-eight seconds down on Nencini in the yellow jersey. With a long time trial of 83 kilometres still to come

– as much a Rivière speciality as it was for Anquetil, as the previous year had established – Rivière was a clear favourite for overall victory. At the start of the 14th stage, from Millau to Avignon, Rivière himself was even moved to say as much with a degree of brio: 'I'm sure to win this Tour, and I may do so even before the last time trial.'

Scarcely has the phrase 'tempting fate' had such unfortunate resonance as on that day. On the rough descent of the Col du Perjuret on the lower slopes of Mont Aigoual, Rivière made the mistake of trying to stick to the wheel of Nencini, the same Nencini who had caused Anquetil to take such risks on the descent of the Passo di Gavia a few weeks earlier in the Giro d'Italia. Rivière was not so lucky, although whether luck played as important a part as oil on his rims – as he originally stated – or his consumption of the painkiller Palfium – as he later admitted in a newspaper – is uncertain. Whatever the exact cause, he misjudged a corner, rode into a block marking the edge of the road and was catapulted ten metres down into the ravine below. Only a carpet of leaves and branches saved his life, but it could not save him completely. The two fractured vertebrae he suffered put an end to both that year's Tour and to his entire career as a cyclist. Indeed, he would remain an invalid until his death, from throat cancer, at the age of 40 in 1976.

The circumstances may not have been those chosen by even the most Machiavellian of rivals, but Rivière's demise meant that by late 1960 Anquetil was temporarily free from a serious adversary, at least within French cycling circles: Bobet and Géminiani had both retired earlier that year, and the promising Gérard Saint was killed in a car crash. Although still not capable of asserting his pre-eminence at the world championships, where he finished eighth, Anquetil did manage to demonstrate his superiority in two end-of-season events.

At the Grand Prix de Lugano, Anquetil took his revenge

on the organisers, as he had previously on Francis Pélissier, after they had offended him by giving the last starting slots, normally reserved for the favourite, to Rolf Graf and Johannes de Haan. His mastery was such that Gilbert Desmet, the rider in second place, owed his finishing position to having been overtaken by Anquetil and, like Gaul, having been able to follow him.

At the Critérium des As in Paris, ridden behind motorbikes, Anquetil was just as dominant, breaking the record set in 1957 by Belgian great Rik Van Steenbergen. The event was also notable for confirming Anquetil's belief in the skills of the 'healer' Jean-Louis Noyès. Already a friend of Anquetil's, Noyès responded to Anquetil's confession that he'd not slept for the past two nights due to a sore throat by suggesting he apply his hands to the problem area. Ten minutes later and the race started with Anquetil feeling as peaky as ever. However, he soon went onto the attack – to test, he said, whether he could cope with the 13-tooth cog at the back – and he felt so good that he decided not to slow down. Everyone else in the race was left in his wake, and Anquetil was converted.

With Jeanine's children Annie and Alain by now regular visitors to the house she shared with Anquetil in Saint-Adrien, 1961 began as promisingly as 1960 had ended. In anticipation of a clear run at the Tour de France as undisputed leader of the French national team, Anquetil began to assert his authority early in the season with overall victory in Paris–Nice. Even better was his victory in the Critérium National, that year run as a one-off race and therefore his first major win in a one-day event since he'd won the amateur French road-race championships back in 1952. The results – Anquetil first, Darrigade second, Stablinski third, all with the same time – suggest he had achieved the unthinkable and beaten them all in a sprint. In fact, he had for once done as his critics suggested he should and taken matters into his own hands. He attacked on his own at one thousand five hundred metres to go and managed to resist the return of the charging peloton by two bike-lengths.

Whether or not victory was even sweeter as a result of an apparent cooling of his relationship with Darrigade, or whether it was simply made possible because they were no longer teammates, is uncertain. Yet the careers of the two men had certainly begun to take different directions, with Anquetil losing his former right-hand man and mentor, who had left to join the Alcyon-Leroux team. According to a gossip column in *Paris-Jour* magazine, and in a scenario as old as time, the cause of the split was not their own relationship but that of their spouses. 'Darrigade and Anquetil Fall Out Because of Their Wives' was the not-so-subtle headline.

'Françoise Darrigade is a straightforward girl, conscious nevertheless of being the wife of a champion,' the story went. 'Jeanine Anquetil is more of the intellectual type. The squabble between the two women began as a result of everything and nothing: the best hotel room that was given to the "other one", the dresses they wore, the people they visited. The two men, their ears burning, were being driven to distraction. Realising they would end up falling out, in spite of their best efforts, they decided – not without regret – to separate. They will now race against each other.'

Philippe Brunel suggests the story of the hotel rooms is not as anodyne as it might appear. 'Anquetil and Darrigade used to travel around the criteriums together, and often, as in the Tour, they shared a room, sometimes with Jeanine as well,' he told me. 'It's funny. When they went into a room, often there would be two beds: one big, one small. Anquetil, as the champion, always took the big bed, and Darrigade took the small one. But then one day he thought, "I'm knackered. I'd really like the big bed this time. I'm fed up it always being me who takes the small bed." But when he got to the room, there was Anquetil, already settled in the big bed. Darrigade had had enough: "Jacques, I'm fed up. From time to time, we should swap beds." Jacques said, "But why do you say that? If you'd come in first, which bed would you have taken?" Darrigade said, "The small one and left you the big one." Anquetil said, "Well, you see, everything's worked out as it should, then."'

Back on the bike, Anquetil beat Baldini by more than four minutes at the Italian's home-town time trial in Forlì and then won the time-trial stage in the Tour de Romandie, his last warm-up race for the Giro. Things looked promising in his second attempt at becoming the first man other than Coppi to do the Giro–Tour double in the same year when he took over the pink jersey of race leader after the time trial on the ninth stage (53 kilometres covered at a mere 46.573 kilometres per hour). Unfortunately, the assertiveness that had served him so well in previous grand tours and in the recent Critérium National deserted him as he let a race-winning escape develop en route for Florence. The beneficiary was Italian rider Arnaldo Pambianco – the same Pambianco who would later cause Anquetil and Ignolin so much trouble after his impromptu escape when apparently going ahead of the peloton to see his wife. Anquetil managed to claw his way back to second, but Pambianco held onto his lead in spite of the fearsome challenge of riding over the Passo dello Stelvio, at 2,757 metres even higher than the Passo di Gavia from the previous year.

Disappointed but in good form, Anquetil vented his frustration by declaring before the upcoming Tour de France that he would win the yellow jersey on the first day of the race and not relinquish it until Paris. With the support of a for-once united French team, Anquetil was as good as his word. The first day was split into two half-stages: a 136-kilometre road stage from Rouen to Versailles (won by Darrigade), followed by a 28-kilometre time trial. Having won the second by nearly three minutes, and having benefited from Charly Gaul losing five minutes in the morning stage, Anquetil had put on the yellow jersey with an already comfortable lead over all his rivals at the end of the first day.

This relative comfort was short-lived, however. The following day, on the stage to Roubaix, the French lost two team members, obliging *directeur sportif* Marcel Bidot to decide on a strategy of attack as the best form of defence. Putting all their resources on the line, the team set out to ride at sufficient pace to stifle all attacks. Initially, this approach was not widely criticised for its deleterious impact on the racing, as it appeared fraught with danger: it was far from certain that the French team would manage to demoralise its rivals before it had worn itself out. The outcome became clearer, however, thanks to Anquetil stamping his personal authority onto the race on the seventh stage from Belfort to Chalon-sur-Saône. Faced with a deficit to a breakaway group that had grown to 17 minutes, and the risk of losing his yellow jersey, albeit to teammate Joseph Groussard, Anquetil took it upon himself to react. According to Chany, Anquetil rode alone at the head of the bunch for 30 kilometres until his position as race leader was once again assured.

With the Alps and Pyrenees still to come, and with Rivière's accident the previous year still fresh in everyone's minds, there was no certainty that Anquetil would win his second Tour. Yet the odds continued to shorten as Gaul fell while leading Anquetil by nearly three minutes on the first serious mountain stage and was unable to cement his advantage. The resultant truce in hostilities lasted throughout the Alps, and the sense of frustration at the perpetuation of the status quo was palpable. When neither the inaugural mountain-top finish at the ski resort of Superbagnères nor the supposedly super-tough 17th stage from Luchon to Pau the following day – featuring the climbs of the Col de Peyresourde, Col d'Aspin, Col du Tourmalet and Col d'Aubisque – conjured any excitement in the race for overall victory, the ire of both spectators and journalists became manifest. Whistled and booed by the crowds on the hills, Anquetil woke the next morning to accusations in the press of having killed the race. Race director and *L'Équipe* journalist Jacques Goddet reprised Henri Desgranges' famous 'Giants of the Road' headline in distinctly less flattering terms. 'Dwarves of the Road' he lamented, going on to say that Anquetil had interrogated his rivals but none of them had been able to respond – the race had stagnated: 'Yes, fearful dwarves, either impotent, as Gaul has become, or resigned to their mediocrity, content simply with a good placing. Little men who have managed to save themselves, to avoid inflicting pain – cowards who above all are scared of suffering.'

In reality, Goddet, at least, should have expected nothing more. Gaul had declared on the radio on the eve of the stage to Pau that his chances of victory had receded: 'If you want the truth, I tried ten times to drop Anquetil and ten times he responded by going faster still. It's true that I can't take off any more, that my attacks are easily anticipated. I've grown old; I've grown old.'

By the time the race reached Paris, with Anquetil having extended his lead, thanks to the final time trial, to the more than comfortable margin of 12 minutes over the Italian Guido Carlesi and just behind him Gaul, he was once again barracked by the Parisian crowd. Even the Anquetil-inspired attack on the last stage, which allowed him to demonstrate his gratitude to his teammate Robert Cazala by presenting him with the stage victory at the Parc des Princes, couldn't appease them.

Yet, while frustration at the relative weakness of his rivals may have been legitimate, Anquetil could hardly be blamed for being a cut above the rest, even if that is precisely what happened. A report written after the race in *L'Équipe* starts by explaining to the holidaymakers who had complained to the paper about the dullness of the racing that it was really the fault of all the riders, before adding:

> Above all, it's Jacques Anquetil and his superior ability that are to blame. Anquetil is at the same time a champion and a phenomenon. That's to say, an example not to follow. He can do everything, and those other riders who are more or less in his wake think they can lead the same life as he does. They're wrong. Anquetil is a unique character. He can race often, no matter where and no matter when. Yet when it comes to the major races, and in particular the Tour, he manages to turn up in perfect condition.

This indicates a subtle metamorphosis in the popular perception of Anquetil. Up to this point, apart from his bad reception after the 1959 Tour – for the more or less justifiable reason of his apparent pact with Rivière in favour of Bahamontes and against Anglade – his success had generally been greeted with a good degree of popular acclaim. Think of his initial victories in the Grand Prix des Nations and then his reception after breaking the hour record. A certain lack of warmth with the public had been noted, as had a taste for provocation, but by far the biggest antagonism came from journalists and rivals opposed to, or exploiting, his seemingly inappropriate lifestyle. Now, however, his continued success and the dominant nature of his victories had more or less put paid to such observations. The other side of the coin, however, was that the apparent ease of this success had served to alienate the public.

Yet this seeming effortlessness was only relative. Anquetil, of course, suffered greatly as a result of his efforts. At the start of the Tour in 1961, he weighed sixty-nine kilograms, but over the next three weeks he lost 4.5 kilograms – the best part of a stone. This, of course, was after exposing himself to a similarly gruelling Giro d'Italia scarcely a month previously. The problem, from the point of view of his public perception, was that he didn't show it. 'He didn't want to show he suffered,' recalls Ignolin. 'He always kept his same tempo, his same position on the bike. He said to us, "You might think I make it look easy on the bike, but it hurts me just as much as it hurts you." He once gave us a little wake-up call: "I'm hurting as much as you. I've got sore legs, a sore back, sore everywhere. When I have to make a real effort . . ." When he was attacked by climbers in the mountains, he couldn't respond straight away, but he always managed to get back to them. He was very courageous.'

Part of this desire to conceal his suffering was to avoid showing any weakness to his rivals. 'Perhaps it was to encourage us as well,' suggests Ignolin. Perhaps the biggest part, however, was simply down to his essential character. 'Ah yes, the descendant of the Vikings. Blond hair, blue eyes, a bit cold, a bit reserved,' he adds. 'He certainly never wanted to show his emotions.'

That this reserve – seen by many as hauteur or arrogance – was an integral part of his make-up is quite certain, at least according to Jeanine: 'Being a star didn't change him. He didn't care for it or for the popularity it brought. We'd go into a restaurant, and I had to go in first to see if we could eat. If yes, then we'd go in, but if people started looking at him, coming up to him, we'd leave. He didn't like being recognised. He wanted a quiet family life. Eating in a restaurant with just me, he wanted to be peaceful. He was very reserved. He never threw his bouquet into the crowd. He said it would have been as if he were saying, "I couldn't give a monkey's for having won this race. I'll chuck away the bouquet." The fact he didn't was out of respect for those who'd given him something, but people took it to be pride.'

Another problem for Anquetil in the court of public opinion was that he also didn't show much emotion in the way he raced. He didn't understand the need to attack and had no desire to do so just to please others. In this, he has an unlikely ally. 'People often reproached him for winning the Tour thanks to the time trials, but I think he wasn't sufficiently recognised for what he did,' his great rival Poulidor asserts. 'I think that if you'd taken out the time trials, he'd have won anyway. He'd have sorted himself to do something special one day or another and won anyway. By emphasising his brilliance in time trials, I don't think we acknowledged what else he achieved. He used time trials, that's all.'

Nevertheless, while he could use time trials to engineer overall victory, he would – at the expense of all other methods, as Ignolin recalls: 'He just didn't want to attack. On one stage, from Angers to Limoges in 1963, I think, we wanted to get him to attack. A large part of the team worked hard for the first 15 kilometres of the stage to create a platform for him to attack. And he went. He got a lead of about 300 metres and then sat up: "I'm not crazy, you know. What do you think I want to go and ride 250 kilometres on my own for?"

'It's not just that it would have been an unnecessary effort. It would have led to 25 or 30 riders being disqualified. He'd have finished – like Merckx one year in the Pyrenees – seven or eight minutes ahead. It would have been a gratuitous effort, and then they would have reproached him, like they did Merckx and Coppi, for having killed the race. For having put a straitjacket on the peloton and saying, "It's me who's in charge."'

This touches on another criticism of Anquetil in general and the 1961 Tour de France in particular: that Anquetil and the French national team exerted their authority in such a way as to dictate the way others raced. Again, Ignolin suggests that this was somewhat at odds with the reality: 'In 1961, he took the yellow jersey the first day in Versailles and held it until the end, but I still won a stage, even though I was in a rival team.' In fact, Ignolin, not noted as a climber, won the prized Alpine stage over the Col de la Croix de Fer and Mont Cenis from Grenoble to Turin. The fact that he could do so, and the remarkable margin of victory over the main bunch of 28 minutes, is used by some as evidence of the extent to which Anquetil's real rivals were intimidated. Still Ignolin demurs: 'In 1963, I was in his team, and I won two stages, but I didn't win them in a sprint. I won from breakaways. One was a solo break and one from a group of five when we'd been away for one hundred and sixty kilometres. He didn't control everything. The overall rankings, maybe, but that's what he was there to win. He didn't block everything.'

Yet his desire for control over the things that were important to him, whether the overall classification or the time gaps in a time trial, was once again apparent at the end of the season. Returning to the Grand Prix des Nations for the first time since 1958, Anquetil surprised no one by taking his seventh victory in seven appearances and breaking his own record for the event. The manner of his victory – more than nine minutes ahead of Gilbert Desmet in second place, with former winner Aldo Moser ten minutes down in third – and the margin by which he broke the record – one minute and twenty-three seconds – gave the crowd no option but to applaud him. Yet Anquetil was furious. He had, in fact, been misled by his *directeur sportif*, Mickey Wiegant. Instead of being given accurate time checks against his schedule, he had been repeatedly told by Wiegant that he was behind.

According to Poulidor, Anquetil was far from happy: 'He said to Wiegant, "You give me the times to see if I'm ahead of the previous year." He didn't want to break his record by too much. His idea was to beat it by a narrow margin – like the pole-vaulter Sergei Bubka. Otherwise, the next year it would be too difficult for him to beat. But one year, Wiegant, as Anquetil was going well, kept saying to him that he was behind, and he pulverised his record. He was furious: "What will I do next year? If I'm not as good as this year, what will they think?"' Maybe the answer was that they would have thought he was a bit more vulnerable and that he would have been a bit more popular as a result. But Anquetil wasn't about to give them the chance to find out.

TWELVE

Just Because I'm Paranoid Doesn't Mean They're Not Out to Get Me

THE CONSIDERABLE LENGTHS TO which Anquetil would go to conceal his occasional weaknesses became clear the following year. The extent to which he had something to hide also became surprisingly apparent at the beginning of the season. Never at home racing in cold and wet conditions – which he dismissively referred to as forced labour rather than competitive sport – he had to abandon both Nice–Genoa and Paris–Nice, his two preferred early season warm-up events. As a result of a fever, he was unable even to start Paris–Roubaix.

It was against this unpromising backdrop, then, that Anquetil arrived at the start of the Vuelta a España for the first time. There was plenty at stake. Were he to win, he would become the first man to have won all three major Tours, a feat not even achieved by Il Campionissimo himself. Were he to lose, of course, the rule of the cycling jungle was that his prestige would fall to an all-time low. This natural reaction would be exaggerated by the expectation heaped on Anquetil coming into the race as a two-times Tour de France winner and one of only a handful to have also won the Giro d'Italia. What's more, the Tour of Spain was, and still is to some degree, considered a poor relation of the much longer established Tours of France and Italy. Certainly, in 1962 it didn't have the history and prestige associated with the other two major Tours: it had only been founded in 1935, compared with 1903 for the Tour de France and 1909 for the Giro, and had only been run on an annual basis since 1955. For Anquetil to not win such an event would be a retrograde step indeed.

Even more serious than Anquetil's usual and widely shared concerns about his contract value and standing in the cycling firmament, however, was the pressure he would come under within his own team. Since his meteoric appearance on the cycling scene, Anquetil had been in a virtuous circle of success breeding strong teams and preferential treatment within these teams – all breeding more success. The importance of the role of 'leader', to Anquetil as well as to all those who pretended to the same position, has already been made clear by the unhappy experiences of the French national teams in the Tours of 1958 and 1959. Too many leaders and the counterproductive rivalry that ensued revealed the less palatable face of competitive sport and also ended in disappointing results.

Not that Anquetil had needed such experiences to inform his behaviour. Ever since his antagonistic reaction to Francis Pélissier's decision to follow Hugo Koblet at his second Grand Prix des Nations, Anquetil had demonstrated an innate understanding of the need to assert his pre-eminence. He had clearly managed to do precisely that within his trade teams to date, but the winter just past had seen the transformation of his 1961 Helyett-Fynsec squad into two new entities: Leroux-Gitane and St Raphaël. Anquetil was now part of the illustrious St Raphaël team and had quickly realised the need to stamp his authority on proceedings, as his soon-to-be *directeur sportif* Raphaël

Géminiani discovered when he joined up with the team for the first time as an assistant in early 1962. 'No cohesion had been established,' he recorded in his book *Les années Anquetil*. 'The *directeur sportif* only had eyes for Anquetil, eating alone with him. He took exaggerated care of some, neglecting others.'

If an excess of leaders can rebound badly on team performance, so too can an exclusive focus on one individual. Anquetil's failings in the early season were mirrored by those of his new teammates. Only one team member made it to the finish of Paris–Nice, while all the St Raphaël riders abandoned the Tour of Germany. By April and the Tour of Spain, things had been going so badly that Géminiani had been promoted to sole *directeur sportif*. Although this was the same Géminiani who had previously fought tooth and nail with Anquetil, Bobet and Rivière for leader status in the Tour in the French national team, he embarked on his career as team manager by making explicit his philosophy of egalitarianism within the team. 'I based my approach on common sense, psychology, confidence, friendship and a sense of equality that I wanted to restore,' he wrote. Sporting reality demanded that there was a leader nominated for the overall classification, however, and Géminiani was happy that this should be Anquetil: 'Jacques Anquetil was our leader. He offered the best guarantee of success over 17 stages.'

Nevertheless, the harsh reality of the road and Géminiani's desire to let his team make the most of their considerable strength in depth quickly exposed Anquetil's relative lack of form. The victory on the second stage by Anquetil's new teammate, and current world pursuit champion, the German Rudi Altig, set the tone. While Anquetil's teammates won a staggering twelve out of the seventeen stages, including the team time trial that would give Altig the leader's jersey thanks to his stage-two win, Anquetil was relegated to the unusual and for him distinctly unpleasant role of spectator.

Languishing in sixth place after the eighth stage, Anquetil's situation deteriorated still further when Altig used an attack by Spanish riders as an excuse to extend his cushion over his erstwhile leader.

Whether Anquetil was now constrained to wait until the individual time trial two days before the end of the race, or simply persisted in his belief that this would suffice and he didn't need to attack beforehand, depends on which account you believe. According to Géminiani in *Les années Anquetil*, in spite of his insistence – and that of his teammates, including Altig – that Anquetil should take the race by the scruff of the neck, he refused to do so. According to Jean-Paul Ollivier, Anquetil's teammates no longer believed in his ability to win overall, and so he was frustrated in his desire to attack by effectively being left on his own.

Whichever, on the eve of the 82-kilometre time trial, Altig still led Anquetil by a minute and a quarter. It was then that Anquetil's insistence on his leadership manifested itself at its most Machiavellian. Not confident that he could rely on the race itself to overhaul Altig, Anquetil asked Géminiani to make sure that the German was not provided with a time-trial bike. This would have the effect of depriving him of the 13-tooth cog fitted to time-trial bikes and effectively limit his top speed. Petulant Formula One racing drivers could teach Anquetil nothing when it came to getting the upper hand, it seems.

Géminiani would hear nothing of it. 'Jacques, you chose to wait until the time trial,' he wrote. 'You wanted this confrontation. It's up to you to face up to that choice. You'll race against Rudi with the same kit.' Ollivier maintains that it was actually Altig who went behind Anquetil's back by insisting on a 13-tooth cog against a prior agreement that only Anquetil would benefit from one.

But surely the point is not the timing of Anquetil trying to enforce an agreement to be able to ride with special kit in order to be able to gain an advantage over a teammate but the fact that this is what he tried to do. What's more, Géminiani's version was corroborated by Altig himself when I spoke to him about his rivalry – and friendship – with Anquetil: 'He'd started the race as nominal leader, but then I took over the lead. There was a long time trial at the end, and as he was very good against the clock he thought he would be able to make up the time on me then. But I was also quite a strong time-triallist, so he didn't want me to have the 13-tooth cog. Perhaps he knew I was going well. Perhaps he felt that he wasn't going to win. But our mechanic said that he'd change my rear wheel anyway and gave me one with a 13-tooth cog.'

The end result was a stage victory by two seconds for Altig – paving the way for overall victory two days later – and an angry and bitter Anquetil, who abandoned before the next day, inspiring press accusations that he had been betrayed by a team that not only won more than two-thirds of the stages but also won the general classification, the green jersey and the team competition. The reasons for this abandonment are again rendered obscure by the various different explanations given. According to Ollivier, Anquetil had for several days been suffering with a temperature that eventually came to a head after the rigours of the time trial. Abandoning was the only option. Géminiani himself recalled no illness, limiting himself to the observation that Anquetil's decision seemed spiteful and worrying. Altig is even more to the point. 'When you lose a race, you're always "ill",' he told me. 'Yet he still finished second. Maybe he was "ill" in the head?'

Whether ill during the Vuelta – another potential explanation for the absence of attacks – or shortly afterwards, Anquetil was diagnosed with viral hepatitis on his return to France. Demonstrating once again the remarkable powers of recovery for which he was justly famed, he lined up at the start of the Dauphiné Libéré ten days later. His physical state may have been diminished by his illness, but his motivation was great. With his reputation both publicly and within his team beginning to fray at the edges, his whole season now rested on his performance in the Tour de France. In turn, his performance – even his participation – in the Tour de France depended on how he fared in the Dauphiné.

The omens weren't good. Géminiani was still the *directeur sportif* and confessed that Anquetil and Altig were barely on speaking terms. He also said Anquetil was in such a poor state that he was scarcely recognisable – even paler and more drawn than he was habitually. Two days of rain and fog made things even worse. Yet Anquetil, surrounded initially by a select coterie of teammates, managed to survive and even show a semblance of form before finishing an improbable seventh overall, a respectable 17 minutes behind the winner Junkermann. Géminiani wrote:

> All he had left was his pride and his courage, which was not much and yet a considerable amount at the same time. Dropped, half-dead, weakened, he rode a time trial each day to try and rebuild his fitness. Slowly, he recovered. He found his rhythm and a level of comfort. I've rarely seen such humility, and once again I had to ask myself where he found this formidable energy.

Anquetil's place on the St Raphaël Tour team – now that the Tour had reverted to trade teams for the first time since 1929 – was guaranteed, even if his actual participation remained in doubt right up to the start of the race. Given his recent health troubles, it should perhaps be little surprise that after the pre-Tour medical inspection Dr Dumas, the official Tour doctor, required a waiver to be signed before he would allow Anquetil to start. Even more serious, however, was the ongoing antipathy between Anquetil and Géminiani.

After his successes in the Vuelta and the Dauphiné, Géminiani had been appointed *directeur sportif* of the St

Raphaël team for the Tour. He had gone so far as to select his Tour team, which included Altig, who was still sparring with his teammate in the press, but would be based, Géminiani maintained, around Anquetil. Yet Anquetil remained unconvinced of the merits of his former rival as team manager and demanded the return of his former manager Paul Wiegant, brother of Mickey, even though Sophie recollects in *Pour l'amour de Jacques* that her father had previously voted against Wiegant after having apparently been led to believe that this was the wish of his teammates. It took a meeting of all ten Tour riders and Géminiani, as well as Anquetil's manager Daniel Dousset and the managing director of St Raphaël, Max Augier, who said he'd had enough of 'Mr Anquetil's caprice', to resolve the issue. In a secret ballot, eight out of ten riders preferred Géminiani.

Anquetil was now faced with two possibilities: yielding to the wishes of others, including Altig, and riding under the guidance of Géminiani; or foregoing the Tour. It was touch and go. As Ollivier points out, 'Never had Anquetil yet been forced to comply with the wishes of another.' According to Géminiani, it took a frank discussion at Anquetil's house before the dispute was resolved. He wrote:

> 'Jacques, Altig didn't usurp you with his victory in Spain. He's in no way involved in your defeat and everybody else in the team knows it, which explains why they voted against you. But all that doesn't matter. I'm here to tell you that they're more than ever confident in you. As for me, I'm convinced you're the only one who can win the Tour.'
>
> 'Great. Let's forget all that, then, and start again from scratch.'

If the relationship with Géminiani had improved, the fractious nature of his rapport with the villainous Rudi was still clear to see. The German won the first stage from Nancy to Spa to put on his first yellow jersey, and then again on stage three from Brussels to Amiens. Ostensibly, Altig was in the team to try and win the green jersey for best sprinter, although his own recollection of the tension with Anquetil suggests his aspirations – or at least Anquetil's perception of them – were higher: 'At the start, it was a bit difficult, but later, when I'd lost some time in the mountains, things got a bit better.'

By the tenth stage and the time trial into La Rochelle, which he won ahead of Baldini and Altig, Anquetil was beginning to dispense with Altig as a rival for the yellow jersey and cement his leadership of his own team. He still had to face up to other contenders for overall victory, however. Initially, the most important of these appeared to be Rik Van Looy. Although renowned as a rider of one-day classics rather than stage races, Van Looy was intent on changing that reputation. To demonstrate his strength, he and his team imposed a record average speed on the peloton as it wound its way through northern and western France to the foothills of the Pyrenees. Even 45 years later, Raymond Poulidor, then in his first Tour, remains impressed: 'Yes, there was Van Looy with his red guard that meant we got to the Pyrenees at a daily average of 44 kilometres per hour. Every day, every day, flat out. He really wanted to be at the front, and he took us at a crazy speed to the foot of the mountains.'

A crash put Van Looy out of the race, however, and it became the turn of Belgian hopeful Joseph Planckaert to threaten Anquetil's supremacy. Demonstrating the form that had already won him Paris–Nice earlier in the season, Planckaert wore the yellow jersey for seven days in the Pyrenees and Alps and earned grudging respect from his French rival, who couldn't drop him: 'He's a real leech.' It took the final sixty-eight-kilometre time trial from Bourgoin to Lyon for Anquetil to finally move into the yellow jersey, turning a deficit of more than one minute into a race-winning margin of four minutes fifty-nine seconds, which he would maintain all the way to Paris.

More significant than all of this, however, was the appearance of Poulidor himself, the first direct confrontation in a rivalry that would endure for the rest of Anquetil's career. Even before the Tour had started, there had been considerable speculation and anticipation in the press as to the level of challenge Poulidor might be able to pose. After all, in only two years as a professional Poulidor had already accomplished two important victories that had as yet eluded Anquetil: the French National Championships – a feat Anquetil would never achieve as a professional – and the Milan–San Remo classic one-day race – it would be another two years before Anquetil won a one-day race abroad. To add more fuel to the fire, it was common knowledge that his absence from the Tour the previous year, when still run in the national teams format, was not down to his relative inexperience or youthfulness – he was only two years younger than Anquetil – but because his manager, Antonin Magne, didn't want him to have to play second fiddle.

'Straight away, journalists set me up as a rival to him, as I'd been noticed right from the start of my career,' Poulidor recalls. 'I'd won or led a lot of races, and the public had also become aware of me. So, that got the journalists talking even more.' Straight away, too, Anquetil took umbrage at this parvenu, a reaction which Poulidor, with typical humility, still finds entirely understandable: 'He didn't react very well, and for good reason. I was set up as a rival, but I didn't have the victories to prove it. I had nothing.'

It looked as if nothing would come of the first confrontation at the Tour, either, after Poulidor broke his left wrist in the run-up to the start in Nancy. He only managed to ride at all in 1962 after being fitted with a special, lightweight plaster cast, immediately throwing doubt on his potential to mount a credible challenge. Far from dampening the potential rivalry, however, this unfortunate turn of events simply proved to be the beginning of Poulidor's love affair with the French public, which in turn would be a major source of antagonism between the two men.

'I had my arm in plaster at the start, so my popularity started from there,' he recalls. 'The first day, I lost nine minutes. I was low in the evening. We went through the feed zone, and it was a jungle. There was only one, so you couldn't miss it, but I only had one arm . . . I couldn't keep up with the first riders through the zone, then there were a few breaks, and I lost nine minutes. It could have been the same the next day, but I managed to catch up the first break, and it was OK.'

Things improved steadily thereafter, and by the time the race came to the Alps Poulidor was lying third overall: 'I did the first eight days with my arm in plaster and only took it off when we arrived at the Pyrenees. Then I won a major mountain stage in the Alps [the 19th stage from Briançon to Aix-les-Bains] and came third in the final time trial behind Anquetil and Baldini, finishing third overall. Our rivalry started from there. When we made it to the Parc des Princes, the crowds were on their feet, and it was all for me.'

This in itself was enough to irk Anquetil: 'How did he react? Certainly it must have been difficult for him. All the adulation was for me, so if I put myself in his place . . .' Yet according to Poulidor it was the practical consequences of this popularity that proved to be the biggest thorn in Anquetil's side: 'What was harmful to his career, I now understand, was this popularity, because I was paid the same rate in the criteriums as him, even though I hadn't won, so for him it was frustrating. I understand. I would have reacted in the same way, and even other rivals reacted in a similar way to Anquetil. I was casting a shadow over all of them, so it was normal that I didn't win. But then the more they didn't let me win, the more they ganged up on me, the more popular I became.'

Yet it was Anquetil who had equalled Philippe Thys and Louison Bobet's achievement of three Tour de France victories, a feat made all the more remarkable by the concerns surrounding his health only a few weeks before the start. Dr Hermier, the doctor who diagnosed the viral hepatitis, was certainly impressed: 'I congratulate you on this new victory, but as far as I'm concerned you should no longer consider me your doctor. You're not made like other people.' Further evidence of this unique constitution came in the form of the tapeworm from which he'd also been suffering during the Tour, and from which he was still recovering when he partnered Rudi Altig, his nemesis from the Tour of Spain, to victory at the Baracchi Trophy in Italy. Once again, Altig proved more than a match for his more illustrious partner, although it was Altig's own hunger for victory and his sense of rage inspired by Anquetil's atypical reluctance to prepare thoroughly that were more significant in his subsequent humiliation than his tapeworm.

'Two or three days before the race, we should have gone out training, but it was raining heavily, so Jacques didn't want to go out,' Altig recalls with a degree of relish. 'So, I went out on my own, and I found a road tunnel that was being repaired, and I rode up and down inside that for three hours. I was angry, because Jacques hadn't prepared as seriously as he normally would. The Baracchi Trophy was an important race, so I said, "If he's not going to train, then he won't forget this race in a hurry, because I want to win."'

This would turn out to be an understatement. After 70 kilometres of the 111-kilometre event, Anquetil cracked, and Altig had to resort to chivvying, haranguing and even pushing his partner. Pictures of the event reveal Altig, riding one-handed but still in the lead, imploring the hapless, glassy-eyed Anquetil to one last effort. By the finish, Anquetil's famous lucidity under duress had for once deserted him, and he was incapable of negotiating the final corner onto the track. Instead, he rode straight ahead into the crowd and crashed so heavily that he had to be immediately taken to hospital. 'Yes, he fell because he was no longer capable of thinking straight,' Altig recalls. 'I had pushed him and pushed him, and then I said, "Turn left, we're going into the stadium," but he just went straight on into the crowd. He had great courage to have held on for so long.' With considerable feeling, demonstrating that he too had the competitive drive inherent in all great champions, Altig adds, 'Fortunately, the time was taken at the entrance to the stadium, so we still won.' A sentiment no doubt shared by Anquetil, if not immediately.

THIRTEEN

An Insatiable Appetite

WINNING, OF COURSE, WAS Anquetil's *raison d'être*. When still a novice, he had been advised that if he raced to make money, he wouldn't win, but that if he raced to win, he would make money. 'He quickly understood that the best way to make money out of riding a bike was to win races,' remembers his friend Dieulois. It may not have been rewarded with great popularity, either with the public or his rivals, but Anquetil did not let this deter him. In fact, his run-in with Altig and the growing threat posed by Poulidor, both on the bike and in terms of the public's affection, only served to encourage Anquetil to even greater achievements – 1963 was to be his most successful year to date.

It should be noted, however, that simply winning any old race wasn't enough – the standing of the event was almost as important as victory. One of the great ironies of Anquetil's rivalry with Poulidor is that it was Poulidor – the eternal second – who ended his career with more professional wins (189 compared with 184). Of course, the vast majority of Anquetil's victories carry far greater prestige than those of Poulidor. Although prepared to go to enormous lengths to assert his authority, he was inspired by pride and a careful assessment of the races that were most important in sustaining his reputation – and contract value – rather than the later all-consuming gluttony of Eddy Merckx, for example. When Merckx was nicknamed 'The Cannibal', Anquetil was dubbed 'The Civilised Cannibal' by Jacques Augendre.

'I think it wasn't in his character to want to win everything,' explains Dieulois. 'The season was long, so he targeted some races and was happy to win those to maintain his status and the commercial value that allowed him to earn his living. He wasn't like Merckx. Jacques could have had a fuller *palmarès* [race record] if he'd really knuckled down to it, but he just based his season on the Tour and the time trials, and that was enough for him. He was quite calculating in this way.'

To this end, starting the season with his third win in Paris–Nice was the best way to demonstrate his form and send out a clear message to his rivals. The victory didn't come without some controversy, however, and once again it involved Altig.

Following the problems surrounding their partnership in the same team the previous season, Géminiani had established a policy of 'horses for courses' at St Raphaël. As a result, Anquetil had been appointed leader for stage races, while Altig, along with Jean Stablinski and Jo de Roo, had been nominated to the same role for the far more numerous one-day races. The distinction was not unique, and in principle would seem to have been a step forward from the previous year's tribalism. Even if both Altig, as winner not just of one-day races but also of the previous year's Vuelta, and Stablinski, one-day man par excellence and himself winner of the Vuelta in 1958, could have justifiably felt aggrieved at the division of labour, Géminiani was moved to describe the mood in the training camp at the beginning of the season as being reminiscent of the musketeers: 'All for one, and one for all.'

At Paris–Nice, Altig was to discover first hand how keen Anquetil was to ensure the first half of that famous motto was adhered to. Shortly afterwards, he would also discover Anquetil's reluctance to fulfil the second half of the pact. First came Paris–Nice, however, and an enterprising Altig took advantage of the tight marking to which Anquetil was subjected to gain a lead of 35 seconds over his teammate. Having learned his lesson from the Tour of Spain, Anquetil swapped high dudgeon for backroom politics and made sure Géminiani was on his side when it came to enforcing the team policy. In *Les années Anquetil*, Géminiani wrote:

> 'I don't like the idea of going into the time trial stage in second place,' he told me. Being the one behind this policy, I couldn't disagree with him. Fortunately, Rudi was as good as his word and didn't balk at the request. A rider with great class and a fine temperament, he made sure he lost some time during a stage, allowing Jacques to put on the leader's jersey that he would then wear all the way to Nice.

Altig's reward for his selfless team work was to finish second in anticipation of Anquetil returning the favour a few days later in Milan–San Remo. This was not to be, as Altig recalls: 'We had an agreement that I would help him in stage races and he would help me in the classics, but it was difficult. I could hardly wait for him at the side of the road. I did it once in Paris–Nice, then three days later he was supposed to help me in Milan–San Remo. But he only did 50 kilometres before stopping and getting into the car with Jeanine, who was parked at the side of the road. I said to myself, "I can't tolerate a teammate like that."' Perhaps revealing the reality behind his claims to be a born-again egalitarian, Géminiani, who places the same incident not in Milan–San Remo but in Paris–Roubaix, dismisses it as no more than a 'hiccup'. Either way, it marked the beginning of the end of Anquetil and Altig's working relationship, although not of their friendship. When I spoke to Altig, he maintained he had always managed to keep a distance between his professional and his private lives, a distance that allowed him to be friends even with rivals: 'In races, he was too selfish, so we decided not to mix racing and friendship. What I can say about Jacques is that since his death he is someone I have missed.' In fact, this is a phrase he repeats several times during our conversation, clearly wanting to underline the warmth of their friendship rather than any lingering bitterness over races won and lost.

Back in 1963, Anquetil was keen to continue to underline his authority. Beating Poulidor in the Critérium National helped, but the next big challenge was to remedy the previous season's failure in the Vuelta. Things started off well. He put on the golden jersey of race leader after the first time-trial stage, and the rest of the team still found time for three stage victories, including one for Guy Ignolin, while helping Anquetil defend his position prior to the next time trial on stage 12. Here, Anquetil was expected to cement his overall victory by extending his lead, but Géminiani records that as early as the 20-kilometre mark he began to look in trouble: 'His face was contorted, and he was sweating more than normal. With a move of his head, he made me understand that things weren't going well and that he felt sick and was spent. The last 20 kilometres were heroic.'

Anquetil indeed achieved the unthinkable in such a state and held onto his leader's jersey, even if he did lose the stage. This was enough to lead to plenty of speculation about his well-being, and Géminiani was fully aware that the rumour mill would run wild if this performance was then followed by any visible signs of weakness. Accordingly, Anquetil was whisked away from the finish area and immediately hidden in his hotel room, where he was in such a state that it took Géminiani and Anquetil's masseur working together to manage to bathe him. Further reclusiveness was impossible, however, as all the teams were sharing the same hotel and, more importantly, the same dining room. Géminiani later wrote:

Sitting down to eat without him would have confirmed their suspicions. Taking advantage of a slight improvement, we dressed him and, surrounded by his teammates and in full sight of everyone, started eating. All except Jacques, of course, who couldn't swallow anything and simply wanted to throw up. Everybody passed their napkins to him to allow him to do this discreetly while all our rivals seemed mesmerised. Having shown himself, Jacques could return to his room.

He could also continue to recuperate, which he did at a remarkable speed: by four in the morning, he had managed to devour a whole cooked chicken and some beer left for him by Géminiani. That his recovery was complete the following morning was confirmed when he became aware of the speculation surrounding his health: 'So, they thought I was out for the count, did they? Well, tell the lads we're off to Valencia [the destination of that day's stage] in top gear.' The fairy tale was complete when teammate Shay Elliot won the stage, and Anquetil held onto his lead until the finish in Madrid two days later.

Unlikely as this may seem, Ignolin was there at the time and confirms the story: 'Yes, he must have eaten something that disagreed with him. He was throwing up, and the masseur was hiding the plate using our napkins. Afterwards, he went up to the room to recover and ate some cold food during the night, and the next day he was going like a motorbike again.'

If the experiences of the Vuelta demonstrate one aspect of Anquetil's remarkable constitution, there are plenty of examples that reveal the more familiar, if sometimes exaggerated, stories about his levels of consumption. In fact, the reality was such that no exaggeration is required, even if he sometimes couldn't help himself. In an article for *Le Cycle* magazine, French journalist and until recently official Tour de France historian Jacques Augendre remembers two favourite Anquetil aphorisms: 'I tried to drink water once. It made me sick'; and 'Health Food? Such an uncivilised phrase will never be uttered in my house.' He also remembers Anquetil's unique way of paying tribute to Pernod for their continued sponsorship of the season-long competition for the rider with the best overall performances, a competition he won four times: 'He won a Baracchi Trophy not with lemon tea in his bottle but with Pernod. Then he got off his bike and offered his bottle to the journalists who were interviewing him and said, "Would you like an aperitif?"'

Even for Anquetil, such indulgence during a major event appears to have been unusual, notwithstanding the regular consumption of alcohol as a pick-me-up and painkiller by cyclists of the time. It should be remembered that beer, wine, champagne and even brandy were frequently consumed after one of the many café raids that supplemented the meagre refreshments provided by race organisers and team cars.

'I never saw him eat excessively during important races,' insists Ignolin. 'But after the Tour, during the criteriums, oh yes. I went on a few trips with him. I remember lots of steak tartare, lots of pepper and lots of champagne – ooh la la. After one race near Reims, there were four of us: me, Jacques, Jeanine and Shay Elliot. We took our supper together after the race at about midnight. What spices there were on the steak, and four bottles of champagne for four people. We raced the next day in Limoges, so we had to drive from Reims to Limoges. I had a sore head the next day.'

His friend Pierre Chany told Sophie of his exasperation at hearing exaggerated stories of Jacques' consumption being repeated so frequently that he came to be seen as a dilettante rather than a serious athlete blessed with unlikely physiological capabilities. Stories such as his victory in the 1967 Critérium National in Rouen after he had been drinking and playing cards until 3 a.m. on the morning of the race and only deciding to participate after finally succumbing to Géminiani's jibes that Poulidor was going to win on his doorstep. Yet it was Chany who inadvertently added grist to the rumour mill when he was involved in one of the most famous of all Anquetil's dietary exploits.

The location was Géminiani's home town of Clermont-Ferrand on the eve of the local Ronde d'Auvergne one-day race. In mid-August, in prime criterium season – and therefore prime money-earning season – it had taken a good deal of persuasion to get Anquetil to the start line. The only persuasion that had worked, in fact, came in the form of a promise from Géminiani of a lavish meal and plenty of liquid refreshment. Given what was consumed, it's perhaps small wonder that Géminiani and Chany's recollections seem a little hazy and in fact differ in the detail of who was there (in *Les années Anquetil*, Géminiani lists Anquetil's teammates for the event as well as a couple of former rugby-playing friends, while in *Pierre Chany, L'homme aux 50 Tours de France* Chany suggests serious contenders for victory in the race such as Stablinski and Van Looy) and also in the exact quantities involved. Nevertheless, both recall that Anquetil stayed up until 5 a.m. drinking champagne, beer and whisky and outlasting all his companions in doing so. For good measure, Chany adds that Anquetil needed to supplement everything he had consumed up to that point by having two fried eggs – washed down with two more whiskies – before going to bed, and was still capable of being taught how to safely eat the glass from which he was drinking (nibble the rim, chew it up and it forms a harmless paste, apparently).

Three hours later, Anquetil required some further persuasion, this time to get out of bed and make it to the start of the race – hardly surprising given the prospect of racing 270 kilometres over the unforgiving terrain of the Massif Central. In spite of puncturing after an hour and considering this the perfect excuse to stop (Géminiani only managed to keep him in the race by saying that it was an excellent way of purging himself of the previous night's indulgences), Anquetil eventually went on to record an extraordinary solo victory. Chany recalled the scene afterwards: 'When Jacques arrived, Raphaël, who was thinking about the purging, asked him, "Have you nothing to say to me?" Jacques replied, "Yes, you can put the champagne on ice."' The following evening, Anquetil won the criterium in the Pyrenean town of Quillan, prompting his British rival Tom Simpson to ask what he had done to be riding so strongly. Had he known, he might not have believed it.

The Ronde d'Auvergne may not have been the most important of races to a multiple Tour de France winner, and this no doubt goes some way to explaining Anquetil's singular preparation for the event, as does the legendary hospitality of the Machiavellian Géminiani. But even without such temptation, he needed little excuse to ignore the dietary rule book or to prove that it had no deleterious impact on his performance. At the Tour du Var in early 1963, Géminiani records how Anquetil was spotted by Antonin Magne, Poulidor's *directeur sportif*, eating a copious breakfast washed down by white wine. 'He may be called Anquetil, but don't be surprised if he's the victim of stomach cramps,' Magne called out to his team, loud enough for Anquetil to hear. Never one to tolerate implied weakness, Anquetil won that day's stage having ridden everybody but Henry Anglade off his wheel. 'By way of cramps, it was us who suffered,' Magne was told by one of his riders.

Anquetil continued to make his rivals suffer at the Dauphiné Libéré, gaining revenge for his tribulations of the previous year with a comfortable overall victory, his first in the race. Next came the Tour de France and the much anticipated rematch with Poulidor, a rematch that was expected to be too close to call, since the organisers had reduced the distance of the time trials and also the time bonuses awarded for winning them. With a very mountainous route and a resurgence in the form of 1959 Tour winner and climbing great Federico Bahamontes (the 'Eagle of Toledo'), Anquetil's dominance was under attack from all sides. Indeed, Anquetil was once again put under considerable pressure from the start, thanks to the incessant attacks of Van Looy (who would eventually finish well out of the picture overall but who managed to win four stages and the green jersey). He nevertheless reassured himself and his teammates with victory in the first time trial, though at only 24 kilometres in length this provided little opportunity for him to establish a race-winning lead.

Instead, and in unusual fashion, he had to wait until the Pyrenees to begin to assert himself. From Pau to Bagnères-de-Bigorre, via the Col d'Aubisque and Col du Tourmalet, Anquetil not only matched Bahamontes but also beat him in the sprint to win the stage.

By the time the race reached the Alps, Poulidor and Bahamontes were left with little option but to attack if they wanted to precede Anquetil in Paris. Bahamontes was at least partially successful, winning the stage into Grenoble and riding into the overall lead at the same time. Still, on the eve of the final mountain stage, from Val-d'Isère to Chamonix, via both the Col du Petit-Saint-Bernard and the Col du Grand-Saint-Bernard, as well as the Col de la Forclaz, Bahamontes led Anquetil by a mere 29 seconds, a clearly insufficient margin to assure overall victory given the 54-kilometre time trial still to come. He would have to try to drop Anquetil again. Poulidor, meanwhile, was behind Anquetil and had even more reason to try and distance his rival. This he duly did, attacking hard on the second climb of the day. He was unable to gain a meaningful advantage, however, and by the time he reached the foot of the Forclaz he was beginning to tire.

What Poulidor appears not to have known, and what Géminiani says he and Anquetil were both aware of, was that the new road over the Forclaz had been closed due to a landslide, obliging the riders to use the old unmade road. At the same time as spelling doom for an already fatigued Poulidor, this allowed the ever-resourceful Géminiani to put into action an illicit plan to facilitate Anquetil keeping up with the inevitable acceleration by Bahamontes. According to Géminiani's recollections in *Les années Anquetil*, he had chanced upon news of the change of route the previous evening. Concerned as to what this would do to Anquetil's morale when combined with an assault by Bahamontes, he planned to reassure his man by effecting a change to a lighter bike at the foot of the climb.

In 1963, however, a rider could only change a bike that had suffered some kind of mechanical failure. This was not enough to deter Géminiani, as Ignolin recalls, even if he appears to cast doubt on this having been a planned move: 'Yes, I remember the Forclaz in 1963. There had been a landslide, so we didn't go up the main road. We went up the old road. It wasn't really a road. It was just a track. It was no longer maintained, and there was no tarmac left. There was mud everywhere: in the chains, on the wheels, in the gears. Jacques was not happy – he was behind Bahamontes at the time. Géminiani said, "Don't worry. We'll sort it." Then he told the mechanic Jacques had a problem. Of course, there was a *commissaire* in the car, but he managed to say to the mechanic to take a pincer and cut the gear cable so that Jacques could have a new, clean bike to finish the stage on.'

Whether Géminiani should be congratulated for having planned all this in advance or for having simply reacted quickly when he saw what was happening, the effect was the same. 'It all happened so quickly, the *commissaire* didn't see anything, and Jacques went on to beat Bahamontes to the stage win in Chamonix,' Ignolin explains.

Following this up with victory in the final time trial, Anquetil ended with a margin of victory over the Spaniard of three and a half minutes. In doing so, he became only the second person, after Bobet, to win three Tours in a row and the first ever to win four overall. Poulidor was a disconsolate eighth.

Anquetil's achievement in having not just won a Tour that had been designed to reduce his advantage over his rivals but in having out-ridden Bahamontes in the mountains (two stage victories to the Spaniard's one) meant he received a far warmer welcome than in the previous two years. 'The most beautiful of his victories!' declared *L'Équipe*, moved also to resurrect the comparisons with Coppi that had littered his earlier career:

> Above all, he demonstrated that he didn't have to rely on the time trials to win, as he also won two mountain stages. All that remains for him to do now in order to be compared with Coppi is to win an important one-day race. At 29, he can still make this dream come true, all the more so having shown this season, through his stage victories, that he's far from having fulfilled his potential. That's no mean feat after such a career.

Yet still not everybody was happy, especially Parisian tabloid *Ici Paris*: 'Jacques Anquetil a superchampion? Everybody agrees this to be the case. It's just a shame that his bored and distant demeanour gives the impression to the public that he's the cat's whiskers, not to say the eighth wonder of the world.' The paper was particularly peeved that Anquetil had rejected its overtures to have him photographed next to Sheila, a pretty pop star of the time. 'What's she doing next to me?' he had asked. 'A charming young lady, who couldn't help but add a touch of glamour to his victory,' was the paper's disingenuous reply. 'He almost flew off the handle. The photographers thought back to another great champion, Louison Bobet, who would never have turned down such a delightful picture opportunity. But Bobet is a gentleman, and therein lies the difference,' it concluded.

This widespread public perception of Anquetil as cold, not to say arrogant, appears to have been at odds with his standing among his peers in the world of professional cycling, who hardly had a bad word to say about him. 'There's always been a "Daddy" in France. First Bobet, of course, and then Anquetil, following on,' recalls Brian Robinson, who rode with both. 'Anquetil was the Daddy then. He was a guy with more star quality than anyone else apart from Coppi. He had a presence, a real good presence. He was a gentleman. If he said something to you, that was it. He was very laid-back.'

Ignolin is similarly complimentary: 'He was a great champion, and I admired him a lot. To find myself in the same team as him was a highlight of my life. I did the three big tours with him, and he won them all.'

Bobet, on the other hand, alienated himself to a degree from his fellow cyclists, as Chany later recalled: 'He had a certain conception of prestige and of life. He was there to be a champion. He had respect for himself. He was proud, verging on being conceited. When he became a star, when he had his plane [at the end of his career, he had a plane that he flew in to races], when he was at his peak, frankly, he was difficult to put up with some days.'

Jean Milesi, another former teammate of Anquetil's, has a favourite anecdote that does much to suggest Anquetil's relative humility compared with his erstwhile rival was genuine: 'It was a stage in the Tour, and I did a café run to pick up some drinks and distribute them around teammates and maybe a few friends from other teams if there were any left. I had a beer left, so I thought I'd give it to Jacques, but we came to a small hill, and to get to him at the front I had to cycle past the whole bunch while climbing this hill. When

I got to him, I offered him the beer, but he said no. He was riding alongside Pierre Everaert, who said, "Do you realise what he's just done, riding past everyone to give that to you? The least you could have done is take the beer from him." By this time, I'd dropped back a bit, but Jacques decided Pierre was right, so he dropped back down the bunch to say thank you for the beer and to drink it. It was a good job I hadn't already given it to someone else.'

Even in the heat of battle of the famous 1964 Tour, the Tour he came closest to losing, and with Poulidor the most likely beneficiary, Anquetil still found time to help out other riders. Profiting from the skirmishes between the two rivals, little-known French rider Georges Groussard had managed to lead the race for eight stages and was still in yellow as the race spent its last day in the Pyrenees. 'The day before I lost the jersey, a stage with four *cols*, Bahamontes had attacked straight away. At the top of the last *col*, the Tourmalet, he still had a five-minute lead, and I'd only had a lead of about two, two and a half minutes on him overall. So we went down as fast as we could, and Anquetil was helping us in the chase. But when we got to within two minutes of Bahamontes, he went to the back of the group, and he didn't want to work any more. He knew he was close enough to him to overhaul him in the time trial the next day, and he wanted to save his energy.

'The result was that we were no longer closing in on Bahamontes, and I was about to lose the jersey, so I went to find Anquetil at the back of the bunch, and I said, "I helped you the other day, so can you help me today? I know full well you're going to take the jersey from me tomorrow, but I'd very much like to keep it tonight." So he came to the front and started to ride again, and he made such an effort that we managed to start closing in on Bahamontes. Everyone else thought that if he was riding, we'd better ride with him, and I kept the jersey. *Voilà*. And I was very happy, as I'd much rather lose the jersey to Anquetil than to Bahamontes, and I had an extra day in yellow. He was very smart. He knew that one day he might need a favour, so he was happy to return one.'

Poulidor, meanwhile, found himself in the unusual position of receiving brickbats rather than plaudits. He was even whistled and booed as the Tour finished in Paris, an experience which he said helped him understand how Anquetil felt when exposed to a similar reaction, even if it was for different reasons: 'Yes, I was whistled for finishing eighth. They whistled me because I'd lost and had been a disappointment. They booed him because he won too much. He was a metronome. All he was interested in was winning, by one second, two seconds – it didn't matter. He had a watch in his head.'

Of course, because Poulidor had been targeted as a result of his failure to win, he had the opportunity to rectify things (Anquetil never felt inclined to lose a race simply to elicit sympathy from the public). This he duly did, taking a comfortable victory in the Grand Prix des Nations. 'The 1963 Tour was a great disappointment to me,' he recalls. 'For that I wanted to ride the Grand Prix des Nations, and I won it with incredible ease. After that, the public loved me even more – this popularity would never leave me. It was revenge for me.' It wasn't vengeance against Anquetil, however: 'No, it was just vengeance against the fans – the same fans who'd whistled me a few months earlier. It was a reconciliation.'

Having also won the Grand Prix de Lugano, another Anquetil speciality, Poulidor was then partnered with his great rival for the Baracchi Trophy, giving him a clear opportunity to become the first man to win all three time trials in the same season. 'The unheralded French pairing of Anquetil and Poulidor condemned to total victory,' trumpeted *L'Équipe*. Yet although Poulidor had the satisfaction of appearing stronger than his rival, with Anquetil not taking turns at the front for the final quarter of the event, this was a pyrrhic victory, as they were beaten into second place – by nine meagre seconds – by the obscure pairing of Joseph Velly and Joseph Novales.

Could Anquetil really stomach the thought of helping his rival to a unique achievement that should by rights have been his? Certainly, Anquetil's apparent insouciance in defeat casts doubt on the assertion by Marcel Bidot that he and Poulidor could have worked together in the Tour to their mutual long-term advantage: 'I regret Antonin Magne being opposed to Poulidor being selected for the national team in 1961. Raymond would have helped Anquetil and most likely they would both have won one or more Tours. Together they would have dominated cycling for ten years.'

With the continuing exception of the world championships – where Benoni Beheyt's controversial victory over teammate Rik Van Looy overshadowed Anquetil inexplicably conceding his own chances by sitting up in sight of the line, even though he was well clear of the bunch – it seems as though Anquetil was not doing a bad job of dominating everything on his own.

FOURTEEN

Fourteen Seconds

FOR ALL THE MASTERY Anquetil could apparently exert over his chosen profession, he was increasingly aware of the uncertainty and fragility of life itself. Maybe it was because he was so intent on being in control of every aspect of his life that he feared the chaos of existence. Maybe it was the other way round, exerting control wherever possible in an attempt to counter the vicissitudes of fate. Certainly, no one should be in any doubt about the extent to which his control of his family life mirrored his mastery on a bike. In *Pour l'amour de Jacques*, Sophie wrote:

> He was Master Jacques, a feudal lord, a sovereign surrounded by his vassals for whom he ensured protection and happiness in the kindest and most generous way. He rarely gave an order, rarely imposed his will, was neither capricious nor moody, but when he made a rule it could never be queried. And it wasn't, of course. The first of these rules was: no one apart from Nanou could tell him what he should or shouldn't do.

Whatever the precise psychology behind this apparent contradiction, Anquetil was confronted with death – the most painful and uncontrollable event of all – just as he was celebrating his most successful season to date. He had already been closely exposed to the death of his idol Coppi in 1960, as well as to those of his fellow Norman Gérard Saint (in a car crash) and most recently his former *soigneur* Robert Pons (another road accident). Now it was the untimely turn of his father, knocked down while crossing the road. Anquetil was on holiday in New Caledonia at the time and flew home immediately for the funeral in Quincampoix. On the way back, he told Jeanine that he was certain he wouldn't live to be as old as his father, who was 56 at the time of his death. 'When his dad died, it was the same year as Kennedy – 1963,' she recalls. 'When we were flying back from holiday in the plane, he told me, "I won't last as long as him."' His later behaviour would go a long way to giving the impression that this had become a self-fulfilling prophecy.

Having recovered from the grief of losing his father, however, Anquetil had his mind firmly set on fulfilling a less ghoulish prediction, one of the few cycling ambitions to have so far escaped him in spite of having made a concerted effort in both 1959 and 1961. The plan was to once again try to become the first man since Coppi to complete victories in the Giro d'Italia and the Tour de France in the same season, a feat Coppi had accomplished twice (in 1949 and 1952).

First, though, Anquetil had to face up to the apparent progress of Poulidor, who beat him in the admittedly hilly time trial in Paris–Nice before losing the chance to take his first overall victory as a result of a fall. Anquetil finished sixth, for once content to let his rival take the limelight while he laid the foundations for the bigger fish he hoped to fry later in the season. Nevertheless, his withdrawal from the Critérium National due to the snowy conditions – and his impotence in the face of another Poulidor victory as a result – seems to have been sufficient to goad him into an unlikely response. Flying in the face of more than ten years of diffidence and indifference to one-day classics, Anquetil surprised both his immediate adversaries and the whole of the cycling world with victory in the Ghent–Wevelgem one-day race.

L'Équipe's headline sums up the amazement: 'Jacques Anquetil Baffles the Belgians in Three Stunning Kilometres'. René de la Tour's race description was almost a eulogy:

> Must we really believe Jacques Anquetil when he so often maintains that, given his prodigious abilities in stage races and time trials, it would be asking too much to expect him to be as successful in one-day races? In those races where he has to confront a plethora of rivals with far more limited horizons? What right do we have to ask this of him? What Jacques achieved before our very eyes in Ghent–Wevelgem was truly exceptional. You have to ask yourself if any other rider in the world could have resisted, as he did, for three kilometres against the massed ranks of the best Belgians, intent on preventing the Norman win in their own backyard. Once Anquetil has decided to give it his all, you need at least two or three dozen riders working together to pull him back. And there were at least this number chasing him, under the urgings of their leaders, Van Looy, Beheyt, [Peter] Post, trying to make up the 40 metres he had acquired after having jumped from the back of the group (a model attack if ever there was one). They might as well have been chasing a rocket launched from Cape Kennedy! When he crossed the line at Wevelgem, utterly relaxed, with a smile on his face and no sign of his efforts, he was still well clear. Sitting bolt upright, he was practically free-wheeling.

If this unheralded victory was designed to seduce the critics, it was a complete success. If the motivation was to unsettle Poulidor, however, it seemed to make no impact. In fact, Poulidor responded with a compelling performance of his own, equalling Anquetil's achievement of winning the Vuelta a España, only for Poulidor this was victory at his first attempt. What's more, he won the race *à l'Anquetil*, that's to say in the final time trial – with a confidence no doubt reinforced by his time-trial performances at the end of the previous season – and then upped the stakes by declaring to the assembled press that he was now on a par with Anquetil in races against the clock: 'Until recently, I suffered from something of a complex with regards to my talents as a time-triallist compared to those of Anquetil. But now that's gone: henceforth I'm no longer afraid of him.'

By May and the start of the Giro, the spotlight was back on Anquetil. As in 1961, Anquetil won the early time trial – this time on stage five, with victory achieved at a staggering forty-eight kilometres per hour – and put on the pink jersey of race leader. Unlike in 1961, Anquetil was fully focused on maintaining this position in spite of the difficulties of being a foreigner leading the most important Italian race. Indeed, Anquetil decided to take a leaf out of their own book – when in Rome, after all – and employ the traditional Italian football philosophy of *catenaccio* (literally the 'door bolt'), mounting a meticulous defence against all attacks. These attacks, of course, came in many forms, and not just on the bike.

First came the conditions of the race itself, as Anquetil's teammate Ignolin recalls: 'There was a hilly, transitional stage, ending with a ten-kilometre climb and a ten-kilometre descent with the finish at the bottom. The last ten kilometres, it was just rocks – there was no tarmac at all, and we were all puncturing. All of us. Suddenly, the team car punctured as well – the front wheel, no less. Géminiani had to do the descent on the rim, but he couldn't keep up with the riders, so he said to Louis de Bruyckere – the team mechanic – take the bike from the roof and try to follow Jacques and give him the bike if he punctures. So Louis set off in his blue overalls on the spare bike and rode to the end of the stage. Géminiani finished the stage on the rim, by which time it was no longer round – it was star-shaped. All of the tyre had disappeared – like in Formula

One. They framed the rim and hung it on the wall of the service workshop.'

Next were the subtle, and not so subtle, attempts by adversaries and organisers alike to encourage Anquetil's demise. Indeed, one of these incidents was so brazen as to inspire the normally reserved Anquetil to lose his cool. 'I only saw him angry once,' says Ignolin. 'It was at the start of a stage south of Naples. The Italians had started riding, but there hadn't been a whistle, a horn, a loud-speaker announcement . . . anything. It wasn't the fault of the riders, it was the organisers – they didn't care. Now the start is more clear cut, but at the time we just got together in a square, and the spectators were in and amongst us. They came to say hello, shake our hands, talk to us . . . So all the Italians had gone, and we were hemmed in by hundreds and hundreds of supporters, and it was impossible to get started. Even the cars couldn't get out. And that was when Jacques got angry. He picked up his bike and spun it round above his head . . . people were being hit on the head by his wheels. Even after we'd set off, the cars couldn't follow, because they were still hemmed in. The effort we had to make to catch the group was quite something.'

Only after all this could Anquetil concentrate on the bicycle race itself, including Pambianco's attempted skulduggery, disguised as affection for his wife. Even this wasn't as straightforward as his uninterrupted wearing of the pink jersey from stage five to the finish in Milan suggests. Ignolin once more: 'He fell on a descent during a short stage, near Genoa, perhaps. It was raining. Another rider slipped in front of him, touched him and they fell into a ditch. We asked Géminiani if we should wait, but he said, "No, he'll be all right." But we did wait at the bottom of the descent, as all the leading Italians – maybe 20 of them – attacked when they realised Jacques was not there. Once he caught us, we embarked on a team time trial to help him regain the lead group, but he dropped all of us one by one, and in the end got back up to them on his own. Then, once he'd caught them up, he didn't content himself with riding with them. Once he was there, he went straight to the front of the breakaway and dragged them all along at 60 kilometres per hour – to show them just how strong he was.'

In fact, even more than forty years later, Ignolin still seems amazed at what they had to endure in the space of three weeks and at how well Anquetil fared: 'In this one Giro, there was Pambianco's trick, the stony descent that wasn't a road, not being able to start at the same time as the others, and the fall Jacques suffered and having to chase back to the lead group on his own after dropping us all. The next day, there was no more attacking. The Italians were asking Jacques if he'd let them win a stage. They realised he was unbeatable.' When you also add in the famous incident of Géminiani's fight with the Italian police as they tried to stop him supporting Anquetil in a break, the arrival on the scene of future winner Gianni Motta and a wrist hurt in the fall remembered by Ignolin, it is no wonder that *L'Équipe* described his overall performance as a 'Giro of attrition'.

And it is no wonder that there was also considerable concern in the St Raphaël team and in the press about the ability of Anquetil to recover from such an ordeal in time for the Tour de France, which started only 15 days later. Poulidor, of course, had had much longer to prepare after his victory in Spain.

He also hadn't had to cope with such distractions as having his death predicted in a national newspaper. Yet this was precisely what Anquetil had to confront as he attempted the already precarious balancing act of physiological recuperation and psychological preparation. Géminiani can hardly conceal his contempt as he records in *Les années Anquetil* the impact of the assertion by the 'seer' Jacques Belline in *France Soir* that Anquetil would die in a fall during the 14th stage of the Tour:

He really must have been a complete degenerate to put such bollocks in a national newspaper. Jacques, hypersensitive, reacted to the article as if he'd been smacked in the face. I tried to pour scorn on the idea of a 'seer', but I couldn't manage to reassure him.

Yet the exact extent of the effect this had on Anquetil seems open to question. Géminiani maintains Anquetil's innate concerns about the fragility of life – brought home so tragically less than a year before by the death of his father – meant he was vulnerable to this type of comment and became a nervous wreck. If the prediction itself wasn't enough, he also says that he had to sort through letters sent to Anquetil, trying to remove those with cuttings from the paper or unpleasant references to his possible fate.

Certainly, it's clear Anquetil had a surprisingly open mind on some practices of dubious scientific merit, in spite of his meticulous and methodical approach to winning bike races. He was already an avowed disciple, for example, of the curious pseudoscience of '*magnetisme*' as practised by the healer Jean-Louis Noyès. It was Noyès who had 'laid his hands' on Anquetil's sore throat prior to him setting a new record in his 1960 victory in the Critérium des As. Ever since, Anquetil had been a regular visitor. 'He never enters a race without having come to see me first,' Noyès 'the man with the golden fingers' told *France Dimanche*. As well as Noyès, Anquetil also made use of the *magnetisme* and 'double-action baths' provided by a certain Marthe Burger. He even went so far as to write her a dedication for an advertisement: 'To Marthe Burger, whose baths have helped me regain form and have supported my efforts, both before and during races.'

'He definitely had a side of him that was easily impressed by certain things – people who'd managed to do things that weren't entirely logical – as with all people who'd managed to do remarkable things, physical or otherwise,' acknowledges Dieulois. 'He wasn't quite credulous, but he was catholic, ready to believe that you could heal yourself in a certain way because someone had said so.' Jeanine simply describes him as being superstitious: 'When he was about to set off on the Tour, he had to see his *magnetiseur*, his hairdresser and suffer behind a Derny for 120 kilometres. If not, he said he felt handicapped.'

Yet equally certain is that others who knew him assert that he wasn't the kind of person to be bothered by a spurious prediction in a newspaper. Bernard Hinault, Anquetil's only rival for the title of best French cyclist ever, became so close to him as to have been asked to be his son Christopher's godfather. When I asked him if he thought Anquetil would have been worried by Belline's prediction, Hinault derided the notion entirely with the same unflinching stare he used to dismiss assaults on his pre-eminence as a cyclist: 'I think he believed in *magnetisme* a bit – a bit. But in the "seer", I don't think so. That wasn't really his style. At least, I don't think so. From what I knew of him, he was more inclined towards astronomy, but as for it making him scared? It's not the sort of thing that would have scared him. No, no, no.'

His former teammate Ignolin is just as adamant that Anquetil would not have been unsettled by astrological gibberish, as is Georges Groussard, his friend and former fellow professional cyclist from the 1960s: 'I don't really think he was scared. He might have said so to the journalists, but I don't think he really felt it himself.'

Groussard, a journeyman professional from Brittany with only a handful of professional victories to his name, exclusively in criteriums, was to play an unlikely but crucial role in the outcome of the 1964 Tour de France, a race that would in many ways come to define Anquetil's career. I met him at his elegant detached house in the attractive Brittany town of Fougères, where he was born and where he returned to work after his eight-year career as a professional cyclist. Now retired, but still busy on the eve of the cyclosportive (a long-distance cycling event for amateurs) organised by the local club in his honour, he was happy to reminisce about his brief spell in the limelight when he rubbed shoulders with cycling superstars thanks to wearing the yellow jersey for ten stages and finishing fifth overall in one of the most famous bicycle races ever. While Anquetil and Poulidor, and other rivals such as Bahamontes, were busy watching each other, the unheralded Groussard stole a march on all of them.

'I took the yellow jersey on the first stage in the Alps, to Briançon over the Col du Télégraphe and the Col du Galibier,' he recalls with an impressive memory for detail. 'I had already been in the breakaway the day before when we took thirty seconds out of Anquetil, and then I was in the breakaway that day and took another four minutes, so I took the yellow jersey in Briançon. The next day was over the Col de Vars and the Col de Restefond [at the time the highest motorable road in Europe], so I kept the yellow jersey in Monaco [when Anquetil beat Simpson in the sprint for stage victory and took a minute out of Poulidor in time bonuses after Poulidor had sprinted a lap too early]. Then there were some flat stages and a short time trial, and I kept the yellow jersey through them – I had four minutes over Anquetil, so I had enough in hand. Then we got to the Pyrenees.'

It was here that the drama really started, though the initial interest was not focused on the race but on Anquetil's activities on the rest day in Andorra – the day before the much anticipated 14th stage. In an attempt, Géminiani maintains, to distract Anquetil from what lay ahead, the pair, along with Jeanine, went to a *mechoui* (a lamb roast) hosted by Radio Andorra. Although even Géminiani maintains Anquetil's consumption was not excessive, this well-publicised – and well-photographed – visit immediately created a furore. Even though the journalists should perhaps have known better, this being Jacques Anquetil, the sight of him tucking into a rare leg of lamb, washed down with a glass of wine while the majority of his rivals would have been out on a training ride, was too much to resist.

The articles the next day once again calling into question Anquetil's professionalism seemed to have been remarkably prescient within a few kilometres of the start of that day's stage – the fateful stage 14. The stage ran from Andorra to Toulouse and was largely flat apart from the ascension, immediately after the start, of the Col d'Envalira. By the top, only the moral support – and strong arms – of Anquetil's teammate Louis Rostollan had prevented him from being any further behind his main rivals than he actually was: five minutes and forty seconds on Poulidor and Bahamontes. Yet the much discussed role of the *mechoui* in this sudden weakness is questioned by those most directly involved in the drama that was to follow.

'I don't think it was the *mechoui*, rather the fact he didn't go for a ride on the rest day and that there was the Envalira straight away the next day,' says Groussard. 'You should always ride for two hours on the rest day – we went and rode up the *col*. Of course, it depends on the riders – there are some for whom it works not to ride – but when you're used to riding every day, you can retain fluid in the legs and the muscles can stiffen up if you don't ride. Maybe it's all right if you have got 40 or 50 kilometres to get going again the next day, but we were straight into a climb, and the Spaniards – Bahamontes and [Julio] Jiménez – and Poulidor attacked from the start. It exploded straight away.'

Poulidor agrees the *mechoui* was of little significance but also disputes the importance of Anquetil not having ridden. 'The *mechoui*? No, no, oh no. That's of no significance. Me, I would have preferred to get out into the countryside than stay in Andorra,' he asserts (although perhaps the difference between the two men was that Anquetil asserted himself at the time rather than lamenting not having done it later). 'In town, it was very hot. You couldn't sleep. There was no air conditioning, nothing. He was in the country to get some air. He had some rare meat. Well, that's nothing, and I didn't ride my bike that day, either.'

The various different ways the riders spent their rest days at the time are captured by *Cycling*'s report of the race. Tom Simpson did go for a ride up the Col d'Envalira, but this was with a friend and was for the purpose of seeing neighbours from Belgium who were camping on the mountain. He then went to a bullfight, hardly a conventional rest-day activity. Fellow British riders Vin Denson and Michael Wright went shopping.

Whatever the cause, Anquetil's tardy arrival at the top of the *col* meant his tilt at overall Tour victory was in serious jeopardy. So, according to Belline, was his life, and the pea-soup fog at the top certainly lent a sinister air to proceedings. In *Les années Anquetil*, Géminiani once again claims to have found just the right words to inspire his man, perhaps also revealing how little anxiety Anquetil had actually suffered as a result of the prediction: 'For God's sake. If you're going to die, you might as well die at the front!'

There is also a more pragmatic explanation for Anquetil's startling recovery in not only making up the time on his rivals but also gaining an advantage of more than two and a half minutes on Poulidor by the end of the stage. Groussard again: 'We heard on the radios of the motorbikes that were near us that Anquetil was behind and that Rostollan was pushing him. We asked each other if he was going to be able to continue – we didn't know. Then on the descent there was a fog you could have cut with a knife. You couldn't see more than ten metres. I remember I went through the first bend of the descent sideways. I don't know how I managed not to fall. We went down carefully, saying there's still 160 kilometres to go, so we can still catch the group ahead – we were a bigger group than those in front. So, we took it easy down the 20 kilometres of the descent. Then, on the descent, we found Anquetil with us.

We were surprised, but there were also lots of cars behind our group, as I had the yellow jersey, and he could use their rear lights as a guide – he could follow the cars. If it hadn't been for the fog, it's certain that he wouldn't have caught us.'

And if it hadn't been for catching the Groussard group, he might not have seen Poulidor and Bahamontes again that day: 'If he was saved, it was thanks to my team – Pelforth – as we were stuck behind the five or six blokes away, Poulidor, Bahamontes and the others, who were two minutes ahead of us. I was in a small group of six or seven with Janssen [his teammate Jan, vying for the green jersey] and Anglade [another teammate, Henry, who finished second in the 1959 Tour], who were not quite such good climbers. But we weren't too worried, as there was still a long way to go, and we said to ourselves we'd catch them. And, of course, it helped him. He was alone. He had no teammates with him.'

I asked Groussard if it wasn't a counterproductive move, riding in such a way as to help his most serious rival for overall victory. Goussard is realistic: 'I never thought I'd keep the jersey to Paris. I knew full well I'd lose it, with the time trial coming. In fact, there were still two time trials to come – one of fifty kilometres – and I only had one and a half, maybe two minutes, so I knew I'd lose it then. I knew my limits. But we wanted to keep the jersey as long as possible, and we were also leading the team classification and helping Janssen with the green jersey. There was no question of not riding with him, not at all.'

The result, therefore, was the two groups coming together. 'When we joined up with Poulidor's group, we still had 40 to 50 kilometres to go, then everything slowed down a bit and Poulidor punctured, changed wheels and his mechanic knocked him off. We heard this on the radio, so we attacked straight away,' Groussard recalls with a hearty chuckle. 'By the finish, he'd lost nearly three minutes. That was in Toulouse.'

Not surprisingly, Poulidor has equally vivid memories of the stage: 'The stage to Toulouse was something else. I had no plans to attack at the foot of the Col d'Envalira, as it would have been pointless – there were another 250 kilometres to go, so it was impossible to make it stick, even if I hadn't fallen. It was the Spaniards who attacked, and I followed Bahamontes – he was a rival, after all. I followed, no more. We had maybe five or six minutes at the top on Anquetil, but because his death had been predicted all the journalists had stayed with him. When we went down the Envalira, we couldn't see more than two metres. He went down with all the cars' headlights. We went down at 20 kilometres per hour; he went down at 60 kilometres per hour. He caught us.

'After the Envalira, he caught up the Pelforth team of Groussard, the yellow-jersey wearer, so they joined up and worked together in the valley, and that was that. But up front, we really weren't forcing it. Then, at 25 kilometres from the finish, I broke a spoke. My wheel was slightly buckled, but I could have continued – we really weren't forcing it, and the peloton was coming back on us, including my teammates. Then Magne – my *directeur sportif* – made me change wheels.'

Tellingly, for all his avuncular nature and apparent acceptance of the surfeit of unfortunate incidents in his career, Poulidor immediately corrects me when I recap what he's just told me and inadvertently say that he had a puncture – which would have obliged him to stop – rather than a broken spoke: 'No, it was Magne who made me change wheels, even though it was only slightly buckled and even though the peloton with all my teammates was closing on us.

'And so I changed the wheel, and it was fine. But just as I was tightening my toe-straps, the mechanic pushed me, upset my balance and I fell, and the chain came off. I couldn't get the rest of the bike straight, either. It took a considerable amount of time. Then they attacked. Not

Anquetil – I was told it was Maurice De Muer [the *directeur sportif* of the Pelforth team] who initiated it. And there was another problem. It was none of his business, but Jacques Goddet blocked the road to stop me taking advantage of the following cars to catch up. He wasn't acting as a race director; he was acting as a journalist. He stopped in the middle of the road to watch, and everyone attacked. So, there was a real scrap, a side wind and my teammates were tired after chasing to get back on. I did one pull at the front of a group of riders and dropped them all. Fortunately, there were only twenty kilometres to go, as otherwise I would have lost five or six minutes.'

Thus a day that began with Anquetil fearing death and seemingly set to lose the Tour de France had turned out to his considerable advantage. Yet Poulidor remains unconvinced that this was the defining moment of a race that would be decided by less than a minute overall: 'So I lost two minutes [actually, two minutes thirty-six seconds], but I don't think it was that that lost me the Tour. If that hadn't happened, I perhaps wouldn't have attacked the next day when I took back all the time I'd lost the previous day. Perhaps I wouldn't have done that. For me, I lost the Tour the first day and certainly during the time trial to Bayonne. In fact, I lost it several times.

'The first day – nobody's ever spoken about it. I lost 47 seconds on the first day. I had a fall with 1.1 kilometres to go to the finish. The last kilometre is neutralised so I was only 100 metres away from being given the same time as the winner. It just wasn't my year.'

Nevertheless, to be foiled once by a panicky *directeur sportif* and a maladroit mechanic may be unfortunate; for it to happen twice appears careless. After the first incident on the road to Toulouse, the second came in the time-trial stage from Peyrehorade to Bayonne, which Poulidor started only nine seconds down on Anquetil. 'I punctured, perhaps losing one minute as a result,' Poulidor recalls. 'Magne braked a bit too quickly in the following car, and my mechanic, who should have given me a replacement bike, ended up in the ditch at the side of the road with the bike. He sprained his ankle, and as the ditch was very deep he couldn't give me the bike, so I had to climb down to get it. But because the ditch was very deep and I had cycling shoes on with no grip, I couldn't get any purchase on the grass, so I couldn't get back out of the ditch. Even when I did get back on the bike, I'd done 50 metres and realised the handlebar was twisted. I got off again, but it was difficult to straighten it, as it was very tight.'

Poulidor pauses, as if to take stock of the significance of the situation. 'You know,' he continues, 'I lost an extraordinary amount of time, and at that point I was leading him on the intermediate time checks – in a time trial. I think that day I would have beaten him, and that would have changed everything. The bonus at the end of the stage, the morale . . . It was several days before the Puy-de-Dôme, and he wouldn't have had the courage to hold on like he did on the Puy. For me, I lost the Tour there. If he'd lost the time trial, it would have been all over. His morale would have disappeared.'

As it was, whether the result of good fortune for Anquetil or bad planning for Poulidor, Anquetil beat Poulidor by thirty-seven seconds and extended his lead overall, thanks to the ten-second bonus for winning the stage, to fifty-six seconds. With Bahamontes now out of the picture, the race would come down to the famous duel on the Puy-de-Dôme and the final 27-kilometre time-trial stage into Paris. Advantage Poulidor on the climb, but advantage Anquetil against the clock. The question was simple – which would weigh most heavily in the balance?

The stage to the Puy started with an attack, once again featuring Groussard. 'I was in a breakaway,' he recalls. 'There were ten or so of us, and we were rejoined just at the bottom of the Puy-de-Dôme, so there'd been a bit of a scrap, and we'd made them work a bit. We'd certainly made Poulidor's team work a bit. They'd led quite a bit on that stage, so perhaps he'd left a lot of energy on the road.'

Poulidor's motivation in restricting attacks even from those not threatening overall victory was to keep open the possibility of not just gaining time over Anquetil but also taking advantage of the time bonuses available for finishing first or second on the stage, giving an extra minute and an extra 30 seconds, respectively. He succeeded to the extent that the race was back together as the leaders reached the punishing final five kilometres. (Perhaps 'punishing' should be put into context here. Although only five kilometres long, this last section of the climb averages 13 per cent and in fact varies very little from this average. The result is a climb that is considerably steeper and certainly a lot more sustained than almost any other used by the Tour. 'There isn't a chance to recuperate,' says Groussard. 'It just keeps going up.')

Unfortunately for Poulidor, the Spanish climbing double act of Julio Jiménez and Federico Bahamontes used the steepening of the road to launch their own attacks – they were still fighting for victory in the king of the mountains competition. Poulidor could neither follow the lead pair nor even drop Anquetil. Instead, he had to battle, elbow-to-elbow, with his great rival simply to keep level with him. According to Géminiani, this was all part of another of his famous plans, a means by which Anquetil could avoid having to respond to Poulidor's inevitable accelerations while also intimidating him into not daring to accelerate in the first place.

Whether Anquetil was really bluffing, however, and whether Poulidor really succumbed to the tactic, remains uncertain. Groussard is certainly sceptical: 'Did Anquetil bluff? I think they were both flat out and neither could go any faster. It was a long stage, maybe 260 kilometres, so they were both tired. I think they were both flat out, and Anquetil just cracked first, but not enough.'

Ignolin is more convinced: 'No, I think Anquetil bluffed a bit by coming level with Poulidor – keeping level with him. He wasn't only a pedalling machine in terms of his muscles; he had the right head on his shoulders, too. He was always lucid, even after 12 hours on the bike, even if he'd ridden for 24 hours.'

Eventually Poulidor did manage to drop Anquetil, but only after they'd entered the final kilometre, finishing the stage 42 seconds ahead of his rival. When Anquetil arrived, he collapsed onto the bonnet of Géminiani's car and managed to ask, 'How much?' Géminiani replied, '14 seconds,' and Anquetil responded by saying, 'That's 13 more than I need.' It was not necessary for Anquetil to spell out to Géminiani that he was asking about the margin by which he had kept the yellow jersey. Indeed, *L'Équipe* chief cycling writer Philippe Brunel insists on the significance of this abbreviated conversation in revealing not just the complicity and level of understanding between Anquetil and Géminiani but also the importance of having kept the famous tunic. Anquetil himself said after the stage, 'If Poulidor had taken the jersey, I'd have gone home tonight.' This is reinforced by Poulidor's only comments to me about the climb: 'When Jacques had the yellow jersey on his back, it was impossible to take it from him.'

And so it would prove in the final time trial, although not without one more twist in the tale. With an estimated five hundred thousand fans lining the road to watch the final twenty-seven kilometres, Poulidor started off well enough to still be within three seconds of Anquetil at the five-kilometres-to-go time check. 'On the last day, we were a couple of kilometres from the finish, and we were even stevens,' he recalls. 'We didn't know who would win.' In fact, if he could make up just eight seconds, the twenty-second bonus for winning the stage would mean he could yet win overall. To add to the drama, contemporary television footage of Poulidor's arrival at the finish and the agonising wait until Anquetil arrived show a man – and a crowd – who believed he had achieved the unthinkable and won. Yet Anquetil once again demonstrated his ability to judge his efforts to perfection, taking eighteen seconds out of Poulidor in the final five kilometres to win the stage and seal overall triumph by a mere fifty-five seconds.

Victory saw him become the first-ever five-times Tour de France winner and the only man other than Coppi to do the Giro–Tour double in the same year. Yet once again, at the zenith of his career, he revealed a humility in victory that contradicts the public perception of his aloofness and arrogance when he acknowledged the scale of Poulidor's challenge: 'I had to give it my all. Rarely have I suffered so much. I had to surpass myself today to beat Poulidor, and I must give him great credit. My pride comes from having beaten a great champion in the hardest Tour I've known.'

FIFTEEN

The Curious Incident of the Race in the Night-time

WHAT NEXT? WHAT COULD possibly top a year in which you'd won twenty-one races, including the two biggest and most prestigious races in the world, both in gripping fashion, and proved your all-round versatility with a stunning first victory in a major one-day race?

This was the dilemma faced by Anquetil on the eve of his 13th season as a professional: how to maintain motivation to continue to exceed expectations if pretty much all expectations had already been exceeded. What's more, even if a sense of sporting desire could be stimulated, what was the point if the rewards for continuing to excel were already as high as they could be? Although Anquetil had probably already earned enough to be comfortable for the rest of his life, and could certainly hope to continue to be paid his going rate for a few years to come, this was of particular importance to someone who never underestimated the importance of money or his own value. After all, being rewarded at a level commensurate with his status as the top rider was not just a practical concern but a matter of pride – hence his frustration at Poulidor earning the same appearance money at criteriums.

Continuing to win became a galling prospect if in doing so

you helped your rival maintain an undeserved equal footing. According to Géminiani in *Les années Anquetil,* Anquetil had already been confronted with the uncomfortable financial reality of his situation in the run-up to the previous year's Tour. Anquetil summoned his *directeur sportif* to his house to tell him, 'I've just had a long conversation with Roger Piel [the rival agent to Anquetil's manager Daniel Dousset]. He made me understand that winning the Tour for the fifth time would be meaningless. The public would still be against me. On the other hand, if Poulidor won, it would be great for me, as I'd become much more popular. Poulidor and Magne know nothing about it, but Piel has guaranteed me 50 very well-paid after-Tour contracts as well as 50,000 francs [France had by then moved to the new franc, so this represented £5,000].' The combination of improved earnings and improved popularity was tempting enough for Anquetil to need Géminiani's reassurance before declining the offer.

If winning a fifth Tour de France had potentially been meaningless in a financial context, then winning a sixth was even more likely to be so. 'He didn't see a victory in the Tour for its intrinsic value or for its contribution to his *palmarès,*' explains Brunel. 'For him, the notion of a *palmarès* was absurd if it didn't add value commercially. That was Anquetil.'

As well as being a gratuitous effort, therefore, it would also have carried a considerable risk. Like all dominant males, Anquetil was subject to constant sniping from younger rivals; like all dominant males, he would eventually have to relinquish his position at the top of the hierarchy. Yet as the Roman general Fabius understood, the art of winning a war is sometimes found in avoiding a head-on battle. Although Anquetil had managed to beat Poulidor in 1964, the margin of victory was so slight as to leave open the prospect of defeat, whether through sporting inferiority or unfortunate circumstance – as had befallen Poulidor that year.

Anquetil was clearly aware of this and, indeed, was sufficiently concerned to want to avoid the confrontation, at least according to his former teammate at the new Ford France-sponsored team, the British rider Vin Denson: 'In my contract with Ford France, it was stated that I was obliged to ride the Tour if selected. Anquetil was also obliged to ride, as they hoped he would win for Ford France. But he couldn't even begin to imagine what it would be like if Poulidor beat him, and he had a funny feeling that he wasn't going to make it that year. You know, that he couldn't do it, that he'd passed his sell-by date.' What's more, Denson maintains that this was down to more than just the innate precariousness of his position: 'I've never known a rider know himself so well. He knew when to ease off, even if he was just having a bad patch for an hour or so. He was unbelievable. He could see it before it came.'

Whatever the precise reason, Anquetil decided on the classic Fabian tactic of avoiding direct confrontation by determining not to ride any of the three major Tours – Spain, Italy or France – in 1965. He still had to conjure up some kind of performance to demonstrate his commitment to his new team, however, and also to improve his standing with the public, or at least provide sufficient distraction for his absence from his normal hunting grounds not to draw adverse comment. Initially, this gap was filled by an unusually early start to the season, leading to a comprehensive victory over both Altig, now in a different team, and Poulidor in Paris–Nice. His first victory in the Mont Faron hill climb, followed by victory over Poulidor in the Critérium National, not to mention three days participating in a Ford car in the Monte Carlo Rally, helped keep his sponsors happy but did little to add to his prestige or dampen fevered expectation. After all, he was by now 'supposed' to win these events. (Even to someone like

Anquetil, this must have become a bit wearing.) They also served merely to delay the inevitable: deciding what would be his big goal for the year.

Once again, it was Géminiani who came up with the answer: 'Looking at the calendar, I noticed something that made me sit up. The Dauphiné Libéré was followed immediately by Bordeaux–Paris. With Jacques having decided to bypass all three grand Tours, an idea sprang into my head. It would have been premature to spell it out there and then, but I let it germinate quietly.' The idea that Géminiani was reluctant to articulate was for Anquetil to race and win both of these events, even though the five-hundred-and-fifty-seven-kilometre Bordeaux–Paris, the longest one-day race in the cycling calendar, was due to start in Bordeaux just seven hours after the Dauphiné was scheduled to finish nearly six hundred kilometres away in Avignon. The question was how to persuade Anquetil to tackle such an improbable challenge. Géminiani wrote:

> I was convinced he could succeed. I'd mentioned it in passing, but he'd hardly been enthusiastic – in fact, that's the best you could say. So, I had to think of another way. I persuaded Jeanine that my idea was well founded and that Jacques could do it if he applied himself fully. 'If you help me we can persuade him. I'm not with him day and night. You are. Suggest it to him and let me know how you get on.'

Even then, it wasn't simply a question of Jeanine suggesting it directly. 'The thing to remember with Jacques was that you shouldn't challenge him,' she recalls. 'You shouldn't say no to him. If you said no to him, he'd do it anyway. It's the same with his daughter. If you say don't do something, she'll go and do it. That's typical Sophie and Jacques. For that reason, Géminiani couldn't tell him to do it. So, he called me to talk about it – I always answered the phone, even to journalists.

Jacques never bothered, unless perhaps it was Chany. If not, I'd ask him the questions, he'd answer and I'd relay them to the person on the other end of the phone. So, Géminiani asked me how we could persuade him to do it, as it would be a great achievement and he'd be really popular. I said that it was quite a task, but Géminiani said that he could do it. I said, "If you think he can do it, we have to tell him that he can't."'

Jeanine still chuckles at the memory and at the predictability of her husband's reaction: 'After a while, Jacques wanted to know what Géminiani had said on the phone. I said, "He's crazy, that Géminiani. You can't imagine what he's got planned for you now. He's mad." Then I explained to Jacques what the idea was, and he said, "What, you think I can't do it?"'

Géminiani was delighted and concluded the deal with a final nod to the publicity to be garnered were he to succeed: 'Imagine what they'll have to write if you succeed. Imagine! There's nothing more to say. You've won five Tours, two Giros, one Vuelta. It's the only thing left for you to do.'

However, there were still some considerable logistical hurdles to overcome. First was the reluctance, not to say downright antipathy, of Georges Cazeneuve, the organiser of the Dauphiné, who sent Anquetil an open letter asking him to renounce his pursuit of his double aspirations, as it was prejudicing the merit of his race. He was eventually won round, though, on the back of the wave of publicity the undertaking had generated and even went so far as to facilitate the crux of the logistical challenge – getting from Avignon to Bordeaux in time – by bringing forward the start of the last stage of the Dauphiné by an hour. Yet the question remained of how this journey could be made. Ford France had initially hoped that one of their new cars could be used, but even with a police escort this would have been cutting things too fine.

Help came from an unlikely source. 'Just before the start of the Dauphiné, a person who wanted to remain anonymous called me on the phone,' Géminiani recalled. 'Monsieur Géminiani, I am with you. A Mystère 20 – a twin-engined business jet – will be waiting for you at the military airfield in Nîmes to take you to Bordeaux. Don't worry about anything. I'll take care of it.' Anquetil legend has it that it was none other than the then French president General de Gaulle who approved the loan of the plane. This may well be true – de Gaulle was an avowed Anquetil fan – although according to *L'Équipe* the person directly in charge was air force general Marcel Dassault.

However, in order to justify the confidence shown by the favours provided by friends in high places, Anquetil first had to win the Dauphiné. Contemporary race reports in *Cycling* reveal that this was no straightforward task. In fact, his overall margin of victory was a slender one minute forty-three seconds, all but thirteen seconds of which had been accrued in time bonuses for stage-finishing positions: Anquetil had beaten Poulidor in the sprints for victory on stages four and six, on both occasions after having been dropped on the last climb, and also the sprint for second place on stage three. Only in the final 38-kilometre time trial had he put any time into his great rival. He also had to confront the terrible weather, in particular during the penultimate stage. *Cycling* recalls a stage with an average speed of a meagre 18 miles per hour and 'an appalling icy sleet which fell all day which reduced the field, while those that remained could hardly pedal. Two hours after the race had finished, Anquetil was still shivering with cold.'

Of course, this was just the hors d'oeuvre. The *plat principal* was still to come – and was 600 kilometres away. *L'Équipe* recorded the timetable for the transition between the two:

16:58 – The Dauphiné finishes in Avignon.

17:00 – Anquetil on the podium, acclaimed by the crowd. He fulfils his obligations as winner – flowers and kisses – but a bit faster than normal.

17:10 – While his mechanic parts the crowds, he runs to the Ford Taunus team car, driven by Géminiani.

17:15 – They leave the car park, surrounded by cheering fans.

17:20 – Arrival at the Hotel Crillon. Anquetil goes to his room – number 18 – for a bath. His *soigneur* Vergani gives him a massage. Next it's dinner time – Anquetil devours a steak tartare, some Camembert, a strawberry tart and drinks two bottles of beer.

17:55 – Departure. In the car with Anquetil, with the Bordeaux–Paris bikes on top, are Géminiani, [Tarcisio] Vergani, de Bruyckere, the mechanic, and Rostollan, a teammate. A police escort clears the way. The scene is staggering: speeds of up to 140 kilometres per hour, screeching tyres. Anquetil and Rostollan have to cling on tightly, and look far from comfortable. Mothers call their children off the streets.

18:30 – Arrival at Nîmes airport, 60 kilometres from Avignon. In the departure lounge, Anquetil is being massaged on a bench by Vergani, surrounded by reporters and photographers. 'I'm completely disoriented. Going from a bike race where I was quite comfortable to this incredible rally is really something.' He checks on the weather.

18:35 – The group walks towards the plane, a Mystère 20, the name of which couldn't be more fitting: Business Jet. Anquetil is slightly concerned by the number of engines. Out of friendliness, he shakes hands with the pilot, René Brigand, a hot shot. Another handshake for the cameras and television crews. Then he sits down and fastens his seat belt.

18:50 – The door is closed. Chocks away. Anquetil smiles and waves through the window. The plane taxis to the end of the runway, where the roar of the engines continues to grow.

18:56 – Take-off, and before long the plane is lost in the setting sun.

18:58 – Rostollan returns alone to the team car. By the time he's back in Avignon, Anquetil will already be in Bordeaux from where he will set off again in the middle of the night – this time on his bike.

The story of the second half of this famous double is best told by one of its leading players, Vin Denson, who along with the ever-faithful Jean Stablinski had been selected as Anquetil's teammate for the 'Derby of the Road'. While Anquetil had been racing the Dauphiné, Denson and Stablinski had been training in Bordeaux: 'Stab and I had been down there training, riding maybe 20 to 30 minutes on our own, then picking up the Dernys for maybe 80 to 90 kilometres. We'd been doing this for a week, living off lovely fillet steaks – the fat of the land, so to speak. We'd been having a good time for a week. While he was flogging himself, we were in bed eating grapes or something.'

It wasn't grapes Anquetil was after when he finally made it to the hotel in Bordeaux, although his craving still bore no relation to the recommendations of any training manual. 'We met him in the hall,' Denson recalls, 'and the first thing he said was, "I'm absolutely knackered." The next thing he said was, "Can you get one of the waiters to get me some glazed cherries?" They were in wine or eau de vie, I think. At first, he just wanted half a kilo of them – he didn't want anything else – but in the end they talked him into eating a main course, so he ordered kidneys in red wine. Then he went to bed to try to sleep, but he said that he couldn't. He just lay there with his eyes closed for a couple of hours. We'd slept in the day, of course, Stab and I, and by the time of the presentation of the riders at the track we began trying to humour him. He did seem a bit tired.'

Things were about to get much worse: 'By 3 or 4 a.m.,

Jacques kept saying, "I'm absolutely knackered. I'm about to fall asleep." I said, "Don't think it's because of the Dauphiné, because I feel like that, too." I didn't, of course. I lied to him, thinking if he falls asleep, I'm gonna lose my wallet. So, I'm pushing him, and he's leaning on Stablinski. Stab's got one arm round his shoulder, and I'm the other side, pushing on his saddle in the dark.'

The effort involved for Anquetil to stay awake and for Denson and Stablinski to keep him going was only tolerable because of the relatively sedate nature of the first few hours of the race. 'The first bit's just like club-run speed at 20 miles per hour,' Denson continues, 'so it was just a question of keeping him moving. But it was only the end of May, so it was still quite a cold night, and it was raining. We all had on arm warmers and leg warmers and ski hats. They weren't Lycra, like today, though – it was all woollen stuff, on this damp drizzly night. We kept going like this until 7 a.m. when we got to the place with the mobile toilets and some food set out.'

According to Géminiani, it was at this point that Anquetil came closest to cracking. In fact, Anquetil actually got into the team car and told his mechanic to pack away his bike, as he wasn't going any further. Until, after having bawled him out to no avail, Géminiani once again found the *mots justes*, that is: 'I should never have put my trust in such a big girl. You're nothing but a big girl, Jacques. A big girl and no more.' Even in such a diminished state, the alpha male in Anquetil couldn't let this insult pass. With an even greater desire to show the world what he was made of, Anquetil resumed the race.

Denson, meanwhile, had missed the near abandon of his leader, as he was one of the first to leave the pit stop, fulfilling his role of responding to early attacks by other riders. In fact, he was to spend very little of the rest of the race with Anquetil. Yet his own experiences reveal just what a gruelling event Bordeaux–Paris was, even without the added inconveniences of sleep deprivation and having ridden a nine-day stage race in the Alps as preparation: 'There was a gentlemen's agreement that you all got changed and went to the loo and no one attacked, but Raymond Delisle, I think it was, in Tom Simpson's team, jumped away. For weeks on end, he'd been practising getting changed on his bike, so that when he stopped all he had to do was put his shorts on. I'd just about come out of the loos, and I suddenly spotted him go. Of course, it was my job to pull everyone back, so I jumped onto my bike, but the *soigneur* had only just put the gunge [to prevent chafing] in my shorts, and I got bits of gravel from my feet into them and into the gunge.'

It's tempting to say Denson's eyes were watering as he recalled the prospect of cycling another 300 or so kilometres in such a state, but this would do him a disservice. If his eyes were at all moist, it was due to the infectious, ribald sense of humour that becomes evident when the tale is recounted and which no doubt went some way to making such an excruciating situation seem tolerable at the time.

Grit in his shorts was merely the beginning of Denson's tribulations, however. 'After such a quick start, I hadn't managed to finish off my pee. I quickly had to jump on my bike to pull him back and make it smooth for Anquetil, to make it like a stepping stone for him, but I was bursting for a pee. Luckily, it was just one guy, but when we got caught, François Mahé, I think it was, attacked, and I had to go again. So, I went with him, and he took me miles up the bloody road. It must have been 80 or 100 kilometres that I sat on him.'

In other words, another couple of hours having to resist the call of nature, a form of purgatory exacerbated by the peculiar nature of the event, run as it was behind motorbikes: 'Because you're behind the Derny, you put on a longer handlebar extension so that you're closer to it for less wind resistance. I don't know if it was that, making me sit more on the tip of my saddle than normal and that I had trapped a nerve, or simply because I hadn't peed and had held it for so long, but I had pains like cramp across the bottom of my stomach, and then they started going down my legs. Luckily, I knew there was a group catching us, so I said to my Derny driver, when they were only one minute down, "I'm gonna stop to pee." He said, "No one stops in Bordeaux–Paris," and I said, "Just watch me." There were radio and television reporters from France, Holland and Luxembourg, and TV cameras, and I was trying to pee against a tree but just couldn't. So, I had to get back on my bike, as Anquetil was coming down the road. I then had to work to pull Mahé back again, and [Tom] Simpson started attacking, and we had to take it in turns to cover him.'

Finally, Simpson broke free of the majority of the bunch, taking only Anquetil and Stablinski with him: 'I was left with the other guys, and I had to stay with them, but then I decided I'd have to stop. As soon as Anquetil and the rest had got two minutes up the road, I said to my Derny rider, "Tell Géminiani I've got to stop to have a pee." So, I stopped behind another tree, but I still couldn't pee. However, the *soigneur* had a brainwave. He pulled my shorts down, poured hot coffee on a sponge and put it on my balls. As soon as he put it on – phew, the relief. I must have trapped a nerve or something. Some journalist was there with a watch, and he said I peed for 38 seconds.'

Oblivious to the specifics of Denson's suffering on his behalf – but not his general commitment to the cause – Anquetil was by now feeling better and better. Taking advantage of their numerical superiority to take it in turns to attack Simpson, Anquetil and his Ford France teammate Stablinski eventually wore down the Englishman's resistance. Inevitably, it was Anquetil who launched the decisive move on the Côte de

Picardie with eight kilometres remaining, riding inexorably away to a famous victory. At the finish in the Parc des Princes, he was 57 seconds clear. Stablinski made it first and second for Ford France by outsprinting Simpson, and a short while later Denson won the prize for fastest lap of the track to add to his victory in the two earlier sprints to give Ford France a clean sweep. The team and Anquetil were delighted with Denson's contribution. 'Anquetil gave me all his prize money, he was so pleased,' he remembers, 'and Stab did as well on this occasion, which was unusual for him, but he was having a good year and on good money. Then I got a special bonus from Ford France, like we all did, and a nice letter, so I think that day was my biggest earner ever, well over £1,000. That's not bad in 1965.'

The money may have been shared, but the glory was all Anquetil's. In Bordeaux–Paris, he had ridden five hundred and fifty-seven kilometres in fifteen hours two minutes three seconds at an average of 37.007 kilometres per hour. That made for a total of two thousand five hundred kilometres and two exceptional victories in ten days. *L'Équipe* called Anquetil's achievement the most 'outrageous' ever and commented, 'The panache shown by Anquetil throughout his double attempt makes him worthy of being considered the greatest *rouleur* of all time.' *Cycling* devoted its entire front page to commemorating his success under the headline 'Incredible Anquetil', adding two more pages of analysis, commentary and editorial. Alan Gayfer, the magazine's editor, wrote:

> Salute, this morning, the greatest cyclist that the world has ever seen, Jacques Anquetil. This marvellous man, who is so gentle in speech and manner, so calm and fastidious in his person, has once more proved that he can break all rules. Whatever Jacques sets out to do, he will do, that is certain, and we must sympathise with Tom Simpson in finding Jacques there in the way of a second Bordeaux–Paris

success for him. To we, who live in Britain, this Norman is particularly dear, for he appeals to all sides of our sport: time trial, road or track, and his mode of living has obviously far more to do with the hard-living and riding cyclist of British tradition than with the monk-like atmosphere we are sometimes encouraged to adopt.

More important even than the unanimous approval of the press was that of the fans, however. 'The welcome which the public at the Parc des Princes reserved for its hero of the day was without precedent,' noted *Cycling*. 'Never in all the time I have been following cycle racing can I remember the Parc shaking so much to the shouts as on Sunday afternoon during his last lap of the track.' Anquetil himself let slip his usual mask of indifference, the report added: 'When he got off his bike, he was marked by his efforts, but he was much more marked by emotion.' Later, he even admitted to being moved to tears, although not until safely ensconced in his car with Jeanine: 'It was the first time since the beginning of my career that I'd cried. And I'm not ashamed to say it, as there and then I was overcome by joy. I was overwhelmed by the public reaction, and I felt as though I'd done something important.'

The significance of this admission was not lost on his friend, the journalist Pierre Chany, as he recalled in *Pierre Chany, L'homme aux 50 Tours de France*: 'The greats – Merckx, Bobet, Coppi – they cried because they had panache. They cried when they'd gone beyond their limits. It's not by chance that you never saw Anquetil cry – he was a functional racer.' Reminded that Anquetil had cried after Bordeaux–Paris, Chany maintained that this proved his point: 'It's true, but he cried away from the crowd, and we'd never have known about it if Jeanine hadn't told us. He cried precisely because this time he'd taken risks, something he never normally did in a stage race.'

After this incredible success, Anquetil felt entirely vindicated in his decision not to race the Tour, even if Poulidor desired his presence. When Poulidor ended up losing to Tour debutant Felice Gimondi, it became clear that his motivation to beat Anquetil was at least the equal of Anquetil's motivation to not let Poulidor beat him. 'All I wanted was for him to be there. The Tour was never the same without Jacques,' he explained.

Meanwhile, Anquetil was explaining Poulidor's failings and the intricacies of the race to readers of none other than *L'Humanité*, the weekly newspaper of the French Communist Party. According to Jeanine, this alliance was an unlikely one. 'He was not interested in politics, but he was Gaullist,' she recalls. 'He knew big Charles. So we were Gaullist. At the moment, he'd be pro-discipline, pro-work. His temperament was to work to earn money. He rode his bike to make money.' Yet for once his motivation appears not to have been purely financial. *L'Humanité* was ideologically and practically limited in the rates it could pay. Instead, Anquetil's benefit from the arrangement came in the form of the access the paper provided to the 'masses', those who attended bike races in person rather than read about them in the office, those who had now begun to show some affection for him. If he wouldn't ride in front of them that year, at the height of his popularity, at least he could continue to cultivate their affinity.

Buoyed, perhaps, by his own success and the failure of his great rival, Anquetil then embarked on a successful end-of-season campaign. He went to the Isle of Man cycling festival and won the Manx Premier Trophy by half a wheel from Eddy Merckx, and then won the Critérium des As and the Grand Prix Forli. He also became the first person to win the Grand Prix des Nations, the Grand Prix de Lugano and the Baracchi Trophy in the same year, winning the Baracchi Trophy with the ever faithful Jean Stablinski.

In the Grand Prix des Nations, on a new, shortened course

of only 73.5 kilometres, Anquetil set a record average of 46.793 kilometres per hour, prompting another flattering *L'Équipe* headline: 'Without Rivals'. Given that Poulidor and that year's Tour winner Gimondi were both riding, and were both beaten by more than three minutes, this was indeed impressive. The paper congratulated him on having the courage to face up to these new pretenders, then concluded that he was 'more imperious, more determined and also more generous than ever'. In spite of another article elsewhere in the paper under the headline 'A Season with Neither Yellow nor Pink Jerseys', cycling's dominant male had lived to ride another year.

SIXTEEN

Anyone but Poulidor

WHEN YOUR ADVERSARIES ARE dead set on a confrontation, Fabian tactics cannot endure for ever. If you're a Roman general, you might get away with passing the responsibility of fighting a rampaging Hannibal to someone else and retiring to Rome for a bout of gladiatorial politics, as Fabius did, but if you're Jacques Anquetil facing up to your would-be nemesis Raymond Poulidor, you can't shirk the challenge. Even the prestige of the previous year's epic double victory in the Dauphiné Libéré and Bordeaux–Paris can't provide shelter for long.

Thus it was that the two inevitably came face to face in a stage race for the first time in nearly a year in Paris–Nice at the beginning of 1966. Even before that, though, Anquetil was beginning to show signs of frustration at his remarkable career being defined solely in relation to his great rival. 'It's diabolical to live in such a symbiotic relationship with a rider who's no worse but no better than many I've encountered in 14 years of racing,' he recalled in *En brûlant les étapes*. He went on to cite the coverage of his victory in the early season Tour of Sardinia stage race as an example, complaining how little of it was about the actual race and how much about the next duel with Poulidor: 'What's that got to do with my victory? Why should Poulidor's name be in any way linked to a race in which he didn't participate? Frankly, it's an aberration.'

Maybe Anquetil himself suffered an aberration by the time Paris–Nice reached Corsica, for he had to give ground – 36 seconds to be precise – to Poulidor in his favourite domain, the time trial. It may have been, as Géminiani pointed out loudly at the time, a tricky, technical route with a significant climb in it that was a long way from favouring Anquetil's superior power and straight-line speed. Yet this hardly mitigated Anquetil's own displeasure at finding himself not only beaten in his speciality, but also relegated to second place in the overall classification by Poulidor.

Clearly, Anquetil had to find a way to react if he wasn't to be seen for the first time in his career as accepting defeat without a fight. The problem was that with only two stages remaining, one of them a flat sprinters' stage with little opportunity to make up time, the opportunities to do so were strictly limited. Worse was the likely reaction to any eventual failure of Anquetil's to overcome his rival, a reaction of which Anquetil was well aware: 'And then I thought what would happen if the results were reversed: first, Poulidor, second, Anquetil. Then, I'd have been written off straight away. One lone defeat would count as much as fifteen or twenty victories. Was that fair? I could already picture the crocodile tears being shed because of my supposed decline.'

In the end, he had little choice but to put all his eggs in one basket and wait until the last stage to attack. This he did to great effect, first through the intermediary of his teammates, dispatched by Géminiani on a series of seemingly suicidal breaks in a bid to wear out Poulidor's Mercier team physically and to heighten the war of nerves already initiated between the two protagonists. After rapidly running out of teammates, Poulidor was eventually required to assume all the responsibility for controlling the race himself and was obliged not just to chase after Anquetil and his team but also attacks from all of his major rivals. Géminiani complimented him on the panache this involved but also said that it was this expenditure of energy that paved the way for Anquetil's decisive move with less than 40 kilometres to go. By the time he arrived at the finish on the Promenade des Anglais in Nice, he had established a lead of one minute forty-four seconds, more than enough to wipe out the deficit incurred in the time trial in Corsica.

The reaction to this success depended on whether you were in the Anquetil or Poulidor camp. In the Anquetil camp, there was nothing but exultation and, according to Anquetil himself, a great sense of pride at one of his most hard-fought victories. In the Poulidor camp, and in the press, there was a sense of outrage at what were perceived to be nefarious manoeuvres – riders ending up in ditches and supposedly rival teams assisting in the wearing out of Poulidor and his teammates, not just with attacks, but also by physically getting in the way of any attempts to counter them. The report in *L'Équipe* went as far as to suggest that the controversy would unleash a civil war in French cycling. Responding to persistent questioning from journalists, Poulidor, although not explicit, left little doubt as to his assessment of events: 'I note simply that Anquetil is still the *patron* of cycling. I don't deny his strengths, nor even his superiority in many domains, but I consider that his teammates did not behave well on the road to Nice. Jacques Anquetil would acknowledge as much if he is honest with himself.'

Anquetil, in fact, did nothing of the sort. 'Poulidor is a cry-baby,' he declared. 'The interview in which he repeated the accusations made by his team to cast a doubt over the correctness and sincerity of my victory, that interview is not worthy of a champion, and I will find it difficult to forgive him.'

More than 40 years later, Poulidor is prepared to be more open about what happened, though he still refuses to blame Anquetil himself. 'The rivalry had grown even fiercer since the Tour in 1964, and it culminated in our confrontation in Paris–Nice,' he recalls, pausing to consider his words carefully. 'He had great difficulty in accepting defeat, especially his entourage, those people around him. So when I'd beaten him by 37 seconds in a time trial, his speciality, he wouldn't accept it. The result was that on the last day, rival teams teamed up, it must be said, and what shocked me the most was that these arrangements happened in front of the race director [Jean Leulliot]. He let it happen, as he was closer to Anquetil than to me. They played tricks on my teammates – [Barry] Hoban and [Jospeh] Spruyt – tipping them into the ditch, and everyone attacked. Orders had been given. Anquetil had done nothing – I've nothing to reproach him for. When he attacked me, I was at the end of my tether. People say I'd wasted too much effort chasing after others, but [Michele] Dancelli attacked – he was only two minutes down – and [Vittorio] Adorni was the same.'

The implication that it was Géminiani, as Anquetil's *directeur sportif*, who had greased the necessary palms to ensure a collusion to dethrone Poulidor is clear. In *Les années Anquetil* Géminiani goes to some considerable lengths to pour scorn on these suggestions and to clear his name, even recording how he offered 10,000 francs (£1,000) to anyone who had any proof of wrongdoing. There were no takers – proof, of course, is hard to come by.

According to Brunel, Géminiani was right – it wasn't the teams ganging up, it was the managers: 'There were two managers – agents, if you like – in France. Roger Piel and Daniel Dousset. Dousset had Anquetil, [Franco] Bitossi, [Lucien] Aimar, Altig and Adorni. Alliances in the peloton were arranged by the managers, not between the teams. Sometimes there were link-ups determined by a race, but there were also alliances to protect the "aristocracy". In this Paris–Nice, there was Adorni, who raced for Anquetil because Dousset told him he had to. He said, "I need to maintain Anquetil's prestige for the critériums [so he could maintain the value of his '10 per cent']." That was the reality until after Bernard Hinault. It was Cyrille Guimard, Hinault's *directeur sportif* and manager, who broke their power off, but it was like that for a long time, and Anquetil was part of the system.'

But no one should be under any illusions as to the fact that collusion between cyclists wasn't also a frequent occurrence and indeed still is. It most often manifests itself in the more acceptable form of several teams with top sprinters pooling their efforts to reel in a breakaway and thus ensure a sprint finish that they will then at least have some chance of winning through their man. And 'acquiring' – that's to say buying – the services of other cyclists was, and is, common practice.

Tom Simpson wrote three exposés of the world of cycling for *The People* newspaper after becoming world champion in 1965, in one of which he admitted to having offered the Irishman Shay Elliot £1,100 to help him win the world title in 1963 and that he had accepted £500 to work for a team other than his own. Anquetil himself was no exception. Later in the year, he would finish third in the Giro d'Italia, ostensibly the result of having lost more than three minutes to seven of his main rivals through a momentary lapse of concentration on the otherwise anodyne descent of the Col de San Bartolomeo on the first stage. Finishing third after such a slip is no mean feat and implies a good degree of determination, but his teammate at the time, Vin Denson, suggests Anquetil's lack of concentration was perhaps less careless than it at first seemed: 'Julio Jiménez [by now a teammate] went away in the break, and the idea was to get him to win. I don't think Jacques was 100 per cent interested in winning the Giro. He was more interested in touching money from others, because there was a lot of money moving about, you know.'

Whether or not Jiménez's presence in and Anquetil's absence from the break was planned, Brunel confirms that once Anquetil was out of the running for overall victory he had another agenda to follow. If not directly about money, this was still the indirect motive – the money associated with the prestige of victory. 'The reality is that Anquetil went to see Géminiani that night and said, "I've lost the Giro. There's still 20-odd stages to go, but I've lost it. I can take three minutes back from six of them, but there'll always be one of them who can keep their advantage,"' says Brunel. 'And then he said, "I've lost, but I can perhaps decide who will win." And that's what he did. He didn't want Gimondi to win, as he'd won the Tour de France and he was a growing rival, so in the end he raced for Motta. In fact, on the last stage he found himself alone with Motta on a climb, and he came out of a bend and dropped him. He turned round and saw Motta dropped. But he waited for him. He had promised to wait for him, so he waited for him, even though he could perhaps have gone on to win the Giro himself. He'd given his word. That's how Motta won the Giro. And he was so appreciative of what Anquetil had done that he arranged for Anquetil to come to a criterium in his home town near Bergamo after the Giro. It was such a small criterium that normally they couldn't have afforded to have Anquetil race, so Motta paid for everything. He paid for the trip, paid for his accommodation, paid for his contract, and Anquetil didn't know.'

According to Denson, there may well have been other even more powerful commercial forces at work behind the scenes: 'We seemed to get a strange bonus – we were told to work for this other team, because as Ford France we were only really riding the Giro to get fit for the Tour de France, and Ford France didn't want to give Ford Italy any publicity, because there was such competition between them on the border around Menton, Monaco, Nice – the cars were cheaper in Italy, apparently. When we finished a stage in the Giro, we were straight away given a hat with a very large Cynar logo on it – a brand of Italian aperitif – and only a very small Ford France logo. As soon as we'd finished, they gave us a hat and a tracksuit with Cynar on it so we covered up Ford France on the rostrum.'

Even after the successful completion of his outrageous Dauphiné Libéré and Bordeaux–Paris double, doubts were cast over the honesty of his victory in the second half of the challenge. As *Cycling* recalled, evidently with some exasperation, Tom Simpson, who eventually finished third, was accused of having sold Bordeaux–Paris to Anquetil:

> 'My own pacemaker came up to me and, before witnesses, accused me of having been bought off by Anquetil. There was nothing I could say. The man was so convinced that he would not have believed a word I said, and I told him this, for what it was worth. Of course, the whole story is ridiculous. I would never have sold, in this race above all, my chance of beating Jacques Anquetil at his own game; it is an insult to Jacques and to me.'

Cycling appears to have been convinced, quoting famous British cycling journalist Jock Wadley, then editor of *Sporting Cyclist* magazine, as an eye witness: '"The three of them, Stablinski, Simpson and Anquetil, were trying so hard that they could not have spoken a word, let alone made an agreement; the whole story is stupid."'

In his own series of provocative articles written for *France Dimanche* in 1967, mirroring those written by Simpson, Anquetil avoids such unsavoury details, but he is candid about collusion being an integral part of the job:

> Everybody knows that the greatest cycling champion can't ride alone. He needs a team. Yet there are still those who whisper, 'Yes, of course, so-and-so won because he "bought" such-and-such a rider.' Once again, this is pure hypocrisy. It's quite clear that we 'buy' riders, and I say that it's quite normal. We pay them for doing their job and that's all. They're the same as any other worker or

employee. They sell themselves to the highest bidder, and it can happen that the auction takes place at the most unlikely moments – at the end of a race, for example.

The point, Anquetil maintains, is that you're buying support in order to win rather than buying the victory itself:

> When I talk about buying riders, I must make one thing clear: you can't buy a victory. That's in your legs, and the best teammate in the world can't sell it to you. In a stage race, if you buy riders it's above all in order not to be constantly attacked, jostled, harried, not to say threatened.

The point also is that a cycling team does not have the same sense of identity or belonging as would a football or rugby club. With winnings from races contributing as much to a rider's income as his basic salary, if not more, and with the cycling tradition of pooling these winnings, a tradition apparently instigated by the self-important Bobet, his first allegiance is to his teammates rather than the team itself. In the best teams, this can make an effective bond, as Brian Robinson's experience makes clear: 'We were young riders, and we all wanted to make money. We were always the team that won the most money, no matter if we won the race or not. We always made the most money in the kitty.'

It's hardly surprising, though, that the entirely unpredictable way a race can develop, with lead groups consisting of *domestiques* rather than stars, may lead to the ad hoc alliances that Anquetil describes. In an interview with *Lui* magazine – a French version of *Playboy* – in 1969, Anquetil explained further:

> 'I've never sold a race, and a champion can't afford the luxury of buying a victory. At my level, I'm in a constant battle for prestige with other champions. What's at stake compels us to confront each other with no holds barred. But it can happen that we pool our resources against others in a breakaway.'

But paying lesser riders for their help was commonplace, even if defining the status of a rider was not without peril: 'You can believe me that a rider only gives up his own chances after having thought about it carefully. It's not always easy to explain to them that they're not capable of winning a race.' The real controversies arise not because these arrangements exist but when their inevitably informal nature leads to them breaking down. The most famous – infamous – example was in the world championships in 1963 when Anquetil apparently gave up victory by sitting up when ahead of the bunch and inside the final kilometre. His own take on events, however, is that he was simply reacting to a perceived feint from favourite Rik Van Looy and was gathering his forces for one last sprint to the line. With Anquetil concentrating solely on Van Looy, and vice versa, neither of them noticed Van Looy's teammate Benoni Beheyt launch his race-winning sprint: 'When we wanted to react, it was too late. Van Looy couldn't get over it. He was mad with rage. In the changing-room, he had to be held back. He wanted to lay in to Beheyt. "I'd paid him to help me," he shouted. But it was too late. Beheyt was world champion.'

If buying riders and collusion between teams is a fact of life, then perhaps the most accurate assessment of Paris–Nice would come from someone who has experienced it first hand. In this respect, the verdict of Guy Ignolin, admittedly Anquetil's former teammate, is clear: 'I think Jacques had a better team and had better teammates than Poulidor. And don't forget, when he got away it was his final attack. He'd said, "If I don't make it this time, that's it." But he really went for it, and Raymond blew up. They found themselves together, then very slowly Jacques was away, and once he was off he was like a train . . . So that's how he won Paris–Nice.'

Nevertheless, the shadow cast over his achievement by this controversy was enough to deprive Anquetil both of the pleasure of victory and of his motivation. He abandoned the Critérium National – won by Poulidor – and even came close to retiring such was the hostility of the reaction. 'After Paris–Nice, he was completely downhearted,' noted Géminiani. It took until the end of the spring classic season was approaching for Anquetil to recover his appetite for battle, and he decided to demonstrate just how strong it still was in typically remarkable fashion.

For a start, the setting – the Liège–Bastogne–Liège one-day race – was unusual. Although the kind of gruelling race that should have favoured such a strong rider as Anquetil, he had done nothing previously to show either an inclination or aptitude for it. What's more, as a one-day race it fell into the category of events he had described in the aftermath of his failed bid for glory in Paris–Roubaix in 1958 as lotteries. In the intervening eight years, a handful of impressive stage victories in the Tour de France and his victory in Ghent–Wevelgem apart, he had done nothing to suggest he had changed his mind.

Yet, his ability to perform in one-day events was not in doubt. Ignolin for one shares the widespread belief that he could have won Paris–Roubaix in 1958, and also suggests victory escaped him in unfortunate circumstances in Paris–Tours in 1965: 'Yes, he could have won Paris–Tours. He had broken away near the end and was following the cars, but when he needed to turn right they went straight on, and he followed them. It was all over. It was in the last kilometre, so he couldn't get going again.' Poulidor agrees, and he was in the race at the time. 'He nearly won it the year we did it without derailleurs,' he recalls, the absence of derailleurs being a throwback to a previous age and restricting the riders to the use of only two gears, one on either side of the rear wheel. 'He was off the front, and I think there was a diversion, and he went slightly the wrong way. As he had a very big gear, 48 or 49 x 13, he couldn't get going again, so he was caught. He had been going very strongly and was well clear, so he could well have won.'

Instead, it was motivation that was lacking, and this was primarily due to the relatively small contribution his performances in these races could make to his financial position. Even victory could add little to his contract value for appearances in criteriums, which was already as high as it could be thanks to the reputation he had built through his performances in stage races and time trials. And even for Anquetil, these contracts were an essential part of his income. 'The real earning power came from the series of contracts after the Tour,' recalls Robinson. 'You'd be riding nearly every day for thirty days, getting as much as £80 per day, so it was pretty good money.' Robinson, of course, would have earned less and had fewer contracts than a star like Anquetil: 'Unlike us, who just rode contracts after the Tour, the stars rode contracts all year round. So, there were those to fit in, and, speaking purely as a professional, he'd be busy enough without worrying too much about the one-day races.'

'In those days, when you won a classic you won hardly anything,' confirms Hinault. 'When I won Liège–Bastogne–Liège, it was about 6,000 francs to share with the team – only 600 francs [£60] each. That's not much. But it helps your *palmarès*. If you can't win the Tour, you can always win the classics, which then helps with the criteriums. And don't forget, base salaries were very small. More than half your income was from the criteriums. If you're thinking about "Père Jacques" . . . if he raced ten criteriums, he could buy a house.'

Then there was the fact that precisely because his reputation – and earning power – derived from stage races and time trials, he was not usually confronted in the one-day arena by the same kind of rivalry that inspired so much of his success. According to Jeanine, the importance of this as a source of motivation for him should not be underestimated: 'Yes, he said that he was not interested in one-day races, that right from the start you could be in the wrong fall, in the wrong break, that one-day races really were too fickle. But he wasn't entirely happy about it, and if Rivière, for example, hadn't crashed and had started to do well in one-day races . . . If it had been Rivière instead of Poulidor, then there would have been a rivalry. Anquetil against Rivière would have been full of panache, as Rivière could have won things Poulidor couldn't. So it would have wound up Jacques, and I'm sure he would have ridden classics to win.'

This is precisely what Anquetil did in Liège–Bastogne–Liège, and his rival for once was not Poulidor but someone who appeared to be about to fulfil the role that had been vacated so unfortunately by Rivière. Walter Godefroot, who would go on to win the race the following year, rode the 1966 race with Anquetil. On the eve of the 2007 event, he told me why he thought Anquetil had finally thrown off the shackles in a one-day race: 'Why did he win Liège–Bastogne–Liège? I think it was because Géminiani, at that time, had said, "Listen, Jacques, you've now got a rival who's young, who wins the Tour and who wins classic races. He's called Felice Gimondi. He's not just won the Tour, but also Paris–Brussels, Paris–Roubaix . . ." I don't think that went down well, and that's why he won.'

L'Équipe agreed:

> Jacques Anquetil dislikes anyone who casts doubt on his supremacy, and he had taken umbrage at the praise that had been heaped on Gimondi every time he won a race. Therefore, in Liège–Bastogne–Liège he decided to make a clear statement of who was boss.

The statement was certainly clear. Attacking initially on the Côte de la Bouquette to leave his immediate companions – no lesser riders than Gimondi, Altig, Motta and Merckx

– he then caught the early break that was still a minute up the road before definitively leaving them behind with another acceleration on the Côte de Mont-Theux. *L'Équipe* was ecstatic:

> For 12 years, we've been waiting for just such an exploit by Jacques Anquetil – to win a classic one-day race. In Liège–Bastogne–Liège, the hardest, most demanding of them all, he finally filled the gap in his *palmarès* in front of impotent rivals, including Eddy Merckx, who expressed his astonishment at the way in which Jacques had built a lead before beating them all home some forty kilometres later by four minutes fifty-three seconds.

The rivalry with Poulidor just wouldn't go away, however. Even his third place in the Giro d'Italia was insufficient to distract attention from their much-awaited Tour de France rematch. Much as Anquetil might complain that 'you can't reduce current cycling simply to us two', that's precisely what the public and the press were inclined to do. There's little doubt that some of the apparent intensity of this rivalry was exaggerated by the press. 'I was in the Anquetil camp, as I was his generation, but then I joined the Poulidor camp, as we went skiing together,' says Brian Robinson. 'They were both different characters and both good fellows. As you probably know, the press make a lot of these things. I think they admired each other. At the end of the day, they respected each other. The rivalry was in the press, really.' Jean Milesi, who has the unusual distinction of having been a teammate for both men, agrees: 'I was with Poulidor during one Tour. I sat with him in the hotel, and he was reading the papers full of articles about him and Anquetil and saying, "I didn't say that. That's not what I said."'

Jeanine, too, points her finger at the press, though for a slightly different reason, one that confirms that Anquetil determined at least some of his actions because of the reputation of his rival: 'The rivalry grew because the journalists talked up Poulidor. But there were other riders who deserved talking up, the proof being that when Jacques didn't ride the Tour it was Gimondi or Merckx who won. Poulidor was a class below the great champions such as Merckx, Gimondi, Baldini – they were real rivals. He didn't understand why Poulidor was placed on the same level.'

Indeed, Anquetil was at times dismissive of Poulidor. In the first of his provocative articles for *France Dimanche* in 1967, entitled 'Why I Don't Like Poulidor', he wrote:

> In my opinion, the simple difference in the number and prestige of our victories contradicts any notion of sporting rivalry. I've ridden in 80 races with Poulidor, and I've won 77. For me, it's quite simple. There has never been a duel Anquetil–Poulidor. The result was decided long ago.

Yet the fascination continued, stimulated in part by the obvious contrast between the two men: the open, vulnerable Poulidor; the cold, calculating Anquetil. Their contemporary, Antoine Blondin, novelist and cycling journalist, wrote in his preface to Pierre Chany's *La fabuleuse histoire du cyclisme*, '*Où Anquetil incarne la partie libre de l'homme, Poulidor incarne la partie fatale.*' (Where Anquetil embodies the part of man free to choose his own destiny, Poulidor embodies the part that accepts his fate.)

Still Anquetil was unmoved. In *En brûlant les étapes*, he wrote:

> I find it quite absurd, this division of sporting France into two camps, with their threats and their passions. I've even received death threats in anonymous letters. It's time to forget this obsession Anquetil–Poulidor, Poulidor–Anquetil. At the risk of stirring up the emotions of my adversaries, I would also add that the key thing for me isn't this duel, in my opinion meaningless, but trying to win the Tour for a sixth time and in doing so fighting

Anquetil in classic time-trial pose during the time-trial stage from Versailles to Versailles on the opening day of the 1961 Tour de France (Offside/*L'Équipe*)

It was for good reason that Anquetil's British teammate Vin Denson likened himself to being Anquetil's valet – Anquetil in Metz, Tour de France, 1957 (Offside/*L'Équipe*)

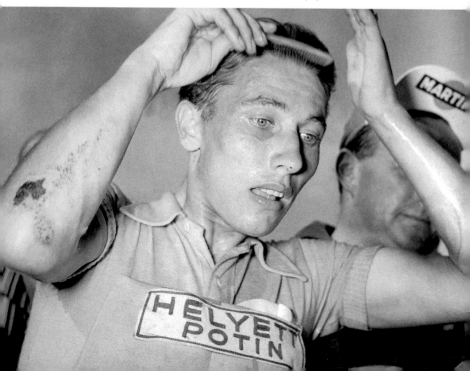

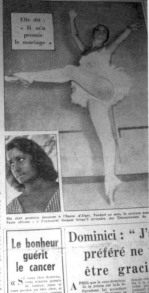

Even inherent French discretion for 'affairs of the heart' couldn't prevent some of Anquetil's private life making it into the papers (Paul Howard)

Jeanine's omnipresence in Anquetil's life is clear from the number of times she appears in his victory celebrations – Paris–Nice, 1965 (Offside/*L'Équipe*)

Anquetil, Jeanine and her children Alain and Annie (Sophie Anquetil)

The chateau at La Neuville-Chant-d'Oisel, known as 'Les Elfes' and previously owned by Maupassant's family, that Anquetil purchased in 1967 (Lionel Fairier)

The state of the roads was almost as big an obstacle as the mountains themselves – Briançon–Aix les Bains, Tour de France, 1957 (Offside/*L'Équipe*)

Anquetil dazed and bloodied after his fall as he entered the velodrome at the end of the Barrachi Trophy in 1962, a race in which he had been humiliated by his friend and rival Rudi Altig (Offside/*L'Équipe*)

Had Annie already caught Anquetil's eye at the age of 16? Her role as surrogate mother and mistress would begin only two years later (Sophie Anquetil)

Parties at Les Elfes with friends were regular occurrences after Anquetil retired – Maurice Dieulois is on the right, playing the tambourine (Sophie Anquetil)

It took a special occasion – such as Sophie's eighth birthday party – to persuade Anquetil back onto the bike once he'd retired (Sophie Anquetil)

Anquetil, Jeanine and
Sophie with their dog
Troika (Sophie Anquetil)

Anquetil and Sophie
in the late 1970s
(Sophie Anquetil)

Jeanine's living room is still dominated by a portrait of her second, late husband (Paul Howard)

Sophie, Annie and Jeanine once again live within a couple of miles of each other, near to the auberge run by Sophie on Corsica (Paul Howard)

The entrance to Les Elfes is marked by a monument to Anquetil's Tour de France achievements (Lionel Fairier)

Anquetil's only cycling club, AC Sottevillais, has added its own tribute to its most famous son on his tombstone at the church in Quincampoix (Lionel Fairier)

against Raymond Poulidor, if he's still in contention, and if not against all of the other serious rivals for victory, because that's what sport is all about. In the next Tour de France, do you not think my greatest rival won't be called Gimondi, Motta, Adorni or Merckx, if he races, rather than Poulidor?

Gimondi, Motta, Adorni and Merckx were all absent from the 1966 Tour, however, and once more it seemed destined to come down to a duel between Anquetil and Poulidor. That was until Anquetil's teammate, Lucien Aimar, took advantage of Poulidor's understandable concentration on his leader and joined a breakaway group on the first stage in the Pyrenees that led to him gaining more than seven minutes on Poulidor. Aimar was no slouch, having already finished second in the 1964 Tour de l'Avenir to eventual 1965 Tour winner Felice Gimondi. More importantly, he had also already been identified by Géminiani as an alternative card to play in the Tour de France as and when Anquetil's hegemony came to an end. According to Géminiani, the two in fact started the race as joint leaders, a situation apparently accepted by Anquetil on the basis of Géminiani's reassurance of his belief in Aimar's ability to fulfil his potential.

The importance of this move would soon become clear. First, Anquetil lost seven seconds to Poulidor in the time trial to Vals-les-Bains. Then he lost 40 more seconds on the stage to Bourg-d'Oisans, leading to him declaring in the immediate aftermath of the stage that he'd also lost the Tour. His spur-of-the-moment assessment seemed all the more accurate the next day when in spite of a show of defiance on the Col du Galibier he could not shake Poulidor, who by now led Anquetil by one place and one minute and eight seconds in the overall classification.

Yet Anquetil having lost the Tour did not mean Poulidor had won it, especially since Anquetil had the alluring prospect of being able to assuage his defeat by facilitating the progress of his teammate Aimar. According to Géminiani, team tactics were thus modified to allow Aimar to attack in order to buy himself sufficient time over Poulidor – poised in sixth place, three and a half minutes down on Aimar – and current yellow-jersey wearer Jan Janssen. This he did with some aplomb on the next stage to Turin, surprising both his rivals – still focused on Anquetil and deprived of Tour Radio to keep them up to speed with events due to the mountainous surroundings – while extending his advantage by just over two minutes and putting on the yellow jersey in the process. The next day, Anquetil turned from passive decoy into active assistant, overcoming the worsening cold from which he'd been suffering for several days to help Aimar contain Poulidor's attack on the Col de la Forclaz, limiting the deficit to a mere 49 seconds.

The mountains were now complete, and the only likely opportunity for change in the overall classification would be the final 51-kilometre time-trial stage, in which Anquetil could no longer help his teammate. At the foot of the otherwise insignificant Côte de Serrières, on the stage from Chamonix to Saint-Étienne, he therefore retired, worn out but once again with his primary goal accomplished: Aimar held on in the time trial to win the race by one minute and seven seconds over Janssen and two minutes and two seconds from Poulidor. The tears – yes, tears from the ice-man Anquetil – that accompanied his descent from his bike as the race disappeared into the distance in front of him made it clear that he knew his career as a Tour de France cyclist was over.

The season was far from finished, however, and nor was France's favourite sporting duel. The final instalment in the saga took place at the world championships on the Nürburgring circuit in Germany, and the controversy of the outcome – Anquetil second, Poulidor third but both beaten by Rudi Altig – even managed to overshadow everything that had gone before. As if the disappointment of having its two cycling greats beaten by a German wasn't enough, France was outraged at the suggestion that Anquetil had actually cooperated with the German to ensure Poulidor wouldn't win.

The suggestion, in the press, was based on a number of factors, notably that Altig, according to some, only caught up to the breakaway containing Anquetil, Poulidor, Motta, Italo Zilioli, Gimondi, Merckx and Martin Van Den Bossche with the help of – you've guessed it – Lucien Aimar, especially since Altig had been seen being sick at the side of the road earlier in the race. Much was also made of the fact that Anquetil and Altig had by now buried the hatchet and were known to be great friends. Anquetil and Jeanine even stayed with the Altigs before the race, and the two reconnoitred the course together. ('We saw it was very hard, designed for cars, not for bikes,' Altig recalls.)

According to Georges Groussard, who was in the French team on the day, the allegations against Aimar don't stack up, even though he admits that it was Aimar who was the catalyst for Altig's unlikely recovery: 'I was there. There were four or five, including Anquetil and Poulidor, in a break, and the peloton was two minutes behind. We, the French team, were doing our job to make sure that as they were ahead one of them would win. Altig was being sick at the side of the road with maybe 50 to 60 kilometres to go, and I said if there's someone who's not going to be champion today, it's him. Then, five kilometres later he was feeling better, and he attacked – or, rather, it was Aimar who attacked to try and get a placing. Altig followed. There were no earpieces, so there was no collusion between Anquetil and Aimar. He knew perhaps they were chasing, but that was it.'

This still doesn't explain why Aimar took the risk of such an attack. The best he could have hoped for was a minor placing, certainly not victory or a podium spot, and in doing so he helped a serious rival from a different national team bridge the gap. Yet Poulidor is adamant that there is no truth in the suggestion he was the victim of anything crooked: 'No, Aimar's not compromised. We were a bit like Claude Criquelion and Stephen Roche in Liège–Bastogne–Liège when they neutralised each other and Moreno Argentin was two minutes down. They messed about; Argentin came and won. It was the same for us. He was scared I would win, and I perhaps didn't want him to win, either. It was our bad blood that allowed Altig to come back. At the finish, Anquetil was upset and disappointed, as after he'd come second he realised he could have won. Then there was a drugs test at the end of a lot of brouhaha, and at first I was the only one on the podium, but then Altig came.'

Yet Hinault is clearly convinced Anquetil was at least prepared to risk losing his own chance of victory if it ensured Poulidor also lost: 'If Jacques had really wanted to race, he could have won it. He could have chased Altig [who attacked on his own after catching the lead group] if he'd wanted, although so could Poulidor, but the first to react might have lost. So, given Anquetil and Altig were friends, he would rather it was Altig than Poulidor. I'm not sure that there wasn't also the thought that because he was a friend – a really good friend – that it wouldn't have given him as much pleasure as if he'd won himself.'

When I spoke to Altig, he would neither confirm nor deny he'd made any arrangements with Anquetil and deliberately left open the intriguing prospect of there being some foundation to the journalists' assertions. 'I don't think the truth will ever come out,' he told me. 'I think the truth is that he was second and Poulidor was third. He was a bit angry, and that's why he didn't come onto the podium. That's all I'm going to say,' he concludes, before nevertheless adding, 'The rest, only he can tell you, but, of course, he can't tell you now.'

It seems that even missing out on probably the best

chance he ever had to fulfil a childhood dream and once again incurring the wrath of a nation in the process was a price Anquetil was prepared to pay to avoid the glory going to Poulidor. For someone who by his own admission was increasingly frustrated with this rivalry, this may seem extraordinary, yet, as Jeanine confirms, it also reveals the extent of the catch-22 situation in which he found himself: 'He said, "If Poulidor beats me one day, they'll kick me out the door. I'll be finished. I can't allow Poulidor to win, because they'll say Anquetil's finished." He understood what he needed to do to be popular, but he couldn't do it.'

SEVENTEEN

Don't Take the P***

INCAPABLE OF BRINGING HIMSELF to lose to Poulidor, Anquetil's unique combination of stubbornness and pride meant he persisted in trying to win hearts and minds by trying to win important races. At the end of 1966, he won his ninth and final Grand Prix des Nations, beating no less than Gimondi and Merckx into second and third place. If nine victories in the unofficial world time-trial championships of the day wasn't sufficient, it should also be remembered that Anquetil had in fact never lost in the race that made his name.

The following year started slowly, however. Rain and, according to Géminiani, disrupted preparations due to changing sponsors from Ford France to Bic meant Anquetil treated the Tour of Sardinia and even Paris–Nice (both events won by Tom Simpson) as training rides, finishing seventh and sixteenth respectively. Only the Critérium National to be held near Rouen – run in 1967 as a single race rather than over three stages – stirred him from his apparent apathy. However, initially even this appeared to have left him cold. Géminiani claims in *Les années Anquetil* only to have heard through the press of Anquetil's decision not to compete, as he was recovering from a cold and had stopped training. When he phoned Anquetil to find out what was going on, he was told, 'Sick as I am, I don't want to make a fool of myself on my own doorstep. You must understand that if I'm only riding to lose, I might as well stay at home.'

By now, of course, Géminiani knew his man better than to tell him he had to race. Yet the journalists were having a field day, implying a diplomatic illness and a fear of losing to Poulidor in his own backyard. Having left him to stew for four days, the night before the race Géminiani eventually went to Anquetil's house, only a stone's throw from the start line. When he arrived, his worst fears appeared confirmed, as he found Anquetil in slippers and a dressing gown, with a scarf wrapped around his neck. Much to Géminiani's satisfaction, however, he also found himself confronted with a considerable meal, indicating that Anquetil had at least recovered his appetite: shellfish, sole meunière, leg of lamb ('nice and rare'), Camemberts ('he had the gift of keeping the best Camemberts') and baked Alaska to finish. 'I shan't mention the wine and Calvados,' Géminiani later wrote. Finally, some time around 3 a.m. while playing a game of cards accompanied by cigars and whisky, Anquetil brought up the subject of the next day's race.

All it took was for Géminiani to insist, with Jeanine's help, that Poulidor was a shoo-in for victory and Anquetil had been converted: 'This race had been bothering him. With the beginnings of his flu and saying he wouldn't ride, he'd managed to avoid any pressure, but he was physically OK. I could feel it. This was the key to the enigma. I knew that in the heat of battle he'd find his form and that his rivals would also be shocked to see him at the start. He had three hours in which to sleep.' It scarcely needs to be added that he beat Poulidor in the uphill sprint to the line. No doubt to the chagrin of the 'Poulidorists', *L'Équipe* declared, 'Poulidor has confirmed himself as indisputably the best French road cyclist after Anquetil. The title is more than honourable, enough even to make others envious.'

The Critérium National apart, Anquetil's approach and his

early season results should not really have been a surprise, however. He had little to gain by chasing victory in either the Tour of Sardinia or Paris–Nice, and the effort expended in doing so may have compromised his plans for the rest of the year. Effectively, he had bigger fish to fry. Even though he had vowed not to return to the Tour de France, a vow made easier to keep thanks to the decision to revert to a national teams formula for 1967, he intended to make the most of the little time remaining to him at the pinnacle of the sport by targeting the Giro d'Italia and the hour record. Although he had already achieved success in both these goals in his career, it was the prospect of him once again attacking the hour record that attracted most headlines. At the age of 33, 11 years after he successfully took the record from Coppi, the prospect of him breaking the remarkable mark of 47.373 kilometres set by Roger Rivière, more than 1,100 metres more than he had covered, seemed incredible and gave the press something other than the rivalry with Poulidor to write about.

Yet first came the Giro, and of course this did not pass off without a degree of scandal. Exactly what happened depends on which source you believe. The most engaging account comes from Géminiani, naturally, who once again complained bitterly about the way the race was organised to the advantage of the local riders and the disadvantage of Anquetil. Still, Anquetil wore the pink jersey of leader for a couple of days after the first time-trial stage, and then looked well placed for overall victory when he was back in pink with only one mountainous stage left to ride. According to Géminiani, it took the combination of a breakaway by a good rider such as Felice Gimondi and illicit assistance in the form of a race car providing a slipstream for him to follow to allow him to drop Anquetil and snatch overall victory. (Lest anyone still thinks this sort of thing was no more than sour grapes, 1984 winner Francesco Moser was accused of benefiting from the downdraught of a helicopter when winning the final time trial and sealing overall victory; a mere slipstream from a car is nothing in comparison.) Anquetil, he says, was so miffed that he deliberately lost second place to Franco Balmamion to register his displeasure.

The most controversial version is Anquetil's own. In one of his articles for *France Dimanche*, in which he described the process of buying help from riders on other teams, he blamed his defeat on the lack of support available to him from teammates, a lack of support curiously ignored by Géminiani:

> For reasons known only to themselves, the company whose colours we were wearing stopped paying my teammates. It rapidly lost interest in a Giro that was still within my reach. The third night that they weren't paid, seven of my teammates abandoned. I was left with only two faithful lieutenants: Lucien Aimar and Jean Milesi. Three against one hundred. I was still in the lead with two stages remaining, but if I couldn't buy other riders to help me, I was cooked.

He tried, and failed, to buy help from a Spanish team, resulting in them adding their support to the massed ranks of the Italians:

> All of a sudden, in addition to the Italian coalition, I had the Spanish against me as well. Throughout the whole stage, they never left me. I knew I'd lost. Gimondi broke away right in front of my eyes, but I was surrounded by a dozen Spaniards who would stop at nothing to prevent me from chasing after him. That's how I lost the last Giro: for want of money to buy riders from another team.

Notwithstanding these two accounts, perhaps the most realistic explanation of his disappointing third place comes, for once, from the journalists, in particular those writing in *L'Équipe*:

During the 20th stage, distanced by Merckx, Gimondi, Adorni and Motta, who made a powerful alliance during the apocalyptic descent of the Brocon pass, he managed to catch up after a long and wearing chase. He then punctured twice and managed to rejoin twice. But the following day, the effort took its toll, and he couldn't recuperate – he was on the edge of exhaustion.

Gimondi's attack the next day with 40 kilometres to go was the final straw. Prosaic this account may be, but it is given great credibility by the pictures that accompany it – pictures that show Anquetil, at the end of the 20th stage, soaking wet and wrapped in a blanket, drawn, vacant almost, looking for all the world like a broken old man.

Even if he was not actually broken, and even if third place in the Giro was a respectable performance, it was hardly enough to convince the by now numerous doubters about his likelihood of succeeding in the planned attempt on the hour record, presumed to be a far stiffer challenge. These doubts only gained momentum when Anquetil engaged in a bit of limelight-stealing during the Tour de France with his deliberately shocking series of articles for *France Dimanche*. Four articles, headlined 'Why I Don't Like Poulidor', 'Yes, I've Taken Drugs', 'The Tragic Death of Tommy Simpson: Anquetil Points the Finger' and 'Yes, I've Bought Riders', earned even someone as used to controversy as Anquetil a new level of notoriety. Worse was to come at the celebratory dinner after the Tour when Anquetil's bitterness at the role his friend Jean Stablinski had played as a teammate for Poulidor – in the French national team, it must be remembered – almost led to the pair coming to blows. It also led to Stablinski leaving Bic and joining Poulidor at Mercier.

Pierre Chany was moved to write an article in *Miroir des Sports* explaining why 'Anquetil has chosen scandal', and the Fédération Française de Cyclisme (FFC) felt compelled to ban him from both the French national championships and the French team for the world championships. Anquetil was not without his supporters, however. 'Here are the nine members of the FFC, who, after three hours of deliberations, took the incredible decision of banning Jacques Anquetil from the French and world championships,' fumed *L'Aurore*. 'Of course, the world number one isn't suspended: he can ride all the other events he's planned, notably his attempt on the hour record. But this year at least he can no longer hope to capture the two titles that are missing from his list of prestigious victories. And all this because he dared write what all cycling fans have known for a long time: that most riders take drugs and that some of them are sometimes bought by champions who need their help.'

In spite of this backing, Anquetil suddenly found himself a leper in the cycling world. He was offered few if any contracts in the lucrative post-Tour round of criteriums – Géminiani says he was reduced to opening a car dealership in Nancy. He also describes him as being like 'Napoleon at Saint Helena', although perhaps Napoleon at Elba would be a better description, as Anquetil was not quite beaten yet. Nevertheless, a successful attempt at the hour record had now become considerably more than just a matter of pride and prestige. It was an essential part of being able to prolong his career and retire on his own terms, rather than as the bitter former champion he was increasingly perceived to be. Preparation came in the form of riding – and winning – the Tour of Catalonia, as well as a series of specially staged criteriums in eastern France. These culminated, three days before the record attempt was due to be held at the famous Vigorelli race track in Milan, in a practice run on the concrete track in Besançon. Due to its construction and to its relatively exposed site, the received wisdom was that Besançon was a slower track than Milan by between one and 1.5 kilometres per hour. When Anquetil managed to record 45.775 kilometres – the eighth-best distance ever at that time, boding well, therefore, for the attempt at the Vigorelli – interest in his attempt suddenly blossomed.

There were still many sceptics, however, among them former Belgian great Rik Van Steenbergen, who had paid his own way to watch 'a miracle, although a miracle I don't believe in', and current record holder Roger Rivière, who said, 'He's too old and hasn't prepared sufficiently.' Their scepticism was only heightened by Anquetil's plan to use an unprecedented gear ratio of 52 x 13 for the attempt, even larger than the already large gear he'd been using in training. This meant that for each complete turn of the pedal, Anquetil would advance 8.54 metres. Rivière, in contrast, had set his record using 53 x 15, a development of only 7.54 metres. In practical terms, this meant that Anquetil would have to pedal at a much lower cadence of 94 pedal strokes a minute (5,640 in the hour) compared with all previous hour records, including his own in 1956, which had been established at a cadence of between 100 and 105 pedal strokes in a minute (6,000 to 6,300 in total). 'He's taking an enormous risk,' Rivière told *L'Équipe*. 'He's constantly going to have to fight against his gearing. If he blows, he'll go backwards rather than forwards. If he succeeds, I'll take my hat off.'

Such a significant change in approach could well have justified their scepticism, but perhaps they should have paid more attention to Anquetil's character and his previous achievements rather than to his specific preparation and his choice of gearing. Poulidor was certainly more optimistic: 'You know, I'm no expert at this type of thing, but when Anquetil says he's going to do something he normally keeps his word.' Poulidor was right. In ideal conditions at 5.38 p.m. local time on 27 September, after a relatively slow start, Anquetil kept meticulously to his timetable, set at a slightly slower pace than that established by Rivière in 1958. After 25 kilometres, covered in just over half an hour, he was 26 seconds down on Rivière's time, but then the gap began to close inexorably. By forty kilometres, he had eked out a lead of just over four seconds, a lead that would continue to grow until the finish. In fact, Anquetil completed a distance of 47.493 kilometres, nearly 150 metres further than Rivière's record of 47.347 kilometres and a massive 1,300 metres further than his own record set 11 years previously.

The crowd went wild, and Anquetil for once let his emotions get the better of him, as made clear by the way he dedicated his victory. After acknowledging the role of Géminiani and his team, as well as his supporters and the 'very sporting' Italian crowd, he told Abel Michea of the *Miroir des Sports*:

> 'For me, the best drug was to think of the reaction of those who had been against me. Oh, I accept that I've not always been universally popular. But I've always done my job as a professional cyclist. I've won five Tours, two Giros and one Vuelta, among others, and that's still not enough for some to rate me as a champion. To be a champion for them would mean riding the races they choose, always agreeing with them, always complying with their expectations. But in the past three or four months, things have got worse. Let's not be afraid of saying it – I've been shot at, made a scapegoat. The Fédération Française de Cyclisme – my federation – banned me from the national and world championships. Well, here he is, the banned, rejected athlete, new world-record holder.'

He wasn't finished yet:

> 'Yes, I was thinking about all those set against me. Yes, Anquetil, the professional who won't ride just for medals, has ridden for a record. And they can say, all these officials, journalists, professional know-it-alls who haven't stopped condemning me, that they were the best form of drug. I was a bad example for young riders? As if every 19 year old who wins the Grand Prix des Nations can become world-record holder 14 years later. Maybe we can stop talking about backhanders, testing procedures, drugs and I don't know what else . . .'

It should come as little surprise that this last desire at least turned out to be wishful thinking. No sooner had Anquetil been lauded for his success than he had it taken away from him. Not deigning to comply with a request from a Dr Marena of the Italian Cycling Federation to submit a urine sample for the purpose of a drugs test, Anquetil effectively forfeited the record, a record that would never be ratified. (Quite right too, says Chris Boardman: 'I think it is perfectly correct that his second record wasn't ratified; pretty clear cut for me, really. I requested blood samples be taken after my hour records and stored for analysis at any time in the future. The UCI wouldn't do it, and in the current climate I am bitterly disappointed by that. The importance of this aspect in ensuring the credibility of a blue-ribbon record can't be underestimated. They did the right thing.')

As the controversy raged, Géminiani blamed everything and everyone other than himself or Anquetil: political intrigue in the Italian Cycling Federation; a specific dislike of him and a general dislike of foreign riders; and a desire for the attempt to have been held at the new track in Rome rather than in Milan. Brunel gives some credence to this last assertion: 'The President of the UCI [an Italian] wanted Anquetil to attempt the record not at the Vigorelli but in Rome – to relaunch the track and give it more prestige – but Anquetil said no. So, initially there wasn't going to be a test, but then all of a sudden there was, and he wasn't expecting it. Perhaps Géminiani knew and didn't tell him before the start, but when he was confronted with it he said, "No. It wasn't planned, so no is no."'

Anquetil was initially outraged: 'I couldn't care less whether the record is ratified. I beat it, full stop. The rest is just talk. And no one can deprive me of my greatest achievement: 14 years as a professional cyclist, always as one of its leading lights. In fact, that's the record I'm proudest of: a career lasting 14 years and the respect of my adversaries.'

Then he began to mock the process: 'After all, I can't very well have a pee in front of everybody. And anyway, straight after a race I couldn't pee even if you paid me.' Finally, he feigned offence at having his word doubted: 'As far as I know, Coppi, Baldini and Rivière weren't required to submit to such a test. Does my word not suffice?'

The question was no doubt rhetorical, but had anybody dared to answer it, it seems unlikely the response would have been favourable. After all, Anquetil had not only used his *France Dimanche* articles some two months previously to admit to taking drugs, he had also gone to some lengths to explain why, and also why he was against drug testing (even though he claimed to be in favour of the idea of reducing drug taking). What's more, Anquetil had form. In the 1966 Tour, he had led a protest by the riders against the introduction of drug-testing procedures. More pertinent still, his victory in Liège–Bastogne–Liège earlier that same year was nearly scrubbed from the record books after he didn't submit to a urine test. Only by adopting the 'scattergun' tactic that has since become the basis of almost all defences against claims of drug use by athletes – that's to say throwing as much mud as possible at the race organisers, the officials involved and the procedure itself and hoping enough of it will stick – was Anquetil reinstated as victor.

Even reading Anquetil's own explanation of his position, you could be forgiven for a degree of confusion (in cycling, it appears, it was ever thus). He confesses to overcoming many a weak moment thanks to amphetamines, and to having caffeine and vitamin injections, even a course of strychnine injections prior to his first Tour de France in 1957 – very invigorating and very popular among professional cyclists in the pre-war years, apparently. He also wrote:

> If you want to accuse me of having doped, it's not difficult.
> All you have to do is look at my thighs and my buttocks

– they're veritable pin cushions. You have to be an imbecile or a hypocrite to imagine that a professional cyclist who races 235 days a year in all weathers can keep going without stimulants.

(It should be noted that Anquetil wasn't always this candid. In a 1961 French television documentary, several professional cyclists were asked what they understood by the phrase *'saler la soupe'* (add salt to your soup), a common euphemism for doping. While several riders looked rather uncomfortable and contrived different ways to avoid answering, and while another tapped his nose and said it was a trade secret, Anquetil didn't even blink and simply denied ever having heard the phrase before.)

However, he then added that he didn't defend doping:

> I don't defend it, but I'm fed up with the hypocrisy surrounding it, one of the most obvious examples being the famous anti-doping law rushed in last year. This is shameful, as it only targets one profession – cyclists. Nobody's worried to know if a student, an overburdened lawyer or a labourer who wants to work overtime takes stimulants. How would you react if a doctor and a police officer turned up at your house and told you to pee into a flask in their presence? The same way as me, I'm sure – that it's an affront to my dignity and my personal freedom.

In a separate article for *Lui* magazine, Anquetil expanded on the reasons for his resistance to being tested:

> I don't want to destroy anything, certainly not cycling, as that's what's allowed me to be 'somebody'. But I must be true to my convictions and my understanding of a man's dignity, and above all of those involved in sport, when confronted with drugs tests carried out in humiliating conditions. We are not animals. We have the right to be treated with respect. I'm not against doping controls, but I am against the conditions in which these tests are undertaken.

Anquetil went on to criticise what he saw as the inconsistencies of the law – all injections were banned, but not caffeine the substance, so you could drink coffee, for example, but you couldn't inject caffeine – and the fact that it was not strictly enforced. He cited the example of a Dutch rider unable to produce a sample after a race who was told he could take a flask home with him and provide one when he was ready; when the sample was returned and tested, there were no traces of doping products, but the rider was pregnant – it was, of course, his wife's urine. Yet the main thrust of his argument was centred on the way cycling as a profession was singled out for special treatment and that this was beneath the dignity of the star riders, whose prestige after all was largely based on their public image.

He reinforced this view with his article the very next week in the immediate aftermath of Tom Simpson's death on the Mont Ventoux in the Tour de France:

> Tom Simpson, my friend Tommy, is dead. He died doing his job, fighting for his sport, in the hardest conditions, in 40-degree heat in the mountains. Later, I'll explain why he was my friend and what a great guy he was. But first of all I want to express my indignation. The very day of his death people thought of only one thing: to cast aspersions on Simpson and through him the whole of cycling. Straight away, people spoke of one thing and one thing only: doping. The police, the judiciary were all involved. Without a thought for his widow or his two daughters, they decided to conduct an autopsy on this family man, who died through overestimating his own strength. In all walks of life, there are men who die when conditions are against them. A roofer can fall, a miner can be run over by a truck, a pilot can crash his plane. But nobody says: ah ha, he was drunk, or he was drugged. Road cycling is a hard and dangerous profession and everybody knows it, although there are fewer deaths than in motor racing, horse riding or climbing. Yet Tommy is dead, and straight away everyone says: it's because he

was doped. They're all doped. What good would it do to know if he had been doped? Leave him in peace. That we should undertake to prevent or manage doping, I agree. But it's through education and training of young riders that we'll succeed, rather than through adopting police methods and treating us like criminals.

If there is anything that justifies Anquetil's stance against measures such as drugs tests that were designed to root out the nefarious practices of professional cycling, it is this notion of going from superstar to criminal without having done anything differently from how you did things in the past. Last year, a few amphetamine tablets and a caffeine injection were accepted as tools of a very arduous trade. This year, drugs tests mean the same activities could earn you a suspension and even a prison sentence (not to mention loss of reputation and income).

What's more, Anquetil was right in seeing cyclists as being singled out. The products used – by and large amphetamines, though steroids and hormones were growing in popularity and would be in widespread use by the 1970s – were both legal and widely available. 'You could buy them over the counter,' remembers Jeanine. 'My husband who was a doctor gave a Maxitot [one of the most famous brands of amphetamine] to my daughter when she was 15 or 16 to help her pass her exams. It was just a little pick-me-up. To keep you alert while driving, you'd take a Corydrane [another brand of amphetamine mixed with aspirin]. Cyclists weren't allowed them, but I could take them for driving, and they were available over the counter.'

Brunel confirms how readily obtainable these products were: 'You couldn't just go and buy them. You needed a prescription, but any doctor could give you one and would give you one. There was no trafficking. It's not the same process as today. There was no criminalisation of the act, where maybe you're in contact with people you wouldn't otherwise want to be in contact with. At the time, everything was easier, more straightforward.'

Jeanine wasn't the only one to use them, and it wasn't all flower power and hippies either. During the Second World War, fighter pilots and naval captains were regularly provided with amphetamines to help them perform for longer, as were workers in Japanese munitions factories. Then there was one of the most famous philosophers of the twentieth century, Jean-Paul Sartre. Asked in an interview with the *New York Review of Books* about the sense of urgency that pervaded his work, he replied, 'I started writing *Critique de la raison dialectique*, and it was this [sense of urgency] that was gnawing at me. I worked on it ten hours a day, taking Corydrane – in the end, I was taking twenty pills a day – and I really felt that this book had to be finished. The amphetamines gave me a quickness of thought and writing that was at least three times my normal rhythm, and I wanted to go fast.'

Anquetil's former teammate Guy Ignolin describes the effect they would have on a cyclist: 'We took amphetamines every now and then. Tiny things, about three milligrams – the stuff you could buy in a chemist's. They lasted about 50 kilometres, an hour, an hour and a half maybe, and then afterwards you'd feel worse than before, so you only took them in the last 50 kilometres. They didn't make you any stronger, but you just saw everything better – the road, bumps, the wheels – everything was clearer.' Poulidor agrees with the idea that the effect and the quantities used were minimal: 'He never hid it. He did it a little, but he certainly didn't exaggerate. He said he took his little pick-me-up. It was nothing like what goes on today, though. It was a little pill to make you feel better, something like students take, that's all. Now it's a medical preparation.'

If this makes the quantities consumed sound reassuringly insignificant, William Fotheringham in *Put Me Back on My*

Bike, his biography of Tom Simpson, suggests otherwise. First, the 'recommended' dose he uncovered was eight milligrams, not three. Even this was likely to be far less than was actually consumed, however. One unidentified former professional he spoke to said 50 milligrams was more usual. The reasons for this apparent discrepancy were twofold: regular amphetamine users acquire resistance over time, meaning more has to be consumed to stimulate the same effect; and cyclists conform to the athletic stereotype of assuming that the more they consume of anything, the better they will perform. The fact is that cyclists are already a self-selected group of individuals with physiological capacities – whether effort expended or substances consumed – far in excess of the norm.

Ignolin also lends support to the assertion that it was the workload that came with being a professional cyclist that was the catalyst for their drug consumption: 'We didn't take them until we were maybe 25 or 26. Until then, we'd always been warned against them and told not to take them. Clearly, Anquetil didn't take anything when he won his first Grand Prix des Nations.' (Maybe, maybe not. It should not be forgotten that while Anquetil was an exceptionally precocious talent who certainly arrived at the top thanks to his natural ability, his *directeur sportif* for his first Grand Prix des Nations, Francis Pélissier, was the epitome of the old pro who knew all there was to know about the trade, warts and all.)

Yet, once again, the argument of pressures of the job seems flawed, as not all cyclists of the time were drug users. Anquetil's teammate Vin Denson, a man capable of cycling Bordeaux–Paris with grit in his shorts and crippled by a trapped nerve in his nether regions, swears he never took anything stronger than sugar. In fact, he went to extreme lengths to ensure he didn't: 'I took rice cakes and rice pudding, apples, sliced up bananas, plus calcium, and I put a lot of glucose in my drinks. I used to take my bottles up to the bedroom and mix my own drinks, then I used to put bike tape round the tops and I put a Rizla paper in the middle, without anyone knowing, so I knew if anyone had tampered with them. I'd give them to the *soigneur* or the mechanic for the feeds on the road, and I'd say, "If anyone touches my bottles, I'll take you right through the courts." To the best of my knowledge, nobody did. They knew I was a bit forthright and totally against it.'

Anquetil knew this as well as anyone. 'One day, he asked me to give him an injection at a criterium, and I refused,' Denson continues. 'I said, "Go out and get someone else. I'll do anything with these legs, and I'll give you a push with my hand, but I won't do anything else like that. I would not encourage you on that side whatsoever. I don't want to get involved." He was a little bit taken aback. The next minute, I saw Stablinski coming round the corner, and he waved him across.' That it was Stablinski who appeared to help out should have come as little surprise. 'The big organiser of products at the heart of the French team was Stablinski,' says Brunel.

Anquetil was right in one aspect, however: all cyclists were being tarred with the same brush. 'It came to a stage when you were taking your kids to school – kindergarten in Belgium – and the kids would say, "Have you been on the drugs again this morning?" and I would say, "Look, I'm pure. I don't take them. I've been through tests 30 or 40 times,"' Denson explains. 'One of the papers latched onto this, and I did an article. I tried to bring in an anti-drug movement.' As the recent history of cycling confirms, however, the attempt was short-lived. 'We had 80 per cent of riders against drugs then in the 1960s. It was in the '70s, '80s and '90s they forgot about it.'

EIGHTEEN

Jacques of All Trades

REGARDLESS OF WHETHER HIS 1967 hour record was ratified or not, Anquetil had achieved his twin goals of cementing his place in cycling folklore and reclaiming his place at the top of the bill, though whether this was a result of popularity or notoriety remained a moot point. In practical and financial terms – the terms that meant the most to him – this restoration of his pre-eminence, even if as something of an elder statesman rather than the dominant rider of previous seasons, afforded Anquetil the luxury of determining his own timetable for retirement, rather than having it imposed upon him by a loss of form or a fall from grace. In fact, Anquetil would end up drawing out his farewell to the world of professional cycling that he'd been immersed in since he was nineteen by another two years until 1969.

'The 8 January next year I'll be 36,' he told *L'Équipe*. 'I always intended to race until I was 34, but I was tempted to carry on a bit longer, and I don't regret it, as I don't think I've made a fool of myself. But enough is enough. It's time to move on.' He certainly didn't make a fool of himself in terms of his race results. The glory days of the early part of the decade may have been definitively behind him, but in 1968 he still found it in him to win the Baracchi Trophy for the third time, this time in partnership with Felice Gimondi.

In 1969, his last year as a rider, he earned a glowing review in *L'Équipe* for his performance in the Tour of the Basque Country, his last major victory: 'A French rider has beaten the Spanish in their own country, and that rider is Jacques Anquetil!'

Even finishing third to Poulidor's second in Paris–Nice (after being caught by Merckx in the time trial up the Col d'Èze) and then losing to his arch-rival in the Circuit des Six Provinces provoked only a measured response. After chasing down a Poulidor break on one stage, he explained his motives: 'I chased to prove something to myself, and I thought I could make it to the lead group, but then I started to get cramps in my legs when we went up the Col de la Forclaz. That hadn't happened to me since the world championships in 1955. Perhaps I was tired after the chase, or perhaps it was a lack of race miles. I haven't raced much this year, and my mind's on other things. I think if I focused exclusively on cycling, I could still be right up there for victory, but, like I say, my mind's on other things, even during a race – on the person behind the rider. It's peculiar, though, that at 35 I'm still acting as if it's up to me to control the race.'

The story was similar in the Critérium des As. Even before the event, Anquetil was talking down his chances: 'I don't think I can win. One hundred kilometres behind a motorbike is no joke, and I know I won't get any presents from the Belgians.' He was right. Walter Godefroot went on to claim victory, while Anquetil came fourth. 'I did what I could. Two laps from the end, I thought I might make it. A few years ago, things would have been a lot more straightforward!'

Seen in the context of the pride and fierce rivalry that inspired so much of his career, this phlegmatic response to defeat, first at the hands of his greatest rival and then in an event he'd won four times previously, raises the question: why was he still racing? Certainly, he'd admitted himself that his mind was elsewhere and that he was short of race miles. In May of his last year, he gave his own explanation in an interview with *Lui* magazine: 'Out of curiosity, no doubt. Out of fear of suddenly being deprived of competitive cycling. Out of pride, also. I'm thirty-five, and I'm constantly facing up to adversaries who are ten or fifteen years younger than me. They can't always show me who's boss, and I'll admit that gives me a degree of pride. For the next generation of riders, Jacques Anquetil is still the man to beat, the public-enemy number one.'

According to Richard Marillier, who describes Anquetil as being more than just a friend to him, and who worked alongside him when he was technical director of the French national cycling team in the 1970s, there was also another more prosaic reason. He wanted the money: 'I hope somebody's told you this. You'd find it somewhere anyway. He had decided to stop racing. He said, "That's it. I'm stopping." He'd bought a farm. It started like that, with something like 400 hectares – it was enormous – but only a few buildings. Then the bloke who looked after his business interests – his solicitor, if you like – said the chateau is for sale, the one by his farm and the one he rode past as a kid. "But how much?" The answer was that it was a price that represented a very good deal. So he rode for two more years solely to pay for the chateau. He borrowed 90,000,000 francs at the time [Marillier still talks in old francs, so this is the equivalent of £90,000]. He paid it off in two years, but he rode solely for that.'

This was towards the end of 1967, and although he may not actually have earned quite enough to completely pay off such a mortgage, Anquetil himself acknowledged the financial benefits of his two-year swansong in his interview with *Lui*: 'The paroxysm of effort in sport is in fact only acceptable through the moral or material satisfaction it provides. I still have a furious desire to race, but I never do it just for pleasure. Pure, unadulterated amateurism is a chimera. It doesn't exist. It can't exist, and everybody knows it. Why this hypocrisy is tolerated, I don't know. I would have been as pure and irreproachable an amateur as the next man as long as one way or another, through whatever detours it took, money was being put into my wallet.'

Nor would this money have been inconsiderable, he claims, suggesting a top amateur was likely to receive in the order of £200 per month plus appearance money, more than double the average salary of the time. Yet Anquetil was more ambitious than that: 'I've been a pure professional for more than 15 years and have never been embarrassed to be one. It's never tarnished my reputation. It's never brought into question what I've achieved.'

He might not have been embarrassed, but his memory appears short. His candid articles two years earlier in *France Dimanche* – including his confessions about buying riders – certainly cast a shadow of sorts on his reputation. Yet as an unabashed professional, he was happy to continue, explaining the comfortable financial situation he was now in: 'I started investing at the end of my military service. On my return to civilian life, I wanted to buy a sports car, a beautiful red one, a car for someone of my age. But instead I chose to buy a small block of flats on rue Malaitre in Rouen. My first property, and my first capital investment. Now I have quite enough money to live comfortably for the rest of my days.'

Two extra years would undoubtedly have helped, however. According to figures Anquetil himself provides in his interview with *Lui* magazine, his basic salary in his last contract with the Bic team was £12,000 per year (although Géminiani suggests he was paid £30,000 per year). He said he could then more than double this through the contracts he was given to race in criteriums (between 50 and 100 of these each year, worth £300 each, giving a total of between £15,000 and £30,000) and other appearance money. On average, he said he declared £36,000 per year for tax purposes, a good reason to keep cycling (even if he chose to ride the Tour de

France route one day ahead of the race in 1969 to provide a stage description for Europe 1 because he earned more from that than from racing).

To put this into context, the average UK wage of the time was £1,300. Anquetil was nearly thirty times better off and could hope to earn more in his two supplementary years than most people would earn in their lifetime. It should be noted, however, that this still doesn't put him into the same stratospheric salary bracket as today's highest-earning sports stars, notably footballers. While the equivalent of Anquetil's earnings today is a very healthy £1,000,000, and this could no doubt be improved considerably by the endorsements and deals that would be available to someone of his status, this is still some way short of Wayne Rooney's latest deal with Manchester United, worth, according to the *Daily Mail* at least, a staggering £35,000,000 over six years – nearly £6,000,000 per year.

Even gravy trains must come to an end, however, and in spite of this earning potential, and in spite of his good showing in the Critérium des As, he decided 1969 would be his last season: 'Even if I'd won the As for a fifth time, it wouldn't have changed anything. It's well and truly over. I shall race the autumn criteriums, and then I'll retire. I'm racing a lot and also working on my farm – there's nothing better to keep you in shape. What's more, as I know I'll be stopping soon, I'm enjoying my racing greatly.' Not even the prospect of a tenth victory in the Grand Prix des Nations could lure him: 'You've got to be joking. If I lost, that's all anyone would remember. Even if I was tempted, I wouldn't fall into such a trap. I'm not even going to participate at the opening of the new track in Grenoble on the first of February for the simple reason that I won't have a racing licence next year.'

He bade farewell to the Parisian crowds in front of a full house of 8,000 at the La Cipale track and received a rapturous reception, a reaction that didn't seem to surprise him: 'The public now appreciate what I've achieved. And, as always, when anybody retires you begin to miss them.' His final race was also on the track, at the Sportpaleis in Antwerp, on 27 December. As befits someone with such an impressive list of victories, he was in exalted company: 'When you're getting ready in the same changing-rooms as Rudi Altig and Eddy Merckx, it's quite something. You don't think about it being your last race. But when the organisers decided to delay the start of the last race by a minute so my wife could set us off, I must admit to having a twinge of regret. That's when it really struck me that I was saying goodbye, and hindsight will surely serve to reinforce that feeling.'

The tributes began to pour in, led by Merckx, Anquetil's heir apparent: 'The ease with which he appears to ride is unprecedented, all the more impressive when you're aware of the hardships involved in riding a bike. The most extraordinary thing is that he still makes it look easy after a career lasting 17 years. I think that's absolutely fantastic, because I know that 17 years as a cyclist is a long, long time. The sum of the hardships that represents is unimaginable.'

According to Brunel, Merckx was more than simply the heir to Anquetil's dominance of cycling. 'Anquetil wanted to challenge Merckx,' he recalls. 'There was a criterium, and at the end of the race he said, "Let's see what Eddy's made of." So they started with a reception by the mayor, where there was champagne, etc. Then they went to a restaurant, eating, drinking more champagne, wine. Then it was off to a nightclub. They started on whisky – double whiskies. And in truth it was Merckx who won – Jacques left first. Merckx won. Jacques left with Jeanine at 5 a.m. to sleep for an hour then met Eddy again at breakfast, and Merckx ordered chicken and pasta . . . They had a rapport that no longer exists today, a very virile rapport.'

Relieved of the hardships Merckx mentions, Anquetil

was not one to sit on his hands. Although happy to distance himself from the effort of racing, he maintained his interest and involvement in the world of cycling. He would eventually become race director for Paris–Nice and the Grand Prix du Midi Libre, a member of the managing committee of the FFC, and made a name for himself as a columnist in *L'Équipe* and co-commentator during the Tour de France and other races, first on radio for Europe 1 and then for the newly created French television channel Antenne 2. He vowed never to become a *directeur sportif*, however. 'He never wanted to be in charge of a team,' recalls Jeanine. 'He could never have said to others not to have a beer when he wanted one himself: "If I told them not to drink, imagine what they'd say to me . . ."'

Yet he was happy to accept his friend Marillier's request to help him with the national team. Formerly a resistance fighter and colonel in the French army during the war in Algeria, now an energetic if slightly ailing octogenarian, Marillier was prepared to go to considerable lengths to meet me and impress upon me his fondness for Anquetil. I ended up taking a train from Paris to meet him in Nevers, as he said it would be too much to ask me to find the old farmhouse he owns, 'lost' – his word – in the surrounding countryside (I would have been delighted to try). I didn't realise until it was too late that this required him corralling a friend into providing a taxi service for the 60-mile round trip, as his fading eyesight meant he was no longer able to drive himself; that he had no trouble in doing this says much about his reputation and his still noticeable military bearing. 'It's the least I can do,' he said when I finally appreciated what had happened. 'I'm obliged to come and speak to you, first because my wife was an English teacher and I'm very fond of *les Britanniques* – I don't speak a word of English, mind you – but mainly because of my friendship with Jacques. And if you can come to France, the least I can do is to come and meet you for lunch in Nevers. And you'll be able to enjoy some decent food.'

To all intents and purposes, Marillier was a one-man team. He was selector of all French national teams – male, female and amateur – manager and *directeur sportif* all in one. Not surprisingly, he felt the need for a bit of extra assistance: 'My first world championships were in Leicester in 1970, and I understood that I needed with me a person, a name that carried some clout on the global stage. At the world championships, when you're abroad, nobody knows who Marillier is; Anquetil is known by everyone. So, I rang Jacques. I asked him, and he said – you have to know him – first he said, "It's kind of you to think of me. I'd say yes, but on certain conditions. Basically, I don't want to be sucked into all the hassle of selection. You select, tell me who you've chosen the evening before so I don't look like a fool in front of the journalists and we'll work like that." And we did work like that for ten years – with him as *directeur sportif*, if you like.'

His duties were not exactly wearing, however: 'What did he do? He didn't do anything! Nothing! He was in the car during the race. There was the driver and Anquetil, and I was at the roadside, linked up by radio. But he never gave any advice. He'd collect the numbers. When we were abroad, they asked who would be collecting the numbers. I'd say, "Jacques Anquetil." They'd say, "What?" "Yes, no joking. He'll be along to get them." I thought French cycling needed a figurehead. Even if I had Poulidor in my team, Anquetil was something else. He was on a pedestal.'

This in itself had benefits for the morale of the team, as Bernard Hinault recalls: 'His most notable achievement was that when he was standing next to you, it was him standing next to you. You'd be full of admiration for him, so it was already a bit of a dream come true. That you could just speak to him like that, when you're only 21, was fantastic, an inspiration. Then when I grew in stature within the team and it was him who came to see me, that also made me happy – the fact that he would ask me for my opinion.'

If Marillier's side of the deal seems distinctly lacking in terms of the practical help you might have thought he'd be looking for, it's clear what Anquetil got out of the arrangement: he could continue his long-standing enjoyment of the camaraderie of cycling with neither responsibility nor great exertion. In fact, being free of these constraints facilitated a remarkable rapprochement with Poulidor.

Anquetil family legend has it that he first became a fan of Poulidor after his daughter Sophie kept repeating '*Vas-y Poupou*' instead of '*Vas-y Papa*' ('Come on Poupou' – Poulidor's nickname – instead of 'Come on Papa'). In fact, the thawing of their relationship had started sometime before Sophie, only born in 1971, was able to make her preferences felt (and, of course, 'Papa' had stopped riding before she came along). This process was only helped by the fact that the two were involved in the same national team. With Poulidor no longer a rival, old enmities could be set to one side. 'At the end, when he'd finished cycling, he talked to friends of mine, and he said to me, "Raymond, we've lost ten years of friendship,"' Poulidor remembers. 'In the end, we became very, very good friends. In fact, he was one of my number-one fans.'

This unlikely turn of events is confirmed from first-hand experience by Marillier: 'I remember a scene from the world championships in France at Gap. It was the eve of the race, and we were in a park on a lawn. All three of us were lying down: Poulidor, me in the middle and Anquetil. Jacques said, "You'd have been in the shit if I'd continued to race. What would you have done when you were choosing – take me or him?" I said, "It's simple, a quick decision – it would have been one or the other. I wouldn't have taken both, except if you'd signed an agreement with me beforehand, but even then . . ." Jacques said, "Yes, but you'd have had half France against you." And Raymond said, "Yes, but you'd have had the other half for you . . ."'

As was the tradition in the cycling caravan, the friendship included plenty of card-playing, one of Anquetil's favourite pastimes, and of course there was only one winner: Poulidor. 'Ah, cards,' he says, smiling. 'Yes, I beat him a lot, but he didn't mind.' Marillier describes one typical confrontation that serves also to reinforce the unique *esprit de corps* that cycling provided at the time: 'It was in 1977, at the world championships in San Cristóbal on the Venezuela–Colombia border. The defending world champion was Freddy Maertens, so the Belgians all rode for him. Then one lap from the end, he abandoned. I can tell you that people like Merckx, who'd worked their backsides off for him, weren't happy. Both teams were in the same hotel, and at dinner time we were eating at opposite ends of the restaurant. Towards the end of the meal, Merckx suddenly got up, and the *directeur sportif* as well, and I thought, "That's it. They're going to fight." But Merckx just came to our table and said, "Commandant," that's what he used to call me, "can I come and sit with you?" I asked, "What's up?" He replied, "I can't stay with those delinquents," so he finished the meal and the evening with us.

'Shortly afterwards, Poulidor said to me that this was his last race for the national team so he'd buy the drinks. Bloody hell. We'd never seen him pay for anything. Never! "You sort it out. Champagne for everyone." I went to find the hotel boss, and I didn't speak any Spanish and he no French, but I understood they didn't have any champagne. "How about whisky?" I asked. Poupou said that this was OK, so we got two bottles, but it was a rip-off – £32 I think. So, they were all there – Anquetil, Merckx, Poulidor – drinking plenty. They'd ridden 260 kilometres that day, after all. After a while, someone suggested playing cards, a game of poker. Anquetil played like a potato but was always happy to play. Poulidor said, "Yes." Merckx said, "Why not?" They all played in Poulidor's room. They started at 11 p.m. I came back at 6 a.m., and they were just finishing. Six in the morning! They hadn't slept a wink. I asked Poulidor how things were going, and he said, "I've taken £34 from one and £36 from the other." In other words, he'd paid £32 for the whisky and had won back double!'

In spite of these occasional financial setbacks against his old adversary, and in spite of Poulidor's retirement, Anquetil continued his functions with the national team even after Marillier left to join the Tour de France organisers. His last attendance was in Villach in Austria, just after he'd had his stomach removed and scarcely three months before he died. The role he had carved out for himself continued to provide unlikely benefits, including discovering the delights of English seaside resorts. 'I remember going to the world championships at Goodwood in 1982,' says Jeanine. 'We both went there. What I remember most are all the slot machines in Brighton.'

There was also the equally unlikely discovery of a new, improved, riding position. For the undisputed master of time-trialling, a man about whose position on a bike people have written poems and eulogies ('Watching Anquetil in the Grand Prix des Nations almost made me cry with admiration' was one of *L'Équipe*'s most notable attempts to characterise his beautiful combination of rhythm and power), this is tantamount to heresy. Had it not come from as competent a judge as Bernard Hinault, it might also seem unbelievable, yet he is adamant: 'It was when we were at the world championships in Colorado Springs in the USA in 1986 – more or less 20 years since he'd been on a bike. He was a bit bored, and he said, "You can't lend me a bike?" So we lent him one and didn't change the set-up at all. It was set up for me, but we didn't change the saddle, handlebars, anything. Then, after we'd started riding, he said he'd never felt so comfortable on a bike.'

This feeling of comfort must have been all the more remarkable given that Anquetil appears to have ridden a bike no more than half a dozen times after he retired. 'When he hung up his wheels, he hung them up for good,' says Sophie. 'I remember him getting back on his bike just three times: once, he climbed the Puy-de-Dôme with Poulidor; once, he rode his bike into the swimming pool on my birthday; and the third time I was twelve. I'd really insisted that he come for a ride with me one weekend. I insisted, insisted, and then finally he capitulated. We went with some friends and did a ride together. But once he'd stopped, that was it. I think that he'd given so much, suffered so much on a bike, that once his career was over that was enough, and he had no reason to keep riding.'

Perhaps the discovery of a better position might have reduced his suffering. 'You must remember, he didn't have a wind tunnel like I had to test his position,' Hinault continues. 'If Père Jacques [the respect implied by this affectionate nickname is quite clear] had been in a wind tunnel, I think he would have changed his position. And when you look at it closely, I've looked at him in photos, he doesn't have the ideal position. Ideal for the time he was riding, yes, but not the best position with hindsight, knowing what we now know. He could have been even more powerful and faster.'

In a similar vein, Poulidor recalls how Anquetil was at ease on almost any bike: 'He was just made to ride a bike. If you gave him a bike, any bike, he was good on it.' Poulidor also repeats the story of Anquetil being asked by his mechanic what gearing he wanted for a big mountain stage during the Tour: 'He just said, "Do as you would for yourself." It was remarkable.'

Yet this may in reality be no more than another facet of the Anquetil myth, another ruse designed to unsettle his rivals. For a start, he was meticulous in preparing his gearing for all his time-trial triumphs – going so far as to work out which gear he needed to be in for each corner on a course – while his attempts on the hour record included the experimentation with different ratios that led to his unprecedented use of 52 x 13. What's more, Vin Denson – the teammate with the closest inside-leg measurement to that of Anquetil – recalls how he was almost as restless as Merckx: 'He had quite long inside legs – he was all leg, in fact – and even though I was quite a bit taller than him I used to have only about a quarter-inch longer inside leg than he did, so they'd build my bike up to his size. On difficult stages, like through the small Brittany villages when you knew the team cars couldn't get through quickly to be able to effect a change if necessary, the team would say I was on Anquetil's bike today, and he was ever so fussy about his saddle position. He'd carry a spanner, and I'd carry one myself, as half the time he'd forget to put his in his pocket. He'd be riding to the start, and he'd say, "Those bloody mechanics have not got my saddle right," and I'd say, "They've probably got it perfectly right. It's just nerves, Jacques; it's just nerves." But he'd insist on stopping, and he'd move it down a quarter-inch, say. And bugger me, after we'd started, just as things were getting a bit frisky, after about 20 kilometres, he'd say, "My saddle's too low," and want it up again. So Stablinski or [Anatole] Novak or someone would be pushing him, and I'd be altering his saddle – it had little notches on it. I'd move it up to what I knew was his position, and he'd be happy then. Then he wanted a comb, then a beer . . .'

Denson was, in fact, referred to by British journalist Geoffrey Nicholson not as Anquetil's 'superdomestique' but as his 'supervalet', a description he still sees as apt: 'I thought, "If you're going to be a valet to anyone, might as well be valet to the Duke of Norfolk." And Anquetil was the star man. Oh yes, he was the top. Nobody to touch him.'

Cycling no longer filled his life, however. As befits a man

with his considerable energy levels, he had various other interests. 'There was a manufacturer who made jerseys, gloves and the rest, all in his name,' recalls his childhood friend Maurice Dieulois. 'There was also a company that made "Anquetil" bikes, and from time to time he did publicity stuff in shopping centres, that sort of thing.' A tête-à-tête with Jacques Anquetil in *L'Équipe* also revealed that he owned a few properties in Cannes, as well as a gravel pit in Normandy, producing some 100,000 tonnes per year. He even found time to dish out road safety advice for a government campaign to reduce road deaths, although his advice wasn't always conventional: 'I've driven 800,000 kilometres, the equivalent of 20 times around the world. Being careful doesn't have to mean being slow.'

His comments on the sometimes uncomfortable relationship between cars and cyclists were perhaps better received – 'When you overtake a cyclist, make sure there's enough space for him if he falls' – and his advice to cyclists themselves was ahead of its time:

> I couldn't recommend highly enough to my cycling friends, those who are passionate about the bike, to use all available means to make sure everyone is aware of them. Even, and I'm not joking, wearing luminous helmets or jackets. Some might laugh at this idea. Others might see it as a chance to start a fashion. Whatever, the important thing is to avert an accident.

But his real passion, going right back to his rural upbringing, was working on his farm, and this he did with abandon. 'How many times did we talk to him with Géminiani about not just buying land but perhaps considering investing in property?' asks Jeanine. 'But no, for him it was land.' In spite of his wealth and his other activities, he was determined that the effort he himself put in on the farm should be appreciated. In an interview with the *Miroir du Cyclisme* headlined 'The

Tour . . . of the Estate with Anquetil', he was asked whether he'd become a gentleman farmer:

> 'Not at all. I'm a farmer. It's not a pleasure garden. Here's where I grow wheat, next door it's oats, further along it's flax – flax is a tricky crop. And the farm can't wait. I've got to spread fertiliser, harrow, sow. I'll take advantage of the good weather and put in some extra hours. They say it might not last, and the barometer suggests a storm's brewing.'

Jeanine's son Alain was nominally in charge of running the farm, but this didn't stop Anquetil from dirtying his own hands. 'Was it just a farm for fun? No, he worked hard at it,' Jeanine asserts. 'We had cows and other animals. Wheat, oats, barley, maize. There were times we'd come back from an evening out in Paris all dressed up with high heels on, and we were in the mud with Jacques if necessary.'

Maybe it was this combination of high society and country living that leads his school friend Dieulois to acknowledge that he was looked on by some as a kind of dandy: 'They said, "Look, he's got a farm, but he must only work there every now and then. Most of the time he must be at his desk, on the phone." But he had the boots, he drove the tractor, he maintained the buildings. Although I don't really know that he made any money from it. On the contrary, at certain points it must have cost him money.'

'He lost lots on the farm, but he liked it,' confirms his last companion Dominique, an assertion that creates an intriguing picture. The man who infamously declared to his friends that he wouldn't ride his bike for 'chocolate medals', whose prime motivation was to use the bike to make as much money as possible in order to improve his lot, was now paying out of his own pocket to reconnect with the rurality of his youth. This was clearly the passion that cycling had never been. 'He just wanted a simple life,' says Sophie. 'He was a peasant, so he went out harvesting, labouring, looking after animals. My image of my father is someone who replanted hectares and hectares of trees, as there had been fires. Someone who took me out on 1 May, as everyone used to, to get wild lily of the valley. Everything followed the rhythm of nature.'

However, this didn't stop him being an innovator, as he had been in cycling. A retrospective in *L'Équipe* after he retired revealed that he was one of the first to import a particular early maturing breed of cattle from Ireland – his success in this venture was enough, the paper claims, to have led to a meeting with the British prime minister. Nevertheless, after a while he moved away from husbandry and became an arable farmer. It was not unusual, the paper said, for him to spend 20 hours consecutively at the wheel of his tractor. 'Like a real farmer, he doesn't hesitate to work from dawn to dusk,' explained his cousin Marcel Bidault. 'He's got farming in his blood.'

Hinault, who until recently had also turned to farming after he'd retired from cycling, doesn't contradict any of these assessments but does suggest another motivation behind Anquetil's desire for land: 'As he was a farmer, we spoke about crops, animals, the farm, long and late into the night. He worked, yes. When he wasn't commentating on cycling, or whatever, he was at the farm working. There was also the fact that having earned lots allowed him to buy a farm – he was no longer the labourer but the landowner. That allowed him to show local people how he had succeeded and succeeded socially. It's not arrogance. That's not how he was. But he wanted to get from the bottom to the top of the social ladder.'

NINETEEN

The Cyclist, the Wife, Her Daughter and His Lover

EXCEPTIONAL, UNCONVENTIONAL, SOMETIMES SHOCKING: if this is an accurate description of Anquetil's life so far, then the way he conducted his family life after his retirement from cycling would only serve to emphasise the picture of a man born to exceed normal constraints, whether physical or social. In fact, the extent and intensity of his off-bike activities – farmer, commentator, race director, unreconstructed bon viveur – were as nothing compared with his domestic arrangements.

The root cause of all the later upheavals was Anquetil's desire, not to say obsession, to have a child of his own. This had been understood right from the outset of his relationship with his then lover Jeanine, as she herself acknowledged when trying to explain her reasons for being willing to give up her own marriage and children for him. The problem was that Jeanine could no longer have children, a fact which had also been clear to both parties long before they married. The inevitable result, although delayed by the duration of his cycling career, was a collision between his desire for his own child and her inability to provide him with one.

When I visited Jeanine in Corsica, she was happy to talk candidly about most aspects of her married life. She was aware of – and unflustered by – the obligation on a biographer to ask sometimes awkward questions on intimate and sensitive subjects. She was nevertheless guarded when talking about some aspects of their relationship – what she felt with regard to asking her daughter to act as a surrogate mother, and the later implosion of the Anquetil family unit as the rivalry between mother and daughter for the love of one man came to a head. Yet although talking to a stranger on such matters may have been uncomfortable, she was quite ready to respond to her granddaughter Sophie's considerably more probing interrogation for her own book about her unique family life. If there is one clear leitmotif for the whole saga, it is that, without a doubt, blood is thicker than water.

It is with reference to Jeanine's comments in *Pour l'amour de Jacques*, then, that the process that led to Anquetil having a daughter with his stepdaughter is best explained:

> 'He'd always wanted to have a child, and I couldn't give him one. I'd had two very difficult Caesarean births with Annie and Alain, and my husband at the time thought it better if I had my tubes cut. While Jacques had been racing, we'd been enough for each other, but I knew him too well to think that his obsession for having his own child wouldn't increase once he'd retired. And that's exactly what happened. As soon as he stopped, his desire to have a kid kept gnawing away at him.'

(The consequences of this desire have obviously been gnawing away at Jeanine ever since. 'If I'd been young now, we'd never have had any problems with having children,' she told me, with evident regret. 'I could have had IVF. In those days, you couldn't do that. I could have had a child of Jacques by IVF, so there wouldn't have been any problems.')

Anquetil, it should be clear by now, was never one to

back away from a challenge, even when others would have baulked at the potential solution:

> 'In 1970, Jacques came back one evening from having been out walking on his own all day in the forest, and he said to me, "I have to find a surrogate mother, even a whore who we have to pay for nine months, but I have to have my own child. We'll go to Paris. That's where we'll find someone."'

Even the resilient and infatuated Jeanine was not enamoured with this plan. The possibility of the mother not wanting to hand over the baby, not to mention the fact that even if she did so it would mean depriving a mother of her child, the difficulty in deciding what to say to that child and the all too real risk of a 'kiss and tell'-style scandal meant that Jeanine resolved to find another way, any other way, as she explained to Sophie:

> 'His sadness – it broke my heart to see your father like that. So, in order that he could be happy, so I could keep him, so that nothing would change, so that the Anquetils could stay together, I had the crazy idea – it was like a deliverance – to ask my daughter to have my husband's child. When I saw that his mental heath was really becoming dependent on having a child, I saw, we all saw, that the only answer was Annie. I know that some people, not to say most people, will find it difficult to believe what I'm about to say, but given the context . . . I had to ask Annie. I had to do it, I felt that, I had to do it, so I did it.'

The idea of a mother offering her daughter to her husband might well be difficult for many people to comprehend, even offensive. Yet Jeanine was happy to confirm this version of events to me. Nevertheless, there are others who maintain that Anquetil himself was far from a passive participant in the drama. Although, as with Jeanine, there were some subjects about which some of the people I interviewed in the course of my research for this book preferred not to speak, others were happy to accept and discuss their erstwhile colleague, friend or rival in his entirety, warts and all. While on occasion this inevitably resulted in the broaching of a subject others would have preferred to have kept quiet, it also reveals the depth of the affection Anquetil inspired in some of his relationships. To remain friends with someone with such a shocking and, it's worth repeating, potentially offensive family life is one thing; to be prepared to discuss that family life publicly and without reservation demonstrates a considerable bond of loyalty, a bond that has to have been hard-earned.

Maurice Dieulois, one of his oldest friends, was only too happy to emphasise the value he placed on Anquetil's friendship: 'Jacques was a chap who was very faithful. He always recognised that I'd introduced him to cycling and that we'd been good friends, and it always stayed the same. He had this character that meant we always stayed friends, and he certainly never took advantage of his stature. At the end of his life, or during races, we always had the same rapport as when we were kids at school. He never spoke about the bike or his career, and if the subject was broached, it was never him who broached it. He never flaunted what he'd achieved. Never. Never. In order to get him to talk about his races, you had to approach the subject indirectly and talk about other things first. He never flaunted himself or told stories to make himself seem grand. And this was in spite of the career he had, being right at the top from 1953 to 1969, the moments of glory and being received in high places, having friends in high places, in the world of art . . . even in politics. He was admired, adulated; people were honoured to receive him. But he never took advantage of that.'

It should be pointed out that a notable exception to this general rule of his friends being content to talk was Raphaël Géminiani. He was initially more than happy to meet and discuss Anquetil – 'there's plenty to tell you'. However, after

I'd visited Jeanine and Sophie in Corsica, a visit he knew about when he agreed to meet me, he changed his mind: 'You've had a good time over there, no doubt, eating and drinking well and talking to women who know nothing about cycling. Leave me alone. Don't bother me any more.' His reputation as a forthright and impetuous character seems justified.

In stark contrast, although perhaps not surprisingly given his plain-speaking, military demeanour, Richard Marillier not only went out of his way to meet me but was unflinching when the subject of Anquetil's domestic arrangements was broached, even if it involved implicating his friend: 'I don't think Jeanine suggested Annie. What I am certain about is that Jeanine was very much in love with Jacques. I don't agree with everything that's happened since, going on tour to explain things, and I've told her. But I do know one thing: she loved him very much, would do anything for him, and if she needed to make sacrifices to keep him, then she would make them. That sacrifice started with her daughter and was taken to such a degree that when Annie was pregnant they both left to hide it and make it seem like Jeanine was pregnant. We, who knew them well, knew it wasn't true. We knew that because she loved him and didn't want to lose him, she accepted that, if that's what it took.'

While it might seem unlikely that Marillier is in a better position to comment on such intimate family details than Jeanine or Sophie, it should be kept in mind that Jeanine's love for Anquetil was – is – so all pervasive that it would inevitably colour her perception of events, even if only subconsciously. It's a common enough trait for those who are fond of someone to paint a rosier picture of them than is justified in reality. The observations of Dominique, Anquetil's second partner, should perhaps be seen in this light, even if they also affirm Jeanine's version of events: 'It's true that he didn't like to be told what to do. Jacques didn't like people deciding for him, especially at work, on the bike. But in his private life, he was quite the opposite – a man who was easily led by others – so he found himself trapped. It's not a question of him not having thought about it, but if he'd taken charge, he would have seen things very differently and things would have happened differently. But he placed a lot of faith in the people with whom he lived, and he let them run the family. So, he no longer took control, and that's how he found himself in the situation in which he did. He could have confronted the issues at the root of the problems if he'd picked up the reins and said, "I want that, and I want that, but not that, so I won't do that like that. I'll do things differently." But because he let other people make the decisions, he found himself caught, as if in a spider's web, in a situation different from that which he would have chosen himself.'

Yet both Sophie, in her book, and Jeanine, when she spoke to me, suggest a man as in charge at home as he was in every other aspect of his life. 'He was the patriarch,' Jeanine says. 'Everything went through him.'

Whatever the exact chain of events, and whoever the initiator was, the end result was the same: Annie consented to have a child with her stepfather. The notion of this relationship being consensual is, of course, central to how it is perceived, as Sophie recognises in her book when she is questioning her grandmother:

> 'You've just said, "I had to do it," to ask your daughter
> from your first marriage to sleep with your second husband
> to give him a daughter you couldn't provide. But was this
> an order or a request? I get the impression it was an order.
> That ought to bother me, but it doesn't, not in the slightest,
> but I want to know.'

Jeanine is adamant that she not only had to convince her husband that this was the right solution but that she left open to her then 18-year-old daughter the possibility of saying no, even if she still perceived her eventual consent as essential:

'Your father had to have a child. You had to be born. As for the freedom of your mother to say no to my plans, she had it, absolutely. That I knew how to be persuasive is a different matter, but, having said that, the best thing to do is to ask your mother what she thinks.'

I, too, would have liked the opportunity to ask Sophie's mother, Annie, directly while I was in Corsica. Sophie had in fact managed to persuade her to speak to me, even though she was initially reluctant. 'She doesn't really like to talk about it all too much now, as she's quite happily built a new life, and she's remarried, so she's no real interest in looking backwards,' Sophie explained. Unfortunately, the meeting was interrupted before it even started when Sophie's son Yan fell off his quad bike and had to go to hospital.

Yet once again Annie's response to the situation is clearly articulated in her daughter's book, even if Sophie says her mother would happily have avoided the subject for the rest of her days:

'No, not talking about it didn't weigh on me, and nor did I feel I was prevented from talking. I wasn't censoring myself, either. It's more that nobody ever asked me about it. Was it a peculiar arrangement? No, I don't think so. Well, perhaps. I don't know. That was the Anquetil universe.'

But what about the thorny issue of consent (not to the act but to the relationship):

'Yes, Jacques and Nanou ensured I was free to do as they wanted . . . You know how your father was. He never insisted on anything he didn't want you to do, but when he wanted something he managed to get it without ever demanding it. As for Nanou, you know how she ruled over Les Elfes. The sultan, her sultan, was Jacques. The grand vizier who could predict his every desire before he even knew it himself – that was Nanou.'

She goes on to point out that she was also only 18 at the time of the proposition and that she felt as though she had been living in a sort of Hollywood fantasy world:

> 'When Nanou came to explain to me that I had to have a child with Jacques . . . I don't know what I thought . . . here's what I want to tell you . . . I was dumbfounded; maybe that makes everything seem anodyne . . . after all, I was part of the Anquetil family unit, of the Anquetil universe where the rules of the outside world didn't apply. They were replaced by those of the man who was the Master of all he surveyed.'

It should perhaps be pointed out that the inevitable inhibition of free will in such intimate relationships is the reason that most legal systems have defined certain rules and responsibilities that should dictate the behaviour of the participants. These are normally called fiduciary duties, and in the United Kingdom and in France they represent the highest standard of care imposed by either equity or law. The duty falls on the person or people in the relationship who are in the position of power. In simple terms, this standard of care consists of not putting their personal interests above their duty to, and the interests of, the less dominant partner. Even more onerous, persons in the position of strength must go so far as to avoid putting themselves in a situation where there is a conflict between their personal interests and their fiduciary responsibilities, let alone then imposing their personal interests. Not surprisingly, the intimacy between parent or step-parent and child – the initial relationship between Anquetil and Annie – is considered sufficient to create a fiduciary duty.

Of course, this means that not only the morality but also the legality of their domestic set-up is open to question. However, of more direct pertinence to a full appreciation of the context in which it happened is an awareness of the paternal relationship between Anquetil and Annie that preceded the sexual one. This remains unclear. At one point, Sophie writes that Annie and her brother Alain lived with Jacques and Jeanine from when she was ten years old – that's to say, in 1962. Later in the book, Alain and Annie are said to have lived definitively with Jacques and Jeanine only from 1967, having initiated the process in around 1964 or 1965. What's clear, however, is that at some point the children broke away from their father.

Sophie says that this rupture was irrevocable, although Dominique, who of course was initially married to Jeanine's son Alain, disagrees. In fact, given Sophie's comments, I expressed my surprise when I met Dominique and she said that she knew Alain's father, Jeanine's first husband. 'Yes, of course I knew him,' she said. Does this mean the children regained contact with him? 'More or less,' she replied, before telling me how the rupture had occurred: 'He remarried, and you know that with women there are often jealousies. They separate their new husbands from their children, push them away, put them in the dustbin, because they're not their own children. So, he was deprived of his children, not by himself, but perhaps because of this woman, who also had her own children and wanted to promote hers at the expense of his. It's a story that's as old as the hills, the story of the nest, even if it's not a nice story.'

If the complicity of their father in the departure of Annie and Alain and their decision to move in with Jacques and Jeanine is uncertain, what is clear is that, whether for only two or three years or whether for the best part of a decade, Anquetil assumed, and didn't shirk, his responsibilities as a father figure. Jeanine has already explained how his rapport with her children, even from before their affair in the mid-1950s, was a determining factor in her seduction. Sophie is equally glowing in her assessment of his role as a father to his two step-children: 'As soon as Annie and Alain went to live permanently with Jeanine and Jacques, he became head of the family, an exemplary father and at the same time a doting dad.'

Annie agrees: 'He took us to the circus and to the fair. He paid close and sometimes critical attention to how we got on at school, but he was very kind. We loved him.'

The question that remains is to determine what it was that allowed Anquetil to either insist on or at least accept a relationship that was possibly illegal and certainly beyond accepted social norms. When I asked Bernard Hinault how he thought people had reacted to the revelations in Sophie's book, he said it would largely depend on how people perceived his motives: 'There will be those who say he was just a *coureur*, in every sense.' The significance of this description comes from the fact that '*coureur*' in French has an unlikely dual meaning. It means both racer, as in racing cyclist – '*coureur cycliste*' – and also womaniser – '*coureur des filles*' (someone who chases after girls – or skirt, as Hinault puts it). This is clearly Hinault's interpretation of his close friend's actions. It is also clear that, in Hinault's eyes, this is an interpretation that doesn't merit great censure. Whether the result of traditional French ambivalence to sexual indiscretions that might make prudish Brits blush, or whether a function of Hinault's own earthy virility, for him Anquetil's stereotypical male appetite for sex should simply be seen as a fact of life. Some people are like that, some people aren't. '*Les problèmes de cul* [loosely interpreted as 'women problems'], as we say, they mean nothing. If you're a very good athlete, a very good politician, you've got to start from the position that it's up to them. It's their private life. *C'est la vie.*'

Yet while this might well be a fact of life, it might not have been a fact of Anquetil's life. Although he was clearly a man with a considerable appetite for many things, his desire to chase after women in general is at best uncertain. He clearly enjoyed his time as a bachelor before marrying Jeanine – at the time of his relationship with Paule Voland, he boasted of the column inches that would be produced if the newspapers wrote about all the girls he saw – but Géminiani, for example, goes to some lengths to spell out to Sophie in *Pour l'amour de Jacques* how faithful he was once married:

> 'Once, we went to Algeria at the end of the season without Nanou. I don't know why. Every day, there was a minor race. We stayed for a week, and, of course, each night we had a party. There wasn't much problem if you didn't want to sleep on your own at night . . . and nobody did sleep alone . . . except Jacques! Yet he was the most sought after, and sometimes there was quite a queue outside his hotel room. It was as if he couldn't see them.'

Dominique paints a similar picture: 'He wasn't a womaniser. It was women who chased after him, not him chasing after them. I've seen him at the Tour. I've seen us arrive somewhere and girls come and say, "Mr Anquetil, I'm on the Tour. I'm working for such and such a company. I hope we'll be able to see each other again during the Tour." That's nice. I'm there, and I'm watching young girls come and try and chat him up in front of me. It's just part and parcel of being a public person. But that wasn't the man.'

Sophie provided an alternative explanation when I asked her how her father came to say yes to the possibility of having a child with his stepdaughter when most people wouldn't consider it, even if they found themselves in the same situation: 'I think it's in his origins and his roots: his proximity to the land; the sense of wonder about and the importance of the family; the desire to stay close to kith and kin. I think he thought it was OK to have a kid with his stepdaughter, as it was the closest he could come to having one with his wife. It was to avoid having recourse to the outside world, for the outside world represented a danger. Someone from the outside could have done a kiss and tell, so it was harder. I think it was truly a desire to stay close to the family.'

This in itself might seem unlikely. Yet Philippe Brunel suggests, with his tongue only partly in his cheek, that in Normandy, at least, similar arrangements were more widespread than might initially be supposed: 'Don't forget, in Normandy it's quite normal. Cases like his, things like the Anquetil family set-up, they happen frequently. If you read Maupassant, you find lots of Anquetil's life in there, lots of blood relationships, lots of relationships within families. It happens. Why, I don't know. It's a region of close-knit communities, in small families, shut off from the outside world, maybe. I'm just saying that in those books you can see it a lot.'

Nevertheless, in addition to the more or less improbable notion of a stepdaughter acting as a surrogate mother for her stepfather, the Anquetil family had also to deal with the fact that their relationship became something more than one of convenience. In fact, Annie and Jacques maintained a sexual relationship, under the same roof as Jeanine, for more than a decade. The result was that Anquetil went to Annie's bed every night before then joining Jeanine. The young Sophie, who initially slept near Jeanine before being transferred to her mother, went in the opposite direction. It's little surprise that Sophie says she referred – and still sometimes refers – to both women as her mother, even though she was fully aware of the biological truth of her situation. Annie explained it to Sophie in *Pour l'amour de Jacques*:

> 'Everybody was quite comfortable with it. That's how it was. We were caught in a sort of gentle madness that didn't actually make anyone crazy. It took me 12 years to realise it wasn't what I wanted. I think I didn't want it right from the start, but without knowing it, without admitting it, it came upon me slowly – very slowly. I should have left after you were born. But I loved him!'

The feeling was apparently reciprocated, again suggesting that Anquetil was more than a mere sleeping partner in the establishment of their relationship. Annie told Sophie:

> 'They were playing with fire. Before Nanou came to explain to me that I had to have a child with Jacques, and that he would find it difficult, but that it was necessary . . . I knew that he wouldn't find it so difficult. He'd started to look at me in a different way. His genuine desire to have a child, had it driven him to prepare me gently to accept him into my bed? With him, it's quite possible.'

Annie even suggests that his desire for a child may have been just the excuse he needed to hide from Nanou his real motivation – to establish a relationship with Annie:

> 'Having me, he had a young Nanou again, without having to lose the old one . . . I'm not their victim. I too played with fire. And once it had happened, instead of spending a few nights with me to make me pregnant, he fell in love with me and stayed for 12 years. You wanted the truth. That's mine, or how I see it, anyway.'

TWENTY

The Cyclist, the Stepson, His Wife and Her Lover

IN TYPICAL ANQUETIL STYLE, even a good old-fashioned *ménage à trois* was too conventional. Only if it involved his stepdaughter as well as his wife could his desire for control, for family intimacy and for progeny be fulfilled. What was perhaps more remarkable still, he managed to make it work, more or less, for 12 years. Certainly, the first few years of Sophie's life passed off without notable antagonism: 'Life was without too many obvious tensions, parties and winter and summer holidays all helping, of course. There were plenty of good times, full of fun and laughter, underpinned by the relaxed atmosphere my father was so good at creating.'

Mostly this involved having a party. 'Every weekend, the whole group of friends would come round. Friends from childhood, some from cycling: they would all come round and have a party,' she told me, surrounded by pictures of the equally frequent festivities that are now held at the auberge she owns with her husband in Corsica. 'Yes, I must have inherited something from them, my father, mother, grandma,' she says with a smile. 'My children like to party, too. My daughter loves to dance – and we all like champagne as well.' Cue more laughter.

Anquetil's schoolmate Dieulois was a regular visitor at this time: 'We quite often went there for meals at birthdays, although, actually, you didn't need a birthday. We just happened to enjoy sitting and eating round a table then going and playing *baby-foot* or going for a walk in the woods to see the birds.'

Jeanine agrees: 'Jacques couldn't be on his own, so any birthday, any weekend, every weekend, once he'd stopped racing, he was the host. He made a fuss if he had to go and eat at a friend's house: "No, come to the house. It's easier." So, every weekend, from Friday to Sunday, there would be 15 or 20 of us. Obviously, my maid left on Saturday, so the wives did their bit – we roasted a lamb, made pasta, did the shopping. It was a laugh, and in the evening we got dressed up and had fun, and Jacques adored that. We were happy like that, every weekend, every weekend, every weekend.'

Whether as a result of these parties or not, Sophie is also adamant that throughout her childhood, in spite of all the later emotional upheaval, she was the beneficiary of the unreserved love and affection of all those around her, in particular her father: 'Yes, he spoiled me. He was away for a part of each year, but when he was there he took me everywhere, although there was no routine. If he wanted to go somewhere in the middle of the night and he wanted to take me with him, then off we'd go. If he needed to wake me up to show me something, he'd wake me up. What I liked most was when we took out his binoculars to look at the moon. He showed me the craters on the moon, Saturn's rings, that a star looked like a huge diamond in a telescope, that you had to follow the trajectory, as it moved all the time. They were wonderful moments. And also night walks in the wood when he would explain the marks made by animals, the noises. I was scared to start with, but he said don't be. He just put the noises into context, and I was fine.'

Even the potentially disorienting fact she had two mothers didn't unsettle her. Although *France Dimanche*, in a commemorative edition brought out after Anquetil died in 1987, either still didn't know or chose not to publicise the fact that Sophie was Annie's rather than Jeanine's daughter – 'And then, in 1971, a miracle: after 13 years of marriage, Jeanine has a daughter: Sophie. Anquetil is over the moon' – Sophie's real parentage was far from a closely guarded secret, as Jeanine recalls: 'Those who were close to us knew our situation. They didn't feel any need to talk about it, but everybody knew. We had journalist friends who knew right from the start that Sophie wasn't my daughter but was my daughter's daughter. But nobody said anything. Everybody accepted it because Jacques had explained things to them and that was that.'

'I grew up quite normally in the middle of all this, where nothing was hidden and where there was lots of love,' Sophie says in her book. 'In fact, there is nothing but love in this story. I experienced it first hand. I know.' Later on, she expresses the ease with which she accepted her situation:

> As soon as I appeared at Les Elfes, life was wonderful. Very quickly, I understood that I had two mothers: no problem. On the contrary, I could give two presents on Mother's Day, and I could play them off against each other. When I fell out with one, I sought solace with the other. Later, at school, I found out that other children didn't have two mums, which seemed a shame for them. Life was great. I was the centre of attention.

That's not to say, though, that Anquetil family life didn't suffer from the stresses and strains inherent in such a set-up; after all, two's company, three's a crowd, and for good reason. The fundamental issue, according to Sophie, was the power struggle between Annie and Jeanine in their mutual desire to be 'first lady'. Even in the first few years, before tensions had had time to take root, a family friend told Sophie that domestic harmony did not always reign: 'There was constant friction in the harem. Sometimes your mothers argued ferociously, even in front of you.'

The catalyst for the inevitable breakdown in the relationship, however, was the arrival at the chateau of Alain's wife Dominique. Although only six at the time, Sophie says she can remember precisely when Dominique came to live with them in 1977: 'From that moment on, there was a different atmosphere among the adults of the house. Straight away, I was convinced, even if I didn't tell anyone, that things would change.' According to Sophie, Jeanine and, even more so, Annie turned against Dominique, a woman too many. A 'foreign body' had been detected in the almost organic Anquetil family unit and needed expelling: 'Above all, Annie accused Dominique of playing Machiavellian games. She was convinced that she had married Alain, her brother, simply to be able to steal Jacques from her once she'd come to live in the chateau.'

Dominique's own recollections of the distance and formality of her interaction with Anquetil at the time suggest otherwise: 'When we knew each other before we became a couple, we used '*vous*' [the formal French form of 'you'] not '*tu*' [the informal equivalent]. We respected each other. If you like, I was his daughter-in-law without being his daughter-in-law. My father-in-law was Dr Boëda. Jacques was no more than the husband of the mother of my husband.' The use of '*vous*' doesn't preclude a warm relationship, of course. After all, it's still relatively common in France for sons-in-law and daughters-in-law to be required to address their parents-in-law as '*vous*', although this is often while being addressed as '*tu*' in return. Yet for both people to use '*vous*' does suggest a degree of distance beyond that which would allow for the seduction of a man already in the middle of a *ménage à trois*.

Certainly, the only initial change in the standings of the three women was that Dominique's stock began to fall. After little more than two years, in 1979, Dominique and a reluctant Alain moved out to a property on the other side of Rouen. Even though he would bring his son Steve to visit the chateau every weekend, Alain also had to give up working alongside Jacques as farm manager. This appears to have been a cruel blow. Anquetil described Alain to Sophie as 'the guy that I loved the most. He was my son,' and the feeling appears to have been reciprocal. Perhaps the perception, rightly or wrongly, that his wife was at fault for this separation was the cause of their own eventual parting of the ways.

Back at the chateau, the imbalance apparently created by Dominique's brief residence would worsen, rather than improve, after her departure. The principal agitator for change was the young pretender, Annie. Sophie wrote:

> With regard to my mum, the more time passed, the more she felt her youth was being spent a prisoner of an impossible situation. She waited years hoping for everything to change, for normal relationships to take over . . . But she knew it was in vain. In fact, she'd known this for a long time, and before she realised it, twelve years had passed. She knew it was now or never to leave Les Elfes.

Yet even though she'd met someone who tried to persuade her to leave with him, she hesitated. Her initial move was not to leave completely but to try and find a job outside the chateau, a move categorically rejected by Anquetil. It took another year of the intolerable status quo before she could be persuaded to leave. Sophie says that she was 12 at the time, so her departure must have been sometime in 1983.

Sophie writes that she was also remarkably sanguine about the fact her mother left her:

> She asked me, before she left, if it was all right that she went.
> She explained that she had to go and that I could go with
> her if I wanted. I told her to go, and to leave me there. We
> knew that Jacques needed me, and he wouldn't have been
> able to cope with losing both of us.

Nevertheless, even with Sophie deciding to stay with her
father, Annie's departure signalled the beginning of the end
of the original Anquetil clan:

> Annie leaving hurt him a lot. He couldn't stop telling me
> how much. He loved Annie. He would do anything for her
> to come back or else . . . On occasion, he seemed to lose
> his mind. I think he was genuinely unwell. His love for her
> made him unwell, as did the fact she was no longer his.

At chateau Anquetil, possession was more than nine-tenths
of the law. It was the law.

According to Sophie, it was Jeanine who attempted to heal
the breach by instigating the return of Alain and Dominique to
the chateau. This only led to further complications, however,
the most notable being her father's decision, several months
after Annie's flight and while still obsessed with getting her
back, to seduce Dominique as a means to this end. 'Tell your
mother I've got my eyes on Dominique. She won't tolerate
that. That'll make her come back,' he told Sophie. Even the
failure of this approach didn't deter him: 'She's not come
back because she knows nothing's going on between me and
Dominique. If she realises she's my mistress . . .'

The day chosen to consecrate the plan was Sophie's First
Communion – Annie's absence confirming Anquetil's worst
fears, as Sophie recalls: 'At the height of his rage, he said
to Nanou and me, "Right, as it's like that, I'm going to take
Dominique!" What an extraordinary thing to say. How did
he know she would succumb to his charms? Had she already
done so in secret? What I do know is that her first official
visit to his bed was that very night.'

The consequences were immediate and stark. Sophie joined her mother, although she would later return to a boarding school in the region and spend weekends with her father, in spite of an uncomfortable relationship with his new companion. Alain left for a woman he had already fallen in love with and, according to Sophie, is still with today. Jeanine moved to a flat in Paris before eventually divorcing Anquetil less than two months before he died. The reasons for this delay are unclear. 'We'd been separated, but as it was my children who would inherit everything and I would end up with nothing we divorced so I would be provided with a pension,' Jeanine told me. Dominique maintained the divorce wasn't confirmed until four years after Jeanine's departure because Jeanine wouldn't consent, making the process much more long-winded than it would have been otherwise.

Not surprisingly, Dominique's recollection of events leading up to her installation at the chateau also differs from Sophie's: 'At the end of the day, I had problems in my relationship, and he had his. He was often out in the woods with my husband to find a bit of peace and quiet, and I called him to say, "Jacques, you're very kind, but I'd prefer it if my husband didn't keep coming back at 4 a.m." He said, "Well, do you want to meet up so we can talk about it?" We still used "*vous*" at the time, but I said it was a good idea. When we met, we spoke about everything except the family. I think we'd both had an overdose of the family. So we found ourselves together, and we found we understood each other because of our own problems. Then we started living together, and after that we never left each other.'

Was she not concerned about hooking up with someone with such a questionable track record? 'No, I knew Jacques when he was married to Jeanine, and I knew his private life. But I also knew that wasn't him – not the real him. He had been sad. He had drawn a line under everything that had happened previously. It still existed, of course – it was part of his life – but we lived something else. We lived our own life.'

This life is recorded in her own book – *Anquetil, Jacques par Dominique* – published only two years after his death. It contains nothing about his previous relationships, an omission that was quite intentional. 'My book is what I lived,' she told me. 'Later, there was Sophie's book, what she felt through her mum, and how that happened. It's a bit like two different stories.'

Her reaction to Sophie's story is revealing: 'It was difficult. When I was asked to appear on television with Jeanine, Sophie and Annie, I said, "Sorry, no, that's nothing to do with my life. It wasn't my life." I was after that. And with Jacques we lived as a couple. We didn't live with the others, then we had a child together.'

Christopher was born on 2 April 1986. 'To start with, I wasn't interested in having another child, making my life even more complicated, and at my age [he was by then 52],' Anquetil told *L'Équipe*. 'But when he arrived, I was smitten. It's truly wonderful. And what's more, everything revolves around me. His only word is "Papa". He says "Papa" when he wants to say "Maman" – he's as contrary as his dad.'

Contrary, perhaps, but Anquetil doted on his son. 'He was an adorable father,' says Dominique. 'No, he didn't change nappies. He said it made him feel sick. But he was quite happy, once the baby was ready – that's to say, clean and dressed – to take him everywhere with him, even in the forest in a papoose. He'd take his hand, walk with him, feed him – he was quite happy doing all those things. He was very practical. But you had to make the baby clean and ready to go.'

Sophie also suggests that he was a natural father: 'I remember him with babies. Often men are a bit gauche with them, but he wasn't. He was happy to pick them up and play with them, even with nurse's baby when she brought him in. He was quite happy to play with him.'

Anquetil himself, in another interview shortly before he died, makes it clear that becoming a father again had helped him move on from all the recent upheavals: 'Christopher is the best present Dominique could have given me. She's 37, I'm 53, but I feel ageless, above all, since I met her.' The picture of domestic normality is underlined when Dominique describes their sleeping habits – the lack of a routine and his increasing insomnia had long been a source of concern for family members and *directeurs sportifs* alike: 'Yes, he slept well and for long enough. We had a normal bed time. We went to bed between 10 p.m. and 11 p.m., but he did leave the television on all night. If I switched it off, he woke up. He liked having the background noise. We didn't get up until 10 a.m. He'd found a way to lead a normal life again.'

TWENTY-ONE

Cycling's James Bond

IT'S QUITE POSSIBLE THAT life with Dominique did indeed mean that Anquetil had finally found the normality required for him to overcome the traumas of the past 12 years. Unfortunately, while this adoption of a routine recognisable to most may have provided him with psychological and emotional solace, his physical well-being was already beyond repair. On 25 May 1987, Anquetil was diagnosed as suffering from the advanced stages of stomach cancer.

The news was broken to him the day after the christening of his son, Christopher. Anquetil's school friend Maurice Dieulois was there at the time: 'I was sitting next to him at the table when he told me he'd been to have some tests during the week and was waiting for the results. He said, "If it's cancer, I've been ill for so long it won't be long before it gets me." In fact, the doctor had the results but didn't want to tell him on the day of the christening, so he came the next day after having rung and said, "I need to see you. I'll come at midday." At that point, Jacques knew it must be something serious. And I remember, we were sitting at the table for lunch when the doctor arrived, and Jacques got up and went off into the study on his own with him. When he came back after the doctor had told him he did indeed have stomach cancer, I'll always remember it, he said "Yes, it's cancer. But the cancer's in for a tough ride, as where it is it's still got its work cut out." Just like that. Just after he'd learned he had cancer.' Even now, Dieulois can't stop himself from chuckling at the memory.

Anquetil's resilience in the face of such devastating news was also appreciated by another friend, his former teammate André Darrigade, who says Anquetil told him he'd had to make life easier for the doctor: 'I was watching the doctor's face when he came with the results of my tests, and he either didn't want to tell me or he was finding it difficult to start, so I decided to help him. I said, "Don't worry. You can tell me. I'm not a little boy."'

Bernard Hinault, who as godfather to Christopher was also there at the time Anquetil learned of his diagnosis, shares this amazement at his friend's reaction, even if his recollection of how he responded is different: 'He said to me, "What should I do? I've got cancer." Just like that. "What should I do? Shoot myself in the head or fight?" I said that it could be treated, so he should go and get himself treated. But then he waited. If he'd been treated earlier . . . In June, he had to go and commentate on the Dauphiné, then there was the Tour. Even in August, he was going to criteriums to get a bit of money. Eventually, he went into hospital, but it was too late.'

Dieulois confirms Anquetil's procrastination: 'He should normally have been operated on as quickly as possible. In the end, he was operated on in August, and the surgeon said it should have been done sooner. But he was committed to commentating on the Tour on television and answering readers' questions every day in *L'Équipe* as well. So, the surgeon said he could start the Tour and go as far as Bordeaux, where he'd do some tests, and then as soon as the Tour had finished he'd operate, maybe around 15 to 20 July. We were there in Bordeaux and spent a couple of hours at least with Jacques after the stage before he went for the tests. To see him, physically, you wouldn't have known that he was ill. He hadn't lost weight; he'd even put a bit on, maybe. But because of the tests, he said, "Sorry, Maurice, I can't even have a drink with you, as I've been told to have nothing in my stomach." So, he didn't have a drink, whereas normally, of course, he was the first to have a drink with a friend. It was then he decided to finish the Tour.'

In fact, the operation – to remove his stomach – didn't take place until 11 August, more than two and a half months after receiving confirmation of the diagnosis.

For once, it seems as if Anquetil was fighting shy of the challenge ahead. Eventually, it was his son who was the catalyst for action. 'One evening, I leaned over Christopher's cot and kissed him on the cheek, which was as warm as life itself,' he was reported as saying in *Paris Match*, just one of the innumerable magazines to carry commemorative articles after his death. 'I felt his little fingers squeezing mine, trying to keep hold of me, and I decided to have the operation.'

The consequences of this delay should not be underestimated, as his daughter Sophie points out: 'Rudi Altig also had a stomach cancer. Before they knew anything was wrong, his wife went to see a clairvoyant, who said, "Your husband is very ill. He has a problem with his stomach." At the time, Rudi felt in fine fettle, but his wife made him go to a doctor. The doctor asked him lots of questions about various things – if he had pain here or pain there – and Rudi said everything was fine, so the doctor said it wasn't worth any more invasive tests. But Rudi insisted: "Take your thingamajig, knock me out and have a look." It turns out that he had cancer, was operated on straight away and is still fine now.'

More serious than the delayed reaction to the diagnosis, however, was his delayed acceptance that anything was wrong. He'd been suffering serious stomach pains for at least four years before his cancer was confirmed – Dominique recalls him being plagued by them from the very beginning of their relationship, which started in 1983. His daughter Sophie acknowledges that he'd ignored the symptoms for longer than he should. 'He just left it,' she says. 'He was very resistant to pain, and when his cancer started he resisted, resisted, resisted, and by the time the pains were really intolerable it was already too late.'

Dieulois agrees: 'He was hardened to suffering. He tried to treat himself with clay masks on the stomach. He thought he'd be able to help himself with that, but to start with he wasn't really being looked after in a medical sense. He was a bit slow before getting himself treated efficiently.'

It would be reasonable to assume that the impact of this delay was exaggerated by his lifestyle. His body had already begun to show signs that the excesses to which it had been subjected were taking their toll. In 1978, he had been diagnosed with cardiac arrhythmia, a complaint that according to some commentators meant he should never have become a competitive sportsman. His daughter, Sophie, is not so sure, suggesting instead that whereas he used to have a heart that could be compared to a Ferrari, it was now more akin to a 2CV.

Then there was his history of amphetamine consumption during his cycling career (and don't forget the caffeine and strychnine injections). Regular and quite possibly excessive amphetamine consumption has been suggested as a contributory factor in the early death of several cyclists of the time, such as Louison Bobet and particularly Gastone Nencini, not to mention Anquetil himself. There appears to be little scientific evidence to support this link, however, and Anquetil certainly didn't give it much credence. 'I stopped riding nearly 20 years ago,' he reminded a local newspaper in Colmar after he was admitted to hospital there. 'If my illness was linked to what I'd done as a sportsman, you'd have to think it had been gestating for an eternity. I really don't think that's the cause.'

Jeanine agrees, and offers an alternative explanation. 'I would have thought if he was going to die young that he'd have died of a heart attack or a lung problem,' she says. 'I never thought of cancer. It's such a cruel illness. But there's no link between the amphetamines and the cancer – it was the stress of his family life. Absolutely. When my daughter left, and then when my son left, Jacques found himself wanting to stick the family back together. He started to get stressed, to get worked up. It was then it started. He was a very nervous character.'

Perhaps this description of Anquetil provides the missing link. There may be little scientific proof of a direct connection between amphetamine consumption and cancer, but there is a clear link between amphetamine consumption and a nervous disposition. Regular amphetamine users are frequently described as being hyperactive, irritable, aggressive, nervous and insomniac – all characteristics displayed by Anquetil during his retirement. (If irritable and aggressive seem at odds with the picture of him as a cool, calculating cyclist and also as the kind of 'gentleman' for whom Vin Denson was happy to act as valet, Richard Marillier assures me he wasn't a man you wanted to cross: 'He was very kind, but you shouldn't wind him up because watch out ... I've seen things I'd better not talk about, but you had to watch out.')

In turn, these traits went a long way to fuelling a lifestyle in which excess continued to be the norm rather than the exception. Indeed, his taste for the high life during his cycling career had already earned him the nickname the James Bond of cycling. He did little to suggest this description wasn't equally valid after his retirement.

Take Marillier's description of his frequent visits to stay with Anquetil at Les Elfes: 'I saw him do things, and I said, "Look, it's none of my business, but you shouldn't carry

on like that. You can't carry on like that. It's not possible."
For example, we'd eat dinner at the house, and we'd have
plenty to drink. Afterwards, we'd go and have a drink at a
night club in Rouen called La Bohème – but for him a drink
wasn't a glass of whisky but a bottle of whisky, and not cheap
whisky, either. We'd get back about 3 a.m., all a bit worse
for wear, and we'd go to bed – but he didn't. He'd have a
shower – hot, then cold, then hot again – put on his overalls,
and go out and start working with the tractor. We wouldn't
see him again until 1 p.m. He was a force of nature. I told
him he was playing games with his health and he'd end up
paying for it.'

Marillier wasn't the only one to notice his penchant for
whisky. One of the journalists Anquetil invited to visit Les
Elfes shortly after he retired records being offered an aperitif
before lunch: 'What would you like? Whisky? Neat? On the
rocks? With water? I always take my first neat . . .' Then two
minutes later: 'Would you like another? I'll have this one
with water, as I'm thirsty . . .'

Of course, Anquetil is not unique in this consumption
pattern. Anyone who's had the good fortune to live in France
will be aware of the tradition – not to say compulsion – to
consume a considerable volume of aperitifs. What's more,
French peasants have for generations used alcohol throughout
the day to ease the rigours of working hard on the land.
Even as fewer and fewer people remain directly involved
in agriculture, the tradition has been adopted by a wider
society keen to keep in touch with its roots. It's still possible
to see cognac and foie gras being consumed by locals at bars
at 9 a.m., locals who now only have a tenuous link to the
peasantry. The point is, though, that the often abbreviated
life expectancy of these locals reflects the extent of this
consumption. For once, Anquetil proved no exception.

His former teammate Guy Ignolin is convinced that it was
his whisky drinking that led to his cancer. 'He used to come to

events I was involved in to help with their profile, and as he was a kind of guest of honour there'd always be a reception with plenty of drink flowing,' he told me. 'After a couple of drinks, Jacques would have eyed somebody up and decided to out-drink him: "You see that guy there? I'm going to bury him." And then they were off – whisky, whisky, whisky.'

Even when those close to him suggested a degree of moderation, Anquetil once again responded as if challenged to consume more. 'We'd say to him to stop drinking so much whisky, that it would make him sick, give him cancer, whatever, but he'd drink a bottle of whisky and say, "Look, there's nothing wrong,"' says Marillier. 'Then someone else would say the same about champagne, so he'd drink three or four bottles of champagne and say, "No problem." It was always a challenge – he challenged himself. He pushed the limits, in everything, everything, everything.' (In 1986, he still let himself be persuaded to participate in the Paris–Dakar rally, losing nearly a stone in weight before eventually being constrained to abandon due to gearbox failure.)

Yet even Anquetil seems to have begun to tire of living up to his own reputation. The more Jeanine organised parties and surrounded him with people, the more he would take himself off into his woods to seek out wild boar or to watch the stars (even if Dieulois says he was always happy for company – or maybe just his company – on these nocturnal sorties). Indeed, he had become a passionate amateur astronomer. 'I remember him following stages of the Tour with me, and he'd get this big book out,' recalls Marillier. 'At first, I wondered what he was going to talk about – gear ratios or something. Not at all. It was his records of the stars. He was crazy about stars. He had a telescope. He was obsessed with them. He'd say Uranus is doing this at the moment or Saturn doing that. I'd say, "What are you bothering me with that for in the middle of the race?" He'd just say it was very interesting. *Ah, ce Jacques.*'

By the time of his relationship with Dominique, the parties may have reduced significantly but not his passion for the outdoors and the night. 'His life was very straightforward,' she insists. 'He liked being outside. He was a man of nature. A lot of cyclists are like that, by the way. When you look at them, they all need to be outside. Look at Bernard Hinault. He likes being outside, and there are lots of others.'

Anquetil himself painted a similar picture when asked by *Lui* magazine on the eve of his retirement how he anticipated growing old: 'In peace and quiet like everyone else, I suppose. Another Anquetil will be born, an Anquetil who will ride 50 kilometres on the bike each week just to prove to himself that he can still do it. An Anquetil who will be able to fulfil his desire for peace and his love of the outdoors. I've always wanted a farm in Normandy. Now I have more land than I ever imagined. I am a man fulfilled.'

Perhaps the most crucial element of this description is the prospect of the birth of a new Anquetil and the implied discontent with elements of his existence to date that this suggests. This sense of dissatisfaction seems to have been exacerbated rather than mitigated by events after he retired, as *L'Équipe*'s Philippe Brunel explains: 'I was in a restaurant with Anquetil and Pierre Chany, and Chany asked Anquetil what would he most like to be if he wasn't who he was. Straight away he said a transvestite: "I'd like to dress up and be someone else, someone who nobody knows, so I could be somebody else." It was quite remarkable. I think by saying that, he wasn't just saying he wanted to be someone else, he was saying how much he wanted to be himself.'

Brunel attributes this desire to the adverse consequences of being so well known: 'His stature and his popularity meant he couldn't be himself. That's why he ended up with this longing to become someone else, wanting to dress up as a transvestite or wanting to go off into the woods and hide himself away. Just to want to be someone else from time to time, to have all the things that we take for granted through being anonymous, the pleasure of being somewhere and not being recognised. That's the true cost of fame. Eddy Merckx tells you the same thing today. You imagine Merckx in Belgium. He can't go anywhere without people coming up to him and saying, "Hello, Eddy." If he goes to the shops, it's in the papers – his wife, his kids, know everything. Anquetil had to live with that too.'

For want of being able to regain his anonymity, Anquetil appears to have succumbed to the stresses and strains created by trying to reconcile two distinct lifestyles – the one dictated by his reputation, a reputation he was too proud not to live up to, and the one dictated by his own desires. For some people, this inability to choose between the two was tantamount to ensuring that his prediction of his own early death, made after his father died, became a self-fulfilling prophecy. 'Yes, maybe,' accepts Marillier. 'He knew he was taking risks. But he was also like the others, like Serge Gainsbourg . . . those who say it's better to live intensely for a few years rather than just hang around. He certainly knew the symptoms. He'd say, "I've got a bad stomach." We'd say, "Of course, it's the whisky." He'd say, "What do you mean?" Then he was off again. There was always this spirit of challenge, of defiance. He defied the bike, he defied death, he defied cancer, he defied everybody – that's Anquetil.'

Dieulois agrees: 'He had certainly been a bit negligent with his health, and, what's more, it was in a domestic context that was a bit difficult and that had affected his morale at the time. It didn't facilitate his determination to look after himself.'

Nevertheless, and perhaps not surprisingly in the light of her being his partner at the time of his death and to some extent a reason for him to want to keep living, Dominique suggests otherwise: 'It's not that he didn't look after himself, at least that's what I think. My understanding is that Jacques was stressed by his life as a cyclist, which was so wearing, so hard. Then, later, he was also worn out by his family life, and when you put yourself under such stress, that's the death of the body. There's only so much a body can take, and when it's been under strain for a whole lifetime . . .'

Dominique even perceives the delay in seeking a diagnosis as normal: 'Of course, he would say he was tired, and he couldn't understand why he was tired, but it was just everyday ailments. It wasn't anything more. He was 50, after all, and with all that he still did in a day, on the farm, with the animals, rushing here and there. I'm also worn out by the end of the day. And you know how it is: you have a bad stomach, then it goes, then you think about something else, life moves on . . . After a while, maybe you say, "Yes, I'll go to the doctor," but then you realise you've things to do, so you say you'll do it next week, and then the same happens the following week. Time passes – one year, two years. That's how it happens. And that's how it happened.'

After his operation to have his stomach removed, Anquetil was initially given the all-clear; at least, the operation itself was deemed a success, even if he did have to be given extra doses of anaesthetic to knock him out. This apparent success was all the excuse Anquetil needed to once again ignore medical advice: 'The day after my operation, the nurse told me I mustn't get out of bed. How on earth could I do that? As soon her back was turned, I went off for a wander.'

According to Darrigade, who went to visit him while he was in hospital, his menu was somewhat modified, however: lemon tea with biscuits when he woke up; porridge and an egg at 10 a.m.; a sole at lunchtime; an artichoke at 4 p.m.; and a saveloy for dinner. Yet only nine days later, he was once again fulfilling his role as *directeur sportif* for the French national team at the world championships in Villach in Austria. 'He was drinking beer and eating his meals with us. He behaved as if nothing had happened,' said one of the riders.

However, normal life only returned for a short period. On 10 October, during a trip to Colmar in eastern France, Anquetil was once more admitted to hospital. Eight days later, he was flown back to the Saint Hilaire Clinic in Rouen. Apart from the occasional afternoon spent at home, he never left the hospital again. He died, with Sophie and Dominique by his side, at 7 a.m. on 18 November 1987. According to *France Dimanche*, Dominique asked him if he needed anything: 'He looked at her, took her hand and didn't respond. His final moments were free from suffering.'

The extent of his suffering prior to that should not be understated, however. He confessed to not being able to tolerate radiotherapy, and in the last month spent in hospital he was covered in bruises, which made even the slightest movement painful. He was frequently given morphine to dull his pain, if not to send him to sleep completely. 'She wants to knock me out,' he told one reporter when a nurse was about to give him his next shot. 'Otherwise it's just too painful all over. I'm convinced it's transferred to the collarbone and to my spinal column as well. I can tell because it hurts to touch them. Tomorrow, I'm having a scan to see if it hasn't also made it to my liver.'

Yet he refused to let this parlous state dampen his spirits. After learning from one of the 3,500 letters he received after his diagnosis that the record for someone to live without a stomach was 42 years, he said, 'If I can keep going that long, I'll have nothing to complain about.' Darrigade also recalls his remarkable strength of character when his son Christopher had to be admitted to hospital following an asthma attack. 'Dominique didn't know where to go, to me or her son, both of us sick but in different rooms,' Anquetil told Darrigade. 'In fact, we lead parallel lives at the moment, Christopher and I. Both of us have a siesta in the afternoon, and we eat our mashed up food from little pots. This can cause problems. When I take one of his, he gets angry and comes and eats half of mine, out of principle.'

In fact, the reserve and distance for which he'd been so chastised as a cyclist had now become a dignity in the face of death that would inspire a whole legion of new admirers. Even in his reduced state, he still managed to be a source of inspiration to others: 'I had 80 calls yesterday, but one that touched me profoundly was from a 60-year-old lady with cancer who said it made her feel better to hear me talk about having cancer – it made her feel as though it wasn't a disease to be ashamed of.'

Anquetil may not have been ashamed, but he certainly had no intention of letting his suffering show. Once again, he was inspired in this by his son: 'I went back to the house, and Christopher came and gave me a big cuddle. He asked why I was sad, and I said it was simply that I was tired, but I vowed that he would never again see me downcast. Mustn't let standards slip!'

Richard Marillier went with Bernard Hinault to see Anquetil for the last time a week before he died. Even at that late stage, he was intent on putting on a brave face. 'I'd called Dominique to say we'd like to see Jacques,' Marillier recalls. 'We could see it was the end. She said, "Yes, but he's in hospital not at the house." We said we'd go to the clinic, but she said he wouldn't have that and that we should go to the chateau anyway. We got there and sat in the living room, from where you could see the steps leading to the front door. Dominique said to wait there and that an ambulance would be bringing him soon. The ambulance came and stopped by the steps. Two guys brought him out and literally had to carry him up the steps. He hadn't seen that we could see him being carried, so he opened the double doors into the living room himself and came in as if he'd seen us just the day before. "Hello, fellas. It's great to see you. Thanks for coming . . ." he said, as if nothing had happened. I'll remember that for the rest of my life. He sat down between us on a settee, and there was a rugby match on TV. He said, "Let's watch that. That'll be great." He had a pain-killing tube going into his arm, but he said, "I'm fine. I've got three cancers, but it'll take more than that to get me. I'll show them. You know me . . ." But you could see he was wearing himself out. Before the end of the first half, he said, "I've got to go, because they're waiting for me back at the clinic. It's been great to see you." And off he went. Eight days later, he was dead.'

Epilogue

CONTROVERSY HAS CONTINUED TO surround Anquetil in death as in life. After being allowed a few years to develop in the French national consciousness into a lamented wise old man of cycling, the publication in 2004 of his daughter's recollections of her childhood and the unique family relationships involved thrust the more contentious aspects of his life back onto the front pages. And not just the front pages. Sophie's book appeared briefly in the best-seller charts, while she and her two mothers – Annie and Jeanine – went on national television to discuss their life with Anquetil. Dozens of articles appeared in both the tabloid and broadsheet newspapers, while Internet chat rooms buzzed with comment.

Although Sophie was sometimes lauded for her honesty, not all of it flattered her or her father. While the more considered comments in the mainstream press hid any disapproval behind discussions of the complexities of Anquetil's character and the apparent consent of all those involved (or whether or not such consent could really exist), the less regulated world of the Internet saw passions soar. Some commentators criticised Anquetil for his 'immoral' behaviour; many more pointed the finger at Sophie for apparently seeking to make money out of her story or for tarnishing her father's reputation.

I asked Sophie how she felt at the sometimes very personal vitriol she had encountered as a result of writing her book: 'There was one thing that I hadn't at all imagined, and that was that when the book came out there was a whole host of other confessional books that came out at the same time [biographies of the controversial family lives of popular French actor Yves Montand and philosopher Bernard-Henri Lévy, for example]. In those, there are stories that are nice and not so nice, difficult to accept and not so difficult to accept, and this coincidence meant that for those who hadn't read my book this media storm implied a pejorative side to it that just doesn't exist in the book itself. That's to say, all those who've bothered to read it realise that I've not at all tarnished the image of my father. On the contrary, it gives him a new dimension. It helps people understand things about him – his life, his reserve, his desire to protect himself, not liking being a public figure, wanting to protect his clan, his private life. It perhaps helped them understand him a bit more, but those who didn't read the book and just read the press got stuck on the bit about how he had a child with the child of his wife. They don't understand his motivations – why or how he got there. And that's why I think it had to be somebody from inside, who lived it, who had to tell the story. Who else can truly understand his motivations if they weren't involved? You can only come at it from outside with judgement, and I didn't want to judge what he did. I just wanted to explain why it happened as it did.'

Yet it shouldn't really have come as a surprise that such revelations would inspire a media frenzy. Even in France, where individual privacy is respected far more than it is in the UK – article nine of the *Code civil* enshrines this right to privacy in French law – a sex scandal or an illegitimate child can still make the headlines. It may not have been until after the death of former president François Mitterrand that the papers felt comfortable discussing his numerous affairs and a hitherto secret daughter, but discuss them they did (even if the most widespread reaction was a Gallic shrug accompanied by the slightly unbelieving and rhetorical question 'only one secret daughter?').

Of course, there are very few stories that can compare to Anquetil's, but those that do have been at the centre of considerable scrutiny. The marriage in 2007 between a 24-year-old Argentinian man and his 82-year-old wife made it all the way round the world. One notable aspect of the relationship, lost behind the headlines stressing their age difference, was that Reinaldo Waveqche claimed to have fallen for Adelfa Volpes after going to live with her after his mother died when he was only 15. As with Anquetil and Annie, the older partner had for some time played the role of parent.

The same is true of Woody Allen and his relationship with his erstwhile stepdaughter, now wife, Soon-Yi Previn. The extent of his role as a father figure has been widely debated. In Marion Meade's biography of Allen – *The Unruly Life of Woody Allen* – Soon-Yi herself is quoted as saying, 'He was never any kind of father figure to me. I never had any dealings with him.' Her brother, Moses Previn, disagreed: 'He was a 12-year boyfriend to my mom, and then he started going out with my sister. How could he do that?'

Regardless of the intricacies of Allen's role as a parent, the criticism of his behaviour has been almost unanimous. Meade suggests that as well as legal fees running into millions of pounds and the loss of his children after a vitriolic custody battle, his audience as a film-maker has also abandoned him. 'There are some things people never forget,' explains one commentator. 'I don't think Woody's scandal will ever go away. It has cost him his primary audience. Women in particular abandoned him. The technical definition of incest doesn't matter so much as the fact that he meddled with the family, and you can't do that.'

Yet although this description could also apply to Anquetil, he has, by and large, escaped such opprobrium. It is not without irony, however, that the very media activity that *Pour l'amour de Jacques* aroused, and the relative lack of condemnation that Sophie suggests is evidence that more people are now able to understand her father, has provoked a degree of frustration, sadness, even outright contempt from those close to Anquetil – often vented towards Sophie.

Dominique is diplomatic when I ask her about it but would clearly rather Sophie's book had never been written: 'When Sophie wrote her book, she called her father a sultan, and I said, "Wait a minute. Your father wasn't a sultan. He didn't have several wives. That's got nothing to do with it." So she changed the title. Yet the journalists and the papers saw sultan and picked up on it, and they had no right to do that. A lot of people took against the book, and a lot of people who were his friends took against Sophie after what she wrote, as it wasn't entirely kind to her father. She should have respected . . . I let her do what she wanted. Perhaps she needed to do it for herself, but I think it was a lack of respect for her father to have written about his life.'

Most of the people I spoke to for this book were happy to discuss all aspects of Anquetil's life – in some cases happy to demonstrate that their friendship transcended his obvious failings – yet were disappointed that *Pour l'amour de Jacques* had brought it all out into the open. A lot of people questioned her motives. She says that there were several reasons for writing the book, including a long-standing desire to write, wanting to quell rumours by having someone from the family to tell the story – but not Annie, her mother, who she says had also thought about writing a book – and because her husband encouraged her. Even Jeanine told me she wasn't greatly enthusiastic about it: 'My son and I didn't like the idea very much.' But then, with what seems to be typical resilience, she brushes all the controversy to one side: 'Hey, when I think about all that, when I'm a bit downcast, I remind myself I didn't waste my time in a factory all day. I just think about the good times. I had an exciting and enjoyable life, and a wonderful place to live. I got to meet de Gaulle, to meet artists. My life was made richer by all that. As for all the little domestic squabbles. Bah!' (This classic, untranslatable French expression of indifference is, of course, accompanied by another Gallic shrug.)

The fact that most of his friends – and they are considerable in number – seem to have found life enriched by their association with Anquetil is crucial. Although Anquetil's *ménage à trois* eventually imploded, he nevertheless succeeded – if that's the right word – in maintaining this unique domestic arrangement for 12 years. What's more, all the formerly antagonistic members of the Anquetil clan now live in a considerable degree of harmony, still united, it seems, by their attachment to Jacques. Sophie, Annie and Jeanine all live near each other in Corsica, of course. Dominique still lives at Les Elfes but is not excluded from this unlikely sorority.

'We all get on fine,' says Sophie. 'We're going to celebrate the 20th anniversary of his death with a reunion for his friends. It will be held at the chateau. My brother runs it with his mother, and we get on fine. We went off to Morocco for five days together. I think the relationship I have with my brother's mother is more like that of a confidante, a friend. We call each other regularly, even if for a period we were separated and had to face up to the fact that several women loved the same man, which can cause difficulties, shall we say . . .

'When he died, there wasn't a great relationship between everyone – far from it. But now, 20 years later, it's as if he's managed to bring us back together, because there's always this link between us. There's lots of love and affection, and the passing of time has healed the negative things and left the positive aspects, with lots of love.'

It is this very evident love and affection that Anquetil managed to inspire from those who knew him that is perhaps his most fitting epitaph. Even those who weren't dazzled by his exceptional talents or blind to his faults were persuaded to like and admire him. Indeed, to many, he was a hero. But the status of hero comes with a caveat, as Anquetil's close friend Pierre Chany explained to Sophie:

'The ancient Greeks used to admire the divinities, the titans, the giants, the demigods and other heroes, but not completely or without reserve: they knew them to be fallible. A hero is above all a man with superior powers to the rest of us mortals but who is nevertheless a man. That's exactly what your father was.'

Palmarès

THE FOLLOWING LIST OF victories and placings in Anquetil's career is designed not to be comprehensive. With 184 career victories and many more podium finishes, a complete list would dilute his major achievements. The aim, instead, is to draw attention to his finest victories – and also occasionally to point out his significant failures. Even such a list may fail to give sufficient precedence to some of his accomplishments, however.

First, there are his numerous victories at track events and in particular at six-day races, including the then prestigious Paris Six Day – not bad for a man often criticised for his lack of all-round talents and his exclusive focus on his strongest events. Then there are his four victories in the Super Prestige Pernod competition (open to all professionals) and three in the Prestige Pernod competition (open only to French riders). These were effectively the predecessors of the World Cup and now the ProTour rankings, with overall success determined by tallying up victories and placings throughout a year in a bid to determine the most consistent performer over a whole season. Another way of putting 'most consistent performer', of course, is best rider. The fact Anquetil won the two competitions seven times between them indicates even more clearly just how much of an all-rounder he was.

Last, but not least, come his time-trial successes. Given that the majority of these races are no longer on the calendar, and those few that are don't have the same prestige as they did in the 1950s and '60s, it can be difficult to gauge the scale of Anquetil's achievements. In which case, it may help to consider the verdict of Brian Robinson: 'The only time trial I rode with him was the Grand Prix de Genève. I got within three minutes of him in eighty miles. I was proud of that – it was the best time trial I ever did. Then they tried to put me in the Grand Prix des Nations, but I wasn't a time-triallist, and at the end of the season, by the time you've ridden all of the grand tours and all the contract races in August, you're absolutely knackered. No way . . .' Anquetil, of course, rode and won most of them.

1951

1st – Grand Prix Maurice Latour (first victory in fourth race)

1st – Overall in *Paris-Normandie*'s year-long *maillot des jeunes* competition for young riders

1st – Normandy team time-trial championships (with Dieulois, Le Ber, Levasseur and Quinet)

12 other victories

1952

1st – French amateur road-race championships (only national road title)

1st – Normandy amateur road-race championships

1st – Grand Prix de France (time trial)

8th – World amateur road-race championships

12th – Olympic Games road race

Bronze medal in Olympic Games team race

1953

1st – Grand Prix des Nations
1st – Grand Prix de Lugano
1st – Tour de la Manche (first race with professionals)
2nd – Barrachi Trophy (with Antonin Rolland)

1954

1st – Grand Prix des Nations
1st – Grand Prix de Lugano
1st – Paris–Nice time-trial stage (the race was in fact called
     Paris–Côte d'Azur that year)
2nd – Barrachi Trophy (with Louison Bobet)
2nd – Critérium des As
3rd – Grand Prix de Genève (also known as the Grand Prix
     Martini)
5th – World professional road-race championships

1955

1st – Grand Prix des Nations
1st – Grand Prix de Genève
1st – Stage six Tour of the South-east Provinces
1st – French pursuit championships
2nd – Barrachi Trophy (with André Darrigade)
6th – World professional road-race championships
First, failed, attempt at world hour record – 45.175 kilometres
     compared with Fausto Coppi's record of 45.848 kilometres

1956

World hour record – 46.159 kilometres
1st – Grand Prix des Nations
1st – Grand Prix de Genève
1st – French pursuit championships
2nd – World pursuit championships

1957

1st – Tour de France (also winner of four stages)
1st – Paris–Nice (also winner of time-trial stage)
1st – Grand Prix des Nations
1st – Grand Prix de Genève
1st – Paris Six Day (with André Darrigade and Fernando
    Terruzzi)
4th – Barrachi Trophy (with André Darrigade)
6th – World professional road-race championships

1958

1st – Grand Prix des Nations
1st – Grand Prix de Lugano
1st – Grand Prix de Genève
1st – Four Days of Dunkerque
1st – Paris Six Day (with André Darrigade and Fernando
    Terruzzi)
2nd – Barrachi Trophy (with André Darrigade)
14th – Paris–Roubaix
Abandoned Tour de France after stage 22 (race won by Charly
    Gaul)

1959

1st – Grand Prix de Lugano
1st – Grand Prix de Genève
1st – Critérium des As
1st – Four Days of Dunkerque
2nd – Tour of Italy
3rd – Tour de France
3rd – Barrachi Trophy (with André Darrigade)
3rd – Ghent–Wevelgem
9th – World championship road race

1960

1st – Tour of Italy (also winner of two time-trial stages)
1st – Grand Prix de Lugano
1st – Grand Prix de Forli (time trial)
1st – Critérium des As
9th – World professional road-race championships

1961

1st – Tour de France (also winner of two time-trial stages and
  race leader from first to last day)
1st – Paris–Nice (also winner of time-trial stage)
1st – Grand Prix des Nations
1st – Grand Prix de Lugano
1st – Grand Prix de Forli
1st – Critérium National (first major victory in a one-day race)
2nd – Tour of Italy
5th – Barrachi Trophy (with Michael Stolker)
Winner of Super Prestige Pernod and Prestige Pernod
  competitions

1962

1st – Tour de France (also winner of two time-trial stages)
1st – Barrachi Trophy (with Rudi Altig – first victory at eighth
  attempt)
6th – Grand Prix de Lugano
15th – World professional road-race championships
Abandoned Tour of Spain after stage 17 (won by Rudi Altig)

1963

1st – Tour de France (also winner of four stages)
1st – Tour of Spain (also winner of two stages and race leader
  from first to last day)

1st – Dauphiné–Libéré (also winner of time-trial stage)
1st – Paris–Nice (also winner of time-trial stage)
1st – Critérium National
1st – Ronde d'Auvergne
1st – Critérium des As
2nd – Barrachi Trophy (with Raymond Poulidor)
3rd – French road-race championships
12th – World professional road-race championships
Winner of Super Prestige Pernod and Prestige Pernod
  competitions

1964

1st – Tour de France (also winner of four stages)
1st – Tour of Italy (also winner of two stages)
1st – Ghent–Wevelgem (first major victory in a one-day race
  abroad)
6th – Paris–Nice
7th – World professional road-race championships
BBC Overseas Sports Personality of the Year

1965

1st – Dauphiné–Libéré (also winner of three stages)
1st – Bordeaux–Paris
1st – Paris–Nice (also winner of one stage)
1st – Critérium National
1st – Grand Prix des Nations
1st – Grand Prix de Lugano
1st – Barrachi Trophy (with Jean Stablinski)
1st – Grand Prix de Forli
1st – Critérium des As
1st – Manx Premier Trophy
Winner of Super Prestige Pernod and Prestige Pernod
  competitions

1966

1st – Liège–Bastogne–Liège (first and only victory in one of the five 'monuments' of cycling)

1st – Paris–Nice (also winner of one stage)

1st – Tour of Sardinia

1st – Grand Prix des Nations

2nd – World professional road-race championships

3rd – Tour of Italy

3rd – Grand Prix de Lugano

Abandoned Tour de France during stage 19 (race won by Lucien Aimar)

Winner of Super Prestige Pernod competition

1967

1st – Critérium National

1st – Tour of Catalonia

2nd – Barrachi Trophy (with Bernard Guyot)

2nd – Critérium des As

2nd – French pursuit championships

3rd – Tour of Italy

World hour record (not ratified due to failure to comply with drug test) – 47.493 kilometres compared with Roger Rivière's record of 47.347 kilometres

1968

1st – Barrachi Trophy (with Felice Gimondi)

4th – Liège–Bastogne–Liège

10th – Paris–Nice

11th – World professional road-race championships

1969

1st – Tour of the Basque Country

3rd – Paris–Nice

Bibliography

Books

Anquetil, Dominique, *Anquetil, Jacques par Dominique* (Editions Denoël, 1989)

Anquetil, Jacques with Joly, Pierre, *En brûlant les étapes* (Calmann-Levy, 1966)

Anquetil, Sophie, *Pour l'amour de Jacques* (Editions Grasset, 2004)

Augendre, Jacques, *Guide historique et culturel du Tour de France* (ASO, 2003, 2007)

Fotheringham, William, *Put Me Back on My Bike* (Yellow Jersey Press, 2002)

Géminiani, Raphaël, *Les années Anquetil: chronique d'une époque bafouée* (Editions Denoël, 1990)

Marchand, Jacques, *Anquetil le Rebelle* (Editions Prolongations, 2007)

Meade, Marion, *The Unruly Life of Woody Allen* (Weidenfeld & Nicolson, 2000)

Ollivier, Jean-Paul, *Jacques Anquetil: la véridique histoire* (Editions Glénat, 1994)

Pélissier, Pierre, *La légende de Jacques Anquetil* (Editions Rageot, 1997)

Penot, Christophe, *Pierre Chany, L'Homme aux 50 Tours de France* (Editions Cristel, 1996)

Poulidor, Raymond with Brouchon, Jean-Paul, *Poulidor intime* (Editions Jacob-Duvernet, 2007)
Yates, Richard, *Master Jacques: The Enigma of Jacques Anquetil* (Mousehold Press, 2001)

Films

Jacques Anquetil – The Man, The Mystery, The Legend (World Cycling Productions, 1998)

Magazines and Newspapers

Almost every francophone newspaper the world over has at some time run articles on Anquetil's career and/or life, and the same is true for the English-language cycling press. As a result, it has been necessary to read so many articles from so many papers to come to terms with Anquetil's achievements that it is impossible to cite them all individually: some have come from scrapbooks, such as the one donated to Sophie Anquetil by a dedicated fan of her father, some have come from the author's own collection, some have come from having been incorporated into the archives of other magazines. The list below merely includes those publications that have been referred to during my research.

Cycle Sport (including 2004 special supplement)
Cycling
Cycling Weekly (including 1987 commemorative edition)
Cyclisme Magazine
Dolce Vita
France Dimanche (including 1987 commemorative edition and Anquetil's own articles written from 4 to 25 July 1967)
France Soir
Ici Paris
L'03
L'Aurore

L'Équipe (including 1969 retirement souvenir edition, 1987 commemorative edition and 2007 special commemorative supplement)

L'Est Republicain

L'Express

L'Humanité

La Voix du Nord

Le Cycle

Le Figaro

Le Monde

Lui

Miroir des Sports

Miroir du Cyclisme

Miroir Sprint

Paris Match (1987 commemorative edition)

Paris-Jour

Paris-Normandie

Paris-Soir

Sport Vedette

Sporting Cyclist

Télé 7 Jours (1987 commemorative edition)

Vélo Magazine